THE COMPLEAT APPLE SPREADSHEETER

Roger E. Clark
Patricia Johnson Swersey

Prentice-Hall, Inc.
Englewood Cliffs, New Jersey

Prentice-Hall International, Inc., London
Prentice-Hall of Australia, Pty. Ltd., Sydney
Prentice-Hall Canada, Inc., Toronto
Prentice-Hall of India Private Ltd., New Delhi
Prentice-Hall of Japan, Inc., Tokyo
Prentice-Hall of Southeast Asia Pte. Ltd., Singapore
Whitehall Books, Ltd., Wellington, New Zealand
Editora Prentice-Hall do Basil Ltda., Rio de Janeiro
Prentice-Hall Hispanoamericana, S.A., Mexico

© 1986 by

PRENTICE-HALL, INC.

Englewood Cliffs, N.J.

All rights reserved. No part of this book
may be reproduced in any form or
by any means, without permission in
writing from the publisher.

Library of Congress Cataloging-in-Publication Data
Clark, Roger E.
   The Compleat Apple Spreadsheeter.

   Includes index.
   1. Business—Data Processing. 2. Electronic
spreadsheets. 3. Apple computer—Programming.
4. Microcomputers—Programming. I. Swersey, Patricia
Johnson. II. Title.
   HF5548.2.C5418 1986   650'.028'55365   85-19241

ISBN 0-13-155094-2

ISBN 0-13-155086-1 {PBK}

Printed in the United States of America

This book is dedicated to the memory of
Mary Louise Tierney Clark,
Roger's loving wife and Tricia's special friend.

PREFACE

We, your authors, talked together about the preface to this book some time ago, when we were planning the "division of labor." Just in case anyone thinks that writers write things in the order in which they eventually get read, forget it! At that time we tried to visualize the circumstances under which it would be read, tried to imagine who the reader might be, had a shot at guessing at the level of expertise we might encounter. We made some notes, and put them aside for later.

Now that we have finished the book, we have pulled out our notes for another discussion—and to our surprise we have ended up writing a book for just exactly the reader we visualized those many months ago!

As we have said in the introduction, you are probably comfortable with one or more of the popular spreadsheet programs. You need to know a bit about our credentials as "experts" in spreadsheeting and as writers, just so that you'll know just how much of the wonderful stuff we are going to tell you about is reliable! Fair's fair, so for the first (and only) time in this book we are going to drop the royal "we" and become "I" for a change—we'll each tell you about ourselves.

I am Roger Clark, a spreadsheet maven. I have been fascinated by this type of software since it first came out. I used to be a computer dealer (primarily Apple)—one of the earliest independently owned "computer stores," then a new kind of retailer. In order to gain the computer awareness necessary to manage a store, I put in many hours as a new computerist—giving me a true insight into the problems that my future customers were to have (and probably some of you readers are having now!).

One day in the fall of 1979 the UPS man brought a package to the store that I had not ordered, from a company we had never heard of—Personal Software. The package contained a diskette and a manual for a program called VisiCalc. After five minutes of watching a free-running demonstration/tutorial about the new program, which was on the flip side of the diskette, I was hooked.

I finally left the computer that night at about midnight. I knew then that a new and significant function had entered the microcomputer world—the spreadsheet program. From that moment on microcomputers could be sold because of an application program—just showing the power of VisiCalc often became enough to sell a desktop system. There is no doubt that the advent of VisiCalc was the reason for the first big surge in Apple sales.

As those of you who are getting comfortable with them know, spreadsheets offer the user a blank program. This tremendous flexibility, this open ended "blankness" to be filled by precisely what the user wants to do, was the reason that as each new computer appeared on the market, the first capability that the manufacturer provided was a spreadsheet.

We guessed that a fraternal spirit would grow up among the men and women using spreadsheets. We felt that as each individual user explored the program and developed his or her own applications, there would be a desire to share the experience—and with whom? Obviously there would be be too few users at that time to have local face-to-face meetings and things—so InterCalc was born.

InterCalc, the International Spreadsheet Users Group, started in the Fall of 1980 and published, bi-monthly, six typewritten pages under the name *SpreadSheet*. Now members contribute to the typeset application newsletter, which is published monthly. The exchange of ideas and applications demonstrates over and over the great facility for creative use of a microcomputer that the program permits. We started a second, more advanced applications newsletter, called *OmniCalc*, in late 1984 which is being well accepted by our readers. The InterCalc publications are how we came to meet Patricia Johnson Swersey, or Tricia as we call her.

Tell 'em about yourself, Trish . . .

I joined InterCalc in 1982. I have been involved with microcomputers since they first obtained the necessary status to be admitted into major corporations as business tools. I saw the resistance of the MIS establishment to their coming (they must have felt a bit threatened at computing becoming accessible to everyone who wanted to get their hands on!), and I was one of the first to get to have one on my desk.

I was a Senior Venture Analyst with International Paper Company. As you can imagine with the amount of "what-iffing" that is characteristic of the evaluation of new ventures, my first exposure to VisiCalc was a revelation! I became a consistent and heavy user and actually trained several others in my own and other departments. (Using VisiCalc, even the first version on a plain APPLE with 48K, was preferable to using my calculator!) Since there lurks in all of us a desire to be independent, and since writing has always been my avocation, it did not take much to get me to to take the plunge. The chance to join InterCalc, and to be able to take consulting assignments and other freelance writing jobs, caused me to happily give up commuting to New York City.

Now that I have "plunged," I have been busily ensconced in my new (a)vocation. I have written a high school training package for word processing and spreadsheets, have been conducting in-house executive training seminars for Fortune 500 companies in the New York and Connecticut area, and have of course been the editor for both *SpreadSheet* and *OmniCalc* (the latter being my baby since I first suggested it).

Roger and I would like to jointly acknowledge several people and companies who contributed their advice and guidance in the writing of this book. John Webster (TeleProducts Corporation), Bob Korngold (co-founder of InterCalc), Phil Chin, the people at Sorcim, MicroSoft, and Software Arts (before Lotus acquired them), who helped with information.

Roger thanks Penny and Alexander, his children, and his wife Mary Lou, for accepting that the back of the neck bent over a computer can radiate love and affection. Tricia thanks her husband Arthur for roughly the same reason—but since the editorial department of InterCalc is sixty miles from their home (in Roger's house), he doesn't even get to see the back of the neck, and is thanked even more for the tolerance to this absence.

We hope that this book will add to the effectiveness and usefulness of spreadsheet programs to computer users of all levels of expertise. All of the applications in this book are actively in use. Some of the applications and tips discussed in this book are based on ideas that have appeared previously in other InterCalc publications, but all models herein have been created and developed by us especially for this book. This reuse and adaptation proves the great adaptability of spreadsheets program applications from machine to machine and program to program.

Welcome to the wonderful world of spreadsheets!

INTRODUCTION

This book is for spreadsheeters, that band of microcomputerists who love and use the ubiquitous spreadsheet programs. It is not for beginners (though even a newcomer to the marvels and benefits of spreadsheets will get a lot from reading it). It is for the person who has started to get comfortable.

We don't spend much time teaching the basics, although since both of us have taught classes on how to use spreadsheet programs, we do have a good idea of some aspects that cause confusion. Therefore we do review some of these areas again for you. When we start to do this, read it even if you are comfortable with the functions under discussion—we have many, many tips and hints on how to use some functions in new and different ways, and you might learn something.

This book is business directed, that is, toward the use in an office or other business environment. We think that everyone will get some ideas from it, however, even the home user. It is impossible to really be *The Compleat APPLE Spreadsheeter* (call our title creative license!) because there is literally no end to the uses to which spreadsheets can be put.

We have carefully selected the models and applications in this book to demonstrate practical *methodologies*, and all of the models here can be adapted to a host of different end-uses. Virtually every function available in a spreadsheet has been used at least once. In addition, we have included five chapters at the end of the book that we have called Utilities. These are models that we think have broader range applications beyond the basic model that is illustrated. Although these chapters contain models that can stand alone, each of the models is really a utility piece that can be inserted into other spreadsheet applications. You will find these Utilities following Chapter 21.

When we started this book there were only two of the major spreadsheet programs available on the Apple—VisiCalc and Multiplan (with a host of lookalikes and act-alikes!). Now, very recently, Sorcim has adapted its program SuperCalc to the Apple world. Over time VisiCalc has improved itself, to the present Advanced Version level. There are yet more spreadsheet programs that model themselves closely on either VisiCalc or SuperCalc—and the situation in the micro world is the same as always: the current status engraved on a marshmallow for permanence!

You'll find that each chapter discusses the function or application concerned running under one of the major programs, but at the end of each is a discussion of any variances or opportunities that others might offer. Just so we are not accused of being lazy, please note that in order to produce this book we had to do each application at least three times. We quickly found that it was easiest (and easiest also to write about afterwards) if we worked "up" from the least featured, rather than "down" from the top. This means that dear old VisiCalc is featured a lot, since in the fast moving micro world there are new features and new capabilities appearing every day—VisiCalc is still the model from where the competitive designers start! Another reason that you will find several chapters dealing with VisiCalc is that we have developed applications in this lowest common denominator program which do many of the things (like date arithmetic) the "more advanced" programs do, that VisiCalc is not supposed to be able to perform! If you don't use VisiCalc though, don't fret—our *OtherCalcs* segments in each chapter explain how to adapt each model to *your* favorite program.

Read this book and then go back to your favorite spreadsheet—we hope that you will enjoy it more!

CONTENTS

Introduction vii

1. If IFs OR ANDs Were Pots and Pans. 1
   Managing a Spreadsheet Database

2. Who's on Top? 11
   Ranking Chart

3. Calling All Coordinates 19
   Checkbook Register

4. Let's LOOKUP Our Local Quick Printer 27
   Estimating and Invoicing

5. There Are Three Sides to Every Question 36
   Triangle Solver

6. Turning a Liability into an Asset 49
   Income Statement and Balance Sheet

7. "The Penalties for Early Withdrawal Are. . ." 60
   IRA Analysis

8. Investment Property—to Buy or Not to Buy 71
   Rental Cash Flow

9. Here's Looking at You, Kid! 78
   Price List

10. Parcels, Unite! 88
    Calculating the United Parcel Service Charges

11. Will I Ever Stop Paying? 99
    Loan Amortization Calculator

12. Making It Come Out Even 108
    Break-even Analysis

13. Making a Score **114**
   Weighted Scoring, Multiparameter Subjective Analysis

14. Where Did All the Money Go? **124**
   Household Expense Register

15. Out of Commission **136**
   Preparing Commission Statements

16. Projecting Is Quite a Project **142**
   Linear Regression Analysis

17. Breaking a Date **149**
   Project Scheduling Application

18. Making the Quota **159**
   Sales Territory Management

19. Keeping the Salaries Secret **168**
   Display Security System and Salary Finder

20. Green Eyeshades and Cuff Protectors **174**
   A Ledger System in a Spreadsheet

21. Automating the Quill Pen **182**
   Automated Mini-Ledger

UTILITIES

U1. Looks Like It's Getting Late! **191**
   Startup Schedule Forecaster

U2. How Much on the Meter? **197**
   Metric/English Measure Conversion

U3. Things Are Looking Up **201**
   Using LOOKUP Tables in Two Dimensions

U4. Doing the Impossible with LOOKUP **205**
   An Automated Invoice System

U5. Finding the Missing Piece **213**
   Interest Calculator

APPENDICES

Appendix I—Function Matrix **221**

Appendix II—Command Matrix **225**

Appendix III—Key Formulas **231**

Index **258**

If IFs OR ANDs Were Pots and Pans

1

SPREADSHEET FUNCTIONS: IF, OR, AND
FEATURED PROGRAM: VisiCalc
TEMPLATE FUNCTION: Managing a Spreadsheet Data Base

BACKGROUNDER

. . . there'd be no work for tinker's hands. That's a computer-pun rendering of the old saying, which originally meant that the wishes of people ("if only . . .") came true so rarely, that if they were pots and pans, tinkers wouldn't have any work to do.

The earliest versions of VisiCalc, the first of the spreadsheet programs that were to proliferate, accumulate, emigrate (to CP/M), and otherwise become the basic tool of business modellers, did not have the logic function, the ability to use Boolean formula structures. We used to wish for them ("If only . . .") and it seems hard to remember that situation now, as the spreadsheets have become increasingly sophisticated and all contain the built-in logic functions of IF, OR, AND, and NOT.

We have a useful utility program in this chapter, and since it uses not only the IF function but also the OR and the AND, it will once again underline and familiarize you with the uses to which the Boolean logic attributes can be used.

The basic function of a logic statement is to produce a TRUE or a FALSE condition after considering a statement presented by the model. Type into a

VisiCalc model the statement "1+1=2" and you will get back TRUE. Type in "1+2=4" and you'll get back FALSE.

In the typical IF statement in a spreadsheet, the program is presented with two options to execute, depending on whether the conditional statement is true or false. In VisiCalc, the syntax of the @IF statement is @IF(logical value statement, comma, if true do this, comma, if false do this) or @IF(lv,v1,v2).

A formula such as @IF(1+2=X,1,0) will produce the more familiar "1" if TRUE and "0" if FALSE, depending on whether X is 3 or not.

OR and AND similarly return TRUE and FALSE but they evaluate more than one conditional statement. Several conditions can be presented and either ANY of them must be true (for OR) or ALL of them must be true (for AND) to render the total statement true.

In the case of OR, the evaluation is of a list of conditional statements, any of which may be TRUE to meet requirements. The following statements will all produce TRUE:

@OR(4+4=8,1+2=3,2+2=4)
@OR(4+4=8,1+2=6,2+2=4)
@OR(4+4=8,1+2=3,2+2=6)

But this statement will produce FALSE:

@OR(4+4=7,1+2=6,2+2=6)

In the case of the first three statements there were correct or true statements among those in the parentheses, but in the fourth none were correct, so FALSE was returned.

The AND logical evaluation is a more stringent statement. It requires that ALL the conditions be met in order to be considered true—near misses win no cigars! Using statements similar to those just used, only the first of the following will return TRUE:

@AND(4+4=8,1+2=3,2+2=4)
@AND(4+4=8,1+2=6,2+2=4)
@AND(4+4=8,1+2=3,2+2=6)
@AND(4+4=7,1+2=6,2+2=6)

There is an easy way to remember the difference between OR and AND. Say to yourself: "EITHER/OR—if either is to be correct choose OR AND the other must be AND."

The syntax of the @OR and @AND statements in VisiCalc is nearly always presented within an IF statement, since it is rare that one wants to have merely the word TRUE or FALSE printed in the model. More often one wants the model to do something depending on whether the conditions are met or not.

If IFs OR ANDs Were Pots and Pans 3

The structure of the typical statements, similar with both OR and AND, would be:

@IF(@OR(list of logical values separated by commas),v1,v2)
@IF(@AND(list of logical values separated by commas),v1,v2)

Needless to say the logical values can be as complex as one wishes, containing formulas that in themselves might contain IF, OR or AND statements. Since they will be in the inside parentheses VisiCalc will evaluate them first in order to take the final look at whether some or all are true or false.

The construction of the IF, OR, and AND statements in the other calc programs covered in this book will be found at the end of the chapter—they are very similar.

APPLICATION SPREADSHEET

Purpose: This model will enable you to find matching sets of information within a kind of data base—a feature not available in regular VisiCalc. Our hypothetical example is a spreadsheet that contains the personnel details of a large number of people. It has been created to enable the financial people in a small company to calculate the cash needs on the weekly paydays and again on the monthly paydays. But our operator decided to add a feature—give the model the ability to provide total salaries based on some selection criteria.

Building the Model

In Figures 1.1 and 1.2 you can see the two segments which make up the complete model, and we will look at it in segments.

Look first at Figure 1.2, the data base portion of the model. The first thing to note is that it appears the model was done in a program that has variable column widths. If your program does, fine, this is how it can look. We actually did the model in VisiCalc with a single column width. We did some judicious juggling of the figure to shrink it down to printable size.

The names of the personnel are listed in columns B and C, with pertinent information about each on their particular rows. These include the birth date, gender, grade level, salary (annual equivalent in the case of hourly paid workers), the year they joined the company (with the length of service in years calculated by taking this from 1984), and some other salary figures that we will come back to in a minute.

In Figure 1.1 you can see the instructions panel that reminds the user how to the model works. Beneath that are the various selection criteria for categories of workers, which will enable the model to display breakdowns of the overall

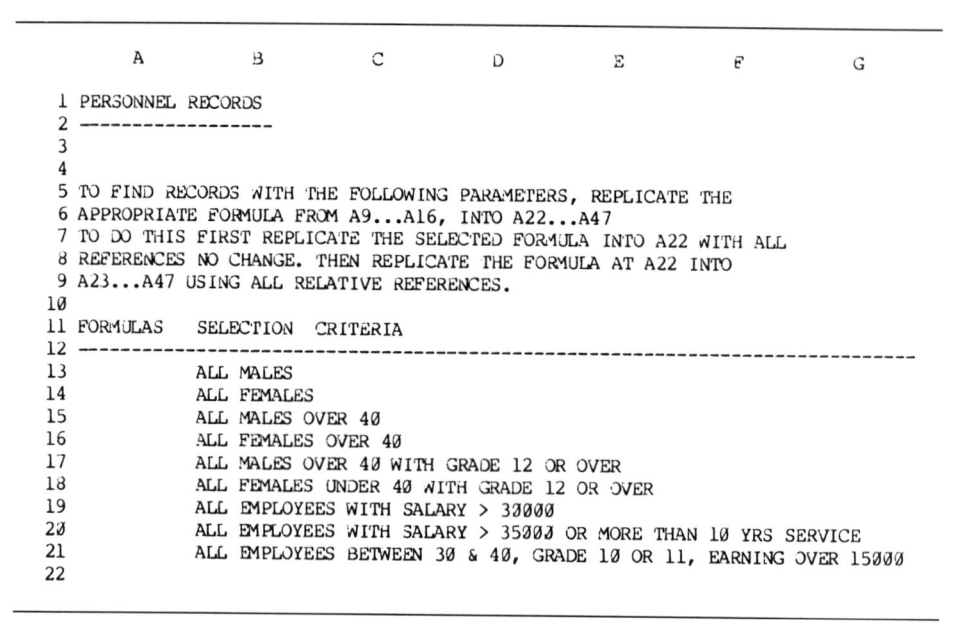

```
                A           B           C           D           E           F           G
     1 PERSONNEL RECORDS
     2 -----------------
     3
     4
     5 TO FIND RECORDS WITH THE FOLLOWING PARAMETERS, REPLICATE THE
     6 APPROPRIATE FORMULA FROM A9...A16, INTO A22...A47
     7 TO DO THIS FIRST REPLICATE THE SELECTED FORMULA INTO A22 WITH ALL
     8 REFERENCES NO CHANGE. THEN REPLICATE THE FORMULA AT A22 INTO
     9 A23...A47 USING ALL RELATIVE REFERENCES.
    10
    11 FORMULAS    SELECTION  CRITERIA
    12 ------------------------------------------------------------------------
    13             ALL MALES
    14             ALL FEMALES
    15             ALL MALES OVER 40
    16             ALL FEMALES OVER 40
    17             ALL MALES OVER 40 WITH GRADE 12 OR OVER
    18             ALL FEMALES UNDER 40 WITH GRADE 12 OR OVER
    19             ALL EMPLOYEES WITH SALARY > 30000
    20             ALL EMPLOYEES WITH SALARY > 35000 OR MORE THAN 10 YRS SERVICE
    21             ALL EMPLOYEES BETWEEN 30 & 40, GRADE 10 OR 11, EARNING OVER 15000
    22
```

Figure 1.1: Criteria and Formulas Area

data. It is this breakout capability that uses the IF, OR, and AND functions in the spreadsheet.

The operator decides which breakout is required, and then /Replicates the formula in to the first person's row, with the relationship as (N)o change. Then the formula is replicated down the column to the last person, with the relationship this time as (R)elative. As the formula is inserted in each row and the model recalculates and an asterisk appears in Column A against each of the personnel that meet the criteria.

The model has a column headed DATA. It is presently set to bring over the salary figure for column J for each of the people selected; thus the total of the column will give the total annual salary budget required for all the people in the category selected.

Let's look at how all this is accomplished.

The Selection Criteria

The first simple conditional formula is in A13 and finds all the males among the personnel (it is similar to that in A14, which identifies the females in the group).

@IF(F27 = 1,1,0) [set asterisk]

SpreadTalk: If the value in F27 equals one, use one, otherwise use zero.

	A	B	C	D	E	F	G	H	I	J	K	L	M	N	O	P	Q
23		LAST	FIRST	MIDDLE					GRADE	SALARY	YRS OF	JOINED	PAID	PAID	PAID	ACTUAL/ AV HOURS	HOURLY
24		NAME	NAME	INITIAL	DATA	SEX	BRTHDTE	AGE	LEVEL	YR/EQIV	SRVCE	CMPNY	MONTHLY	WEEKLY	HOURLY	WORKED	TOTAL
25																	
26																	
27		ADAMS	CHARLES	A.	0	1	2/29	40	4	13500	4	1984	0.00	0.00	7.42	28	207.69
28		BISSET	JACQUELIN	B.	0	2	4/13	38	15	50000	14	1970	4166.67	0.00	0.00		0.00
29		CLARKE	ROGER	C.	0	1	8/04	35	16	55000	12	1972	4583.33	0.00	0.00		0.00
30		DUNN	IRENE	D.	0	2	12/25	21	12	35000	8	1976	2916.67	0.00	0.00		0.00
31		EDGARS	MEDGAR	E.	0	1	7/07	30	10	27000	15	1969	2250.00	0.00	0.00		0.00
32		FRANKLIN	BENJAMIN	F.	0	1	3/15	64	7	19000	4	1980	0.00	365.38	0.00		0.00
33		GRETZKY	WAYNE	G.	0	1	4/20	29	5	15000	2	1982	0.00	288.46	7.42	20	148.35
34		HANCOCK	JOHN	H.	0	1	5/01	35	4	13500	6	1978	0.00	0.00	0.00		0.00
35		ITO	HIRO	I.	0	1	10/12	30	10	27000	12	1972	2250.00	0.00	0.00		0.00
36		JOHNSON	PATRICIA	J.	0	2	6/30	35	10	26000	11	1973	2166.67	0.00	0.00		0.00
37		KOCH	EDWIN	K.	0	1	11/02	22	6	17000	1	1983	0.00	326.92	0.00		0.00
38		LISTON	SONNY	L.	0	1	1/01	27	4	13500	5	1979	0.00	0.00	7.42	15	111.26
39		MENCKEN	H.L.	M.	0	1	9/20	56	4	13500	15	1969	0.00	0.00	7.42	15	111.26
40		NIXON	RICHARD	N.	0	1	6/02	19	3	12500	1	1983	0.00	240.38	0.00		0.00
41		O'NEILL	TIP	O.	0	1	8/18	26	10	20000	5	1979	1666.67	0.00	0.00		0.00
42		POLDARK	ROSS	P.	0	1	1/12	44	6	17000	10	1974	0.00	326.92	0.00		0.00
43		QUINN	SALLY	Q.	0	2	9/13	60	12	35000	17	1967	2916.67	0.00	0.00		0.00
44		REAGAN	NANCY	R.	0	2	5/26	43	7	19000	5	1979	0.00	365.38	0.00		0.00
45	*	STEPHENSON	ADLAI	S.	35500	1	7/18	32	10	35500	10	1974	2958.33	0.00	0.00		0.00
46		TOSCANINI	ARTURO	T.	0	1	11/14	27	4	18500	5	1979	0.00	0.00	10.16	25	254.12
47		UDALL	MORRIS	U.	0	1	4/05	23	4	13500	2	1982	0.00	0.00	7.42	25	185.44
48		VANDERBILT	AMY	V.	0	2	7/23	21	6	17000	3	1981	0.00	326.92	0.00		0.00
49		WEST	JERALD	W.	0	1	2/03	49	4	13500	6	1978	0.00	0.00	7.42	15	111.26
50		XERXES	KING	X.	0	1	3/17	54	7	19000	7	1977	0.00	365.38	0.00		0.00
51		YAEGER	ANDREA	Y.	0	2	8/22	57	13	40000	17	1967	3333.33	0.00	0.00		0.00
52		ZIEGFELD	FLORENCE	Z.	0	1	9/18	31	4	13500	10	1974	0.00	0.00	7.42	15	111.26
53					-----								-------	-------			-------
54				TOTAL	35500								29208.33	10423.03			4962.64
55																	
56									CASH REQUIRED MONTHLY-->44594.05								
57												WEEKLY->15386.71					

Figure 1.2: Data Base

As you will have surmised, this formula, although in A13, is designed to be used in row 27. Once it is /Replicated down to row 27, no change, and then re-replicated from there down to the bottom of the model, relative, it has the desired effect: it places a one in column A on each row that it finds a male, which appears as an asterisk.

Over in the DATA column there is the formula:

(J27*A27)

SpreadTalk: Multiply the value in J27 by the value in A27.

This will work on the salary figure, multiplying it by the value in column A. In the case of a male there is a "1" there, so it effectively repeats the salary figure. In the case of a female there is a "0" in column A, therefore nothing appears. We have the effect we want—a sublist of the salaries so that they can be added for a sum of the male salaries we pay.

Now that the principle of the extraction method has been covered, we can look at the different formulas, and how other conditions have been applied in selection criteria.

Suppose we want to find all males (and in the next criterion, females) over 40. This means a one or a two in the SEX column and a figure of forty or more in the AGE column. So that is what we tell VisiCalc:

@IF(@AND(F26=1,H27>=40),1,0)

SpreadTalk: IF SEX=1 AND AGE is greater than, or equal to, 40, you found an over-forty male, then insert 1, but if even one of these criteria is false, insert zero.

Next we want to find all women who are younger than forty with a grade level higher than 12

IF(@AND(D27=2,H27<40,I27>=12),1,0)

No need to SpreadTalk this one—there are three AND conditions, all of which must be met to qualify. The other criteria are similar in principle, except for the last one:

@IF(@AND(H27>=30,H27<=40,
    @OR(I27=10,I27=11),J27=35000),1,0)

Here we are looking for someone like Mr. Stevenson—anyone between 30 and 40, grade 10 or 11, and earning over $35,000.

Once again SpreadTalk is unnecessary but notice that since VisiCalc will evaluate the innermost set of parentheses first, it will solve the OR in the middle first, and if it is TRUE will have that item "checked" off as it evaluates to see if all the other items are also TRUE, as required by the AND statement.

If IFs OR ANDs Were Pots and Pans

There are a few more IF, OR, and AND statements over in the right-hand side of the model. There are some columns over there that the financial department needed for their weekly and monthly cash requirements. This time the whole column is a "selection criterion" and an entry will only appear if a person meets the requirements of the column heading.

Essentially each column heading has a definition, and that definition is the construction of the formula. Look at the first one, headed PAID MONTHLY. In this company only people who earn $20,000 or more or are grade 10 or higher get a monthly check. So the formula says just that:

@IF(@AND(J27>=20000,I27>=10),J27/12,0)

and in the column appears one-twelfth of the annual salary if the person meets the definition, otherwise zero.

The next column, PAID WEEKLY is defined as people who earn less than 20,000, are less than a grade 10 but not a grade 4. In order to get a "BUT" in there you must define your conditions carefully, so that VisiCalc knows what you want:

@IF(@AND(J27<19999,I27<10,I27<>4),J25/52,0)

SpreadTalk: If the salary is under 1999 ALSO the grade level is less than 10 ALSO the grade level is not 4, then . . .

All PAID HOURLY employees are grade 4, but they earn different hourly rates. The hourly rate is carried in the budget as an annual figure equivalent (so as to make annual budgeting easier), so we have to compute it out the figure in column J. The formula is simple enough:

@IF(I27=4,(J27/52)/35,0)

As can be seen, the hourly workers are paid for 35 hours a week at straight time, so in this column will appear their hourly rate.

The next column is for the bookkeeper to enter the actual hours worked in the week under consideration (or in the case of a forecasting process, an average figure), so that the last column can compute the actual cash required by multiplying O and P.

QUICK SUMMARY

Just remember this "aide memoire": "If either is acceptable, choose OR, AND the other must be AND."

OtherCalcs

Multiplan

The model will be able to use the identical construction to that explained earlier for VisiCalc, but of course without the leading @ sign for the expressions. Similarly, the functions AND and OR are usually contained within an IF statement.

When replicating the conditional formula from the top into the data base segment, you have to take some additional steps in Multiplan. This is because of the way in which Multiplan handles Absolute and Relative references. When you set up the formulas in the instructions area, it is best to use Named cells. In doing this you will avoid the bother of having to edit or rewrite formulas once they are moved from the conditions area to the data base.

The first step to take then is to name the cells in some of the data base columns. The columns to name in this example are SEX, AGE, GRADE, SALARY, and YRS OF SERVICE. To name the column containing the Grade Level information, for example, you would press N to begin the Name command, type Grade (or any meaningful abbreviation), TAB and enter R27C9:R52C9, then RETURN. Now all of the cells in this column are named GRADE.

To use this name in a formula that finds everyone who is Grade Level 6 to 10, you would write:

IF(OR(GRADE>=6,GRADE<=10),1,0)

This is a nice feature of Multiplan, in that your formulas are more meaningful to other people trying to use the model.

Names will work in any of the formulas in this model, which should make formula writing easier, and the formulas much more understandable.

SuperCalc³

This model in SuperCalc³ would be identical to Multiplan in that the formulas are not written with the leading @ sign. There is no naming feature in SuperCalc³, however, so the formulas and the replicating instructions are more like VisiCalc. Although this type of application would likely be done in SuperCalc³'s //Data Management command, the concepts for using the IF, AND, and OR functions remain true in SuperCalc. True results are represented by a 1 and False results represented by a 0, rather than the TRUE and FALSE statements achieved in VisiCalc.

Even though two of our featured programs, VisiCalc and Multiplan, do not have a true data base manager (the application we have shown you in this chapter tries to simulate one), SuperCalc³ does have a data base management segment. We are not going to give you all of the details for using this complex program segment, but will go through the basics and show you how the application detailed in this chapter would look.

A data base in SuperCalc³ consists of information usually entered in a formatted way. There should be a row of Field Names above the information or records. In our figure, the data base records begin at row 27. To use the //Data Management command we would place our field names in the row immediately above the rows of data. The field names would have to be abbreviated from those shown in our model. They can be on only one line, so we would use LAST for last name, FIRST for first name, etc.

Once the data are entered into the data base we can use some commands to highlight the records we are interested in (as in our VisiCalc and Multiplan models), or actually extract the information to another location on the data base.

To use the data base to extract information you must enter the //D command in SuperCalc³. Once you press //D then your first step is to specify an Input range. This range is the data base range including the row of field names. You must include the field names or the extract will not work. The data base records should start in the second row of the input range. This means you probably should not have a row of underlines, or a blank row separating the field names from the data. You also must specify the Input range before you can continue with the //D commands.

Once you have specified the Input range, you need to specify the Criterion range. This is the range where you put the selection criteria that you want to use to find the records that you are interested in. In our model we have put several selection criteria formulas in the area shown in Figure 1.1. We can leave this area almost as is, if we edit the formulas somewhat. While our explanation of how best to use the AND and OR functions says they are normally used within an IF statement, in the case of data base management functions, they are usually used by themselves.

If we edit the formulas to remove the IF statements, we can use these formulas as our criteria ranges. For example, our formula at A13 selects all the males by determining whether the F column value equals one. The formula reads:

$$IF(F27=1,1,0)$$

We can edit this formula to read:

$$(F27=0)$$

and specify A13 as our C(riterion) range. This formula will be evaluated for each of the records in our data base and the matching records will either be highlighted, if we are using the Find command, or extracted to another location, if we are using the Extract command.

Another example of an edited formula would be the one in Row 18 that selects all women younger than forty whose grade level is 12 or greater. The formula reads:

IF(AND(F27=2,H27<40,I27>=12),1,0)

This would be edited to read simply:

AND(F27=2,H27<40,I27>=12)

All records which match these criteria will be selected.

Once the formulas have been edited to delete the IFs, we can choose which condition we wish to evaluate, and then specify this formula as our Criterion range. Then we can use the Find command to simply highlight all matching records.

If we wish to extract the records or portions of the matching records, we must specify an Output range before using the Extract command. The Output range should be large enough to contain all the records that we think will be extracted, or we will get an error message. The Output range should also contain the field names as its first row. These field names can be placed in any order and may be all of the fields from the data base or just a select few containing information you are interested in. If, for example, we were interested in looking at the totals for salaries for each of our criteria categories, as we were in our VisiCalc data base, we would not have to use a column DATA (column E in the model). We could simply specify only the SALARY field name in our Output range and then sum up all of the extracted records.

Once the Output range has been specified (along with the criterion and input ranges) you can proceed to extract the information you are interested in.

This is by no means a detailed lesson on using the SuperCalc[3] //Data Management commands, but you should get an idea (at least) of what can be accomplished.

2

Who's on Top?

SPREADSHEET FUNCTIONS: MIN, MAX
FEATURED PROGRAM: SuperCalc³
TEMPLATE FUNCTION: Ranking Chart

BACKGROUNDER

As their names imply, the MIN and MAX functions in spreadsheets are used to find (and use) the highest and lowest values in a range or list. As usual at the end of the chapter we will detail for you any differences that exist in the way the others of our three key programs use the function.

In SuperCalc³ the format of the formula used to establish the high and low values are formatted:

MIN(range and/or list)
MAX(range and/or list)

All of the following are valid formulas, and would be identical for MAX formulas, too:

MIN(A1:A42)
MIN(A1:A42,B9,B42,AZ100)
MIN(A1,G60,B9,B42,AZ100)

Each will return the lowest or highest value found as the list and/or range is checked.

There are various valuable uses for the MIN/MAX pair, and we find that the function is often forgotten, even by "expert" spreadsheeters. After reading this chapter, uses may spring to mind when next you are trying to formulate a spreadsheet for a particular purpose.

APPLICATION SPREADSHEET

Ranker

There are times when using the sorting function in a spreadsheet, covered elsewhere in this book, is unsuitable. For instance, since the sorting involves an actual rearrangement of the full rows or columns involved, there may be surrounding material that will be inappropriately placed after such a rearrangement. This would be particularly true if textual material, required to clarify a part of a model, was rearranged— it may not only become unreadable, it could convey false information! Our first simple utility model uses the MAX and MIN functions to "sort"—not into a new order, but to label a series of entries from highest to lowest.

In Figure 2.1 you can see a product scoreboard. We had the sales figures for each product size, and we wanted to rank each of them, so that additional analysis could be done with the results. Notice that the scoreboard is placed

```
           R           S          T          U

22   "SCOREBOARD"
23                                       PERCENT
24   PRODUCT    QUANTITY      RANK        TOTAL
25
26   MICRO      1000.13         1         18.51
27   MINI        900.34         2         16.66
28   REGULAR     800.44         3         14.81
29   SMALL       700.16         4         12.96
30   MEDIUM      600.12         5         11.11
31   LARGE       500.88         6          9.27
32   SUPER       400.45         7          7.41
33   JUMBO       300.21         8          5.56
34   ULTRABIG    200.03         9          3.70
35   MAGNUM           1        10          0.02
```

Figure 2.1:   Results Screen

down in the matrix and over to the right. The reason for this will become evident. Obviously this information is coming from somewhere—each number must have been evaluated against its fellows and a decision made as to its order in the scheme of things. The "somewhere" is shown in Figure 2.2 which is the top part of the model. It is here that all the work takes place.

Positioning the Components of the Model

The reason the scoreboard is placed to the right of the work area is to avoid the forward references, which would have necessitated a second recalc had the scoreboard been placed elsewhere. In this model one cannot avoid the forward references by setting the order of recalculation to (R)ows, (as is sometimes possible) since most of the calculations and evaluations are oriented vertically.

In Figure 2.3 columns A and B are the raw data that must be evaluated. Against each Product Name is the sales figure for the "last period," whatever that was. From this data we are going to produce the ranking.

Going to Work

In the first work column, F, headed "FIND .00001," we establish which of the full list of sales figures is the largest, replace it with another number (the one at the head of the column), and then copy into the column all the other numbers that are less than the largest. The formula for this first appears in E13

IF(D13 = MAX(D13:D22),E8,D13)

replicated down the column with the relationships as Ask,YNNNY.

SpreadTalk: If D13 is the largest number in the column, pick up the value at the head of the column, otherwise just write D13 in this location.

You can see that the formula has the desired effect on the first entry. (We "rigged" the entries for this first figure by entering sample data in descending order, so that you could see the model really working!) The value .00001 appears opposite the first value to be ranked because the MICRO size was indeed the top selling, or MAXimum figure in the column.

The next column, G (FIND .00002), is going to produce the second largest figure. Since it is going to be working on the column of values just created in E by the formula we just reviewed, it is a straight replication, and you can do it in one go all the way across. How far? Well we have just ten numbers to sort so a ten-column total would be enough, but if you are going to be using this model as a utility (discussed at the end of this chapter) then make a few more (up to the maximum number of values you will wish to rank).

	E	F	G	H	I	J	K	L	M	N	O	P	Q
5	WORK AREA DO NOT DISTURB					WORK AREA DO NOT DISTURB					WORK AREA DO NOT DISTURB		
6		.0001	.0002	.0003	.0004	.0005	.0006	.0007	.0008	.0009	.0001		
7		HIGH	HIGH	HIGH	HIGH	HIGH	HIGH	HIGH	HIGH	HIGH	HIGH	RANK	SORT
8	LIST												
9	----												
10													
11	1000.13	.0001	.0001	.0001	.0001	.0001	.0001	.0001	.0001	.0001	.0001	1	1000.13
12	900.34	900.34	.0002	.0002	.0002	.0002	.0002	.0002	.0002	.0002	.0002	2	900.34
13	800.44	800.44	800.44	.0003	.0003	.0003	.0003	.0003	.0003	.0003	.0003	3	800.44
14	700.16	700.16	700.16	700.16	.0004	.0004	.0004	.0004	.0004	.0004	.0004	4	700.16
15	600.12	600.12	600.12	600.12	600.12	.0005	.0005	.0005	.0005	.0005	.0005	5	600.12
16	500.88	500.88	500.88	500.88	500.88	500.88	.0006	.0006	.0006	.0006	.0006	6	500.88
17	400.45	400.45	400.45	400.45	400.45	400.45	400.45	.0007	.0007	.0007	.0007	7	400.45
18	300.21	300.21	300.21	300.21	300.21	300.21	300.21	300.21	.0008	.0008	.0008	8	300.21
19	200.03	200.03	200.03	200.03	200.03	200.03	200.03	200.03	200.03	.0009	.0009	9	200.03
20	1	1	1	1	1	1	1	1	1	1	.0001	10	1

Figure 2.2: Sort and Rank Area

Who's on Top ?

```
             A         B
     1 RANKING NUMBERS
     2 ----------------
     3 ENTER VALUES AND
     4 RE-CALC TWICE
     5 FOR RESULT DISPLAY
     6 GOTO <U22.....
     7
     8 ENTER DATA HERE
     9 NAMES       SALES
    10 -------    -------
    11 MICRO      1000.13
    12 MINI        900.34
    13 REGULAR     800.44
    14 SMALL       700.16
    15 MEDIUM      600.12
    16 LARGE       500.88
    17 SUPER       400.45
    18 JUMBO       300.21
    19 ULTRABIG    200.03
    20 MAGNUM            1
```

Figure 2.3:   Data Entry Area

You can see from the figure that the neat progression of ".0000" values marching across the model proves that the ranking is taking place—each column that is designed to "FIND" a rank has indeed done so.

Incidentally, it is worth mentioning why we chose the ".0000" values as our indicators in the model (we could have used regular integers for each rank and saved ourselves the conversion step, after all). It was simply so that the model could rank all kinds of values down to single integers and even decimal values. If your application requires smaller values than five decimal places, then just make the column "finder" values really small— like .00000000000001 and so on.

Now we want to make the ranking numbers into integers. It would appear that all we have to do, in the column headed RANK, is multiply each of the values that have arrived in the column before by 100,000

+N11*100000

This would work fine except in the case of ties. If two or more values in the list are the same, then each gets the same rank, the correct procedure. But this produces a small problem with all those that come after them in the rankings, particularly the last ones. We therefore substituted the formula:

MIN(F11:O11)*100000

SpreadTalk: Multiply the minimum figure in the range by 100,000. In Figure 2.4 we have entered some more realistic numbers for the sales figures so that

16 Who's on Top ?

	E	F	G	H	I	J	K	L	M	N	O	P	Q
5	WORK AREA DO NOT DISTURB				WORK AREA DO NOT DISTURB				WORK AREA DO NOT DISTURB				
6													
7		.0001	.0002	.0003	.0004	.0005	.0006	.0007	.0008	.0009	.0001		SORT
8	LIST	HIGH	HIGH	HIGH	HIGH	HIGH	HIGH	HIGH	HIGH	HIGH	CONVERT		
9													
10													
11	4977.34	4977.34	.0002	.0002	.0002	.0002	.0002	.0002	.0002	.0002	.0002	2	5000.87
12	500.23	500.23	500.23	500.23	500.23	500.23	500.23	500.23	500.23	.0006	.0006	6	4977.34
13	500.23	500.23	500.23	500.23	500.23	500.23	.0005	.0005	.0005	.0005	.0006	6	3005.72
14	1754.3	1754.3	1754.3	1754.3	1754.3	.0005	.0005	.0005	.0005	.0005	.0005	5	2343.54
15	2343.54	2343.54	2343.54	2343.54	.0004	.0004	.0004	.0004	0.304	.0004	.0004	4	1754.3
16	500.23	500.23	500.23	500.23	500.23	500.23	.0006	.0006	.0006	.0006	.0006	6	500.23
17	10.87	10.87	10.87	10.87	10.87	10.87	10.87	10.87	.0008	.0008	.0008	8	64.49
18	5000.87	.0001	.0001	.0001	.0001	.0001	.0001	.0001	.0001	.0001	.0001	1	10.87
19	64.49	64.49	64.49	64.49	64.49	64.49	64.49	.0007	.0007	.0007	.0007	7	.0008
20	3005.72	3005.72	3005.72	.0003	.0003	.0003	.0003	.0003	.0003	.0003	.0003	3	.0009

Figure 2.4: Sort and Rank Area for Nonordered Entries with Some Tie Scores

you can see some real ranking. Notice that there is a three-way tie for sixth place and it is handled correctly—the three tieing values are classified as sixth place and the last place is therefore ninth—the way it is usually done.

The scoreboard in Figure 2.1 is there to demonstrate how one might pull out the figures into an analysis area. (It also shows how you might even use this model for actually managing a sporting event, say a race of some kind. Mental images of an Apple connected to a projection TV!).

MAKING AND USING A RANKING UTILITY

SpreadTip: While this model is an active application in itself, you might want to save a "bare bones" version to a utilities diskette so that it can be brought into any model that needs a ranking feature. We use utilities a lot in our work at InterCalc, and there's a procedure we use that makes it easy. It's simple but very specific.

Always save your utility components with a legend in the filename that indicates the columns by rows that it occupies. For instance, using this model as an example, you might call it RANK9X25.

When you are ready to transfer the utility into your current model, arrange things so that there is space for it (a rectangle nine columns by fifteen rows), positioned just exactly where you want it. Then note on a piece of paper this "hole" you have left, into which the utility will be placed. Save the model to disk. Load the utility and modify it so that it occupies the same coordinates in the matrix that fit the "hole," and be sure that there is no extraneous material that might interfere with the original main model.

Now reload the main model over the utility, and they will have been combined, ready for some editing to call the figures to be ranked from their place in the main model. Needless to say, if this model is done as a utility it can be compacted significantly when all our "window dressing" is taken out.

OtherCalcs

VisiCalc

This model will work exactly as shown in VisiCalc. The only difference is in the formula construction, as VisiCalc uses the leading @ symbol before the built-in function names (@MAX, @MIN, etc.

Multiplan

This model, which demonstrates advanced use of the Max and Min functions will work in Multiplan as shown. You may wish to take advantage of the Sort command in Multiplan to do this type of ranking however.

To do this, you would specify a Sort by column 2 on rows 11:20 in ascending or (>) order. Only the specified rows within the worksheet will be reordered.

Calling All Coordinates 3

SPREADSHEET FUNCTIONS: Coordinate Calls
FEATURED PROGRAM: VisiCalc
TEMPLATE FUNCTION: Checkbook Register

BACKGROUNDER

Even the newest spreadsheet user is familiar with the concept of moving data around the template. If you enter +C1 or (C1) anywhere in the model, the value stored in C1, even if it is in itself the product of other calculations or calls, will appear and be shown. But the straight call, using a plus sign or parentheses is not required as often as the ability to call selectively: call based on some predetermined criteria.

Remember when you were thinking of buying a computer, the salesperson said that one of the very useful things the computer could do for you was to balance your checkbook? Well here it is! A spreadsheet template that is in fact a checkbook register (throw away the paper one!). This one is a bit different, however, since *it automatically reconciles the bank statement to the checkbook register!* All it needs to know is if all the transactions you have executed have appeared at the bank yet.

APPLICATION SPREADSHEET

In Figure 3.1 you can see what looks like a pretty standard template. It has the date column, a space for the check number, the payee, the amount, and then some columns for various items.

20   Calling All Coordinates

	A	B	C	D	E	F	G	H	
1						ENTER	CHECK-	STATE-	CURRENT
2	1	MONTH	CHECK	TO/	AMOUNT	1 IF	BOOK	MENT	BALANCE
3	1984	YEAR	NUMBER	FROM	CHK/DEP	CLEARED	BALANCE	BALANCE	**DO NOT
4	--								TOUCH**
5	1	1		OPENING BALANCE.	4032.56	1	4032.56	4032.56	
6	1	4	101	RENTCO	675.00	1	3357.56	3357.56	0.00
7	1	6	102	GIANT FO	135.76	1	3221.80	3221.80	0.00
8	1	7	103	VISA	175.00	1	3046.80	3046.80	0.00
9	1	7	104	RED CROS	250.00	1	2796.80	2796.80	0.00
10	1	7	105	NE UTILI	35.76	1	2761.04	2761.04	0.00
11	1	7	106	NYNEX TE	47.84	1	2713.20	2713.20	0.00
12	1	14	107	MARSHALL	32.43	1	2680.77	2680.77	0.00
13	1	24	108	DR. MOLA	75.00	1	2605.77	2605.77	0.00
14	1	30	D	DEPOSIT	1873.24	1	4479.01	4479.01	0.00
15	1	31	109	BLOOMING	25.00	1	4454.01	4454.01	0.00
16	2	1	1	SERVICE	6.00	1	4448.01	4448.01	0.00
17	2	1	INT	INTEREST	23.40	1	4471.41	4471.41	0.00
18	2	4	110	RENTCO.	675.00	1	3796.41	3796.41	0.00
19	2	10	111	VISA	78.42	1	3717.99	3717.99	0.00
20	2	10	112	GLOBE IN	172.13	1	3545.86	3545.86	0.00
21	2	10	113	NE UTILI	37.23		3508.63	3545.86	0.00
22	2	10	114	NYNEX TE	42.01	1	3466.62	3503.85	0.00
23	2	13	115	GIANT FO	124.28		3342.34	3503.85	0.00
24	2	15	116	GUS' AMO	56.91	1	3285.43	3446.94	0.00
25	2	19	117	IRS	478.29		2807.14	3446.94	0.00
26	2	19	1	CASH MAC	100.00		2707.14	3446.94	0.00
27									2707.14
28									0.00
29									0.00
30									0.00
31									0.00
32									0.00
33									0.00
34									0.00
35									0.00
36									0.00
37									0.00
38	--								
39	TOTALS						BALANCE: 2707.14		

Figure 3.1:   VisiCalc Checkbook

In this figure the first two columns handle the date. Both the month and the day are values, so that we can do things with them. VisiCalc and Multiplan do not have a date arithmetic feature, so to work with the calendar in these programs takes more calculations. In SuperCalc[3] we can manage the date differently, as we shall see.

At the top of the model is an entry for the number of the month in which the register starts. This is so that you don't have to type the month in each time—the value is carried down to the first row of the month column, and then replicated down (about far enough to manage a month's entries but it's not critical). When you start a new month you just add one to the value on the first entry, then replicate that down, and so on.

The next column is headed Check Number but it serves a greater purpose than just ordering the checks—this column will be used for the model to decide

Calling All Coordinates

if a transaction is a payment (outgoing funds) or a receipt (deposits, interest earned, etc). We shall see how this is done shortly. It is enough for now to notice that all payments or deductions from the account get a numeric designation (we have arbitrarily selected a "1" for debit memos, machine withdrawals, and so on). Checks get the number on the check, of course. Other transactions, such as deposits or other income, get an abbreviated word or legend: D for deposit, INT for interest payment, and so on. The alphabetic description of the transaction goes in the next column.

SpreadTip: There is a useful spreadsheeting trick here: You may notice that the column width for Description is not very wide. You do not have to use a wide column width, or more than one column to enter a lengthy description. Most spreadsheets will retain the entire contents of a text cell, even if the cell width is too narrow to display it all. If you have a long entry that is abbreviated in the display, and you forgot what the entry was, run the cursor over to it and the whole entry will be revealed on the prompt line. If the entry is still too long to read in the prompt line, enter the Edit command (/E in VisiCalc) and use the edit cursor keys to read to the end of the entry.

The next column, Amount (column E), is the dollars involved in the transaction, and they are all entered as positives—we will have the template take care of debits and credits.

The bank reconciliation process starts with the next column, column F, which is designed to have a "1" entered in it when a transaction appears on the bank statement—i.e., when your cancelled checks are returned.

The next two columns (G and H) look similar but they are different—the first, Checkbook Balance, replaces the running total that you have in your present (soon to be discarded!) checkbook register and is of course the uncommitted funds you have at your disposal. Column H is the running statement reconciliation. Each month, when you get your statement, all you have to do is mark in Column F the items that have cleared the bank, and the amount which appears as the last entry in this column should equal the bank statement's claims about your liquidity.

The Formulas

The spreadsheet technique we are demonstrating in this chapter is called "coordinate calls," the movement of data from one place to another in the template. We are going to look at the various ways this is done. Since most things are happening across columns, we will place all our example formulas in Row 7, that of the first transaction of the period.

First let's look at the column headed Checkbook Balance (Column G), in which a running total is kept of the money you haven't spent yet. The formula in this column is:

@IF(C7<1,+G6+E7,+G6−E7)

SpreadTalk: If the value in column C, the check number or transaction code, is less than one, which it will be if it is anything but a number, it must be a deposit or other form of income, so add it to the preceding balance. Conversely, if it is a number, it must be a check or other payment, so deduct it from the balance.

It is a pleasure not to have to remember to enter the amounts of transactions as pluses or minuses. Even some of the expensive bookkeeping programs require this (sometimes calling the darn stuff "debits" or "credits"!). This model takes care of that annoying necessity as a by-product of simply entering identification information in columns C and D, that you will perhaps need one day in order to trace a transaction.

Now look at column H, the Statement Balance. For most of us, this is only of interest once a month, when you get the bank's statement of your account. Of course, it might be critical if you are a sophisticated money manager working the "float," the amount of money that you have spent that the bank hasn't heard of yet. In this case you will be maintaining the column daily (and calling the bank to get news of the transactions clearing their books each day).

When the statement comes in you will go down column F putting a single digit "1" against each item, income or "outgo," that appears on the statement. When this is done, one recalculation and column H should show the same amount as the bank's close-of-period statement.

The formula that does the trick in this column is looking at the "if cleared" column, in the formula:

@IF(F7=1,@IF(C7<1,H6+E7,H6−E7),H6)

SpreadTalk: If the item has cleared, look at column C and see what kind of item it was. Then add to the preceding balance if a deposit, deduct if not. If it has not cleared, carry forward the current balance.

Entering the Data

The frequency with which you update the checkbook register is a matter of choice, but you will certainly enter the transactions from the check stubs at least once a month. You will know roughly how many checks and deposits you make each month, but unless you intend to keep a separate model for each month, there will be no "bottom" to the model, and the entries will keep on running down the template until either memory runs out or you decide to start a new one.

Our model has a totalling line in it at row 39. As we enter each transaction the area above the total fills and we add more formulas for the new data when necessary. This is done by /Replicating the formulas into the appropriate locations. When we reach the arbitrary line (row 39), and we want to continue entering data on this model, we move this total row down by inserting rows.

SpreadTip: In order to keep the Total formulas correct, our @SUM() formula includes the dotted lines in row 38 that separate the formulas from the total. It also includes the dotted line in row 4 that separates the titles from the data. As long as you insert rows between these two dotted lines, the @SUM() formula will automatically update itself to include the new rows.

Remember that spreadsheet programs automatically update for added rows and columns *but only for formulas appearing to the right and/or below the added material.* Always try and arrange things in a way that an added new row at the top or bottom of an existing range will be certain to be included, as we have done.

You may want to replicate all the formulas in every location between the two dotted lines from the titles to the total line to be ready, but if not you will periodically replicate the last horizontal row down a few more rows (always above the total line!) to accommodate the next entries.

Tricks of the Trade

That is really all there is to the check register, but there are a couple more tricks of the trade we have built that are worth looking at—they will be useful in other models too. They, too, call values from different places in the model, but have their unique characteristics.

Notice that on the TOTALS row there is a simple entry BALANCE. It matches the last entry in the column that has been running down the model as we entered checks and deposits, adjusting to the current situation as it went. To get the BALANCE on the Totals row all we have to do is call that last location, which is H26 in our illustration, right? Right, but. . . if you add rows below H26 as new transactions are entered, you are, of course, calling the wrong location for current balance.

Another solution might be to run the formula in this column all the way down to the dotted-line, which would mean that the last transaction row entry would be repeated, then pick up the last entry before the line. That would work, even though it would look ugly.

But there would be another problem. While spreadsheets adjust the formulas for an added (or moved) column or row, they only do it for locations to the right or below the addition. Calls to locations above or to the left of the inserted space are left unchanged. So if you were calling the location immediately above the dotted line, then finally got to the point that you had to move the dotted line down for more entries, the call in BALANCE would not change.

Our solution is a neat one that can be used in lots of other applications—and it is in the far right column (column K), called (strangely enough!) BALANCE. The formula on each row of the model is (this example is the location showing a value in the model, K27)

@IF(H27+H26=H26,H26,0)

SpreadTalk: If current row plus last row equals last row, enter last row value, otherwise zero. Note that this calculation has produced a value only on the row that *follows* the actual current balance. Obviously this formula will only contain a value other than zero if the coordinate immediately following the last is zero.

This formula works just fine in virtually all running total columns, because even if a zero appears in the total column as a result of the operations used, the effect in column K is correct —in order to produce that zero the column would have to be "zeroed out" by entering a transaction that offset the balance (a check written for the balance in the account, for instance).

Now we can go back to the entry on the totals row called BALANCE (H39 in our model). The formula that gives the value is

@MAX(K4...K38)

VisiCalc looks up the column and brings back the largest number it finds—and since there is only one that is not zero, we have our current balance.

Naturally the column that does this work for us, in our case K, is placed in the matrix out of the way and is never printed out. But it has very valuable functions, because now we can call and use a figure that is constantly changing as entries are made with absolute confidence that we will have the current last figure. This will be useful in all kinds of situations.

SUMMING UP

In this model you have learned how to move data about the spreadsheet using several different Calling techniques. You have moved data simply by referencing one cell, you have data using IF statements, you have called data into a vertical column from a horizontal row, and you have learned how to have your Calling formulas automatically update themselves (inserting rows between the two @Sum ranges, and using the Running Total and @Max column in the Current Balance formula). We bet you never knew there were so many ways to call on data!

OtherCalcs

Multiplan

This model will work in much the same way in Multiplan. There are some ways in which the instructions would be different in this program, though. The Replicating process in Multiplan is done with the Copy command. To replicate the formulas in the model down the columns you would either use the Copy From command to copy all of the cells in the first row into the rest of the data section, or you would use the Copy Down command to copy the first cell in a column Down into the rest of the column. You have to take care when constructing your formulas because you have to specify whether a reference is Relative or Absolute when you construct the first formula.

One final refinement in Multiplan will allow you to protect the Running Total column (Column K or 11). You can use the Lock command to protect all of the formulas in the column, so that they are not ever inadvertently written over. You can also use the Lock command to protect all of the other formulas in the model to prevent disasters from happening when other people use your model.

SuperCalc[3]

There are no special differences between the VisiCalc model outlined above and SuperCalc[3], with the exception of how the transactions are dated. In SuperCalc[3] you can use the formula

DATE(MM,DD,YY)

to enter the date in a cell. You can then use this cell in other formulas to write the next dates. For example, if you put the formula

DATE(01,01,85)

in cell A5, you can enter the next date (January 4) in cell A6 be writing the formula

A5 + 3

You can see how this would look in Figure 3.2.

	A	B	C	D	E	F	G	H	I	K
1						ENTER	CHECK-	STATE-		CURRENT
2			CHECK	TO/	AMOUNT	1 IF	BOOK	MENT		BALANCE
3	YEAR 1985		NUMBER	FROM	CHK/DEP	CLEARED	BALANCE	BALANCE		**DO NOT
4	-------		-------	--------	-------	-------	--------	--------		TOUCH**
5	1/ 1/85		OPENING	BALANCE	4032.56		4032.56	4032.56		
6	1/ 4/85		101	RENTCO	675.00	1	3357.56	3357.56		0.00
7	1/ 6/85		102	GIANT FO	135.76	1	3221.80	3221.80		0.00
8	1/ 7/85		103	VISA	175.00	1	3046.80	3046.80		0.00
9	1/ 7/85		104	RED CROS	250.00	1	2796.80	2796.80		0.00
10	1/ 7/85		105	NE UTILI	35.76	1	2761.04	2761.04		0.00
11	1/ 7/85		106	NYNEX TE	47.84	1	2713.20	2713.20		0.00
12	1/14/85		107	MARSHALL	32.43	1	2680.77	2680.77		0.00
13	1/24/85		108	DR. MOLA	75.00	1	2605.77	2605.77		0.00
14	1/30/85		D	DEPOSIT	1873.24	1	4479.01	4479.01		0.00
15	1/31/85		109	BLOOMING	25.00	1	4454.01	4454.01		0.00
16	2/ 1/85		1	SERVICE	6.00	1	4448.01	4448.01		0.00
17	2/ 1/85		INT	INTEREST	23.40	1	4471.41	4471.41		0.00
18	2/ 4/85		110	RENTCO.	675.00	1	3796.41	3796.41		0.00
19	2/10/85		111	VISA	78.42	1	3717.99	3717.99		0.00
20	2/10/85		112	GLOBE IN	172.13	1	3545.86	3545.86		0.00
21	2/10/85		113	NE UTILI	37.23		3508.63	3545.86		0.00
22	2/10/85		114	NYNEX TE	42.01	1	3466.62	3503.85		0.00
23	2/13/85		115	GIANT FO	124.28		3342.34	3503.85		0.00
24	2/15/85		116	GUS' AMO	56.91	1	3285.43	3446.94		0.00
25	2/19/85		117	IRS	478.29		2807.14	3446.94		0.00
26	2/19/85		1	CASH MAC	100.00		2707.14	3446.94		0.00
27										2707.14
28										0.00
29										0.00
30										0.00
31										0.00
32										0.00
33										0.00
34										0.00
35										0.00
36										0.00
37										0.00
38	-------									
39	TOTALS						BALANCE:	2707.14		

Figure 3.2: SuperCalc³ Checkbook

You might also wish to use the /Protect command to prevent those disastrous mistakes that can happen when you don't pay attention to the cursor location. Just hit /P, enter the range of formulas that you want to protect, and hit return. No more accidents!

Let's LOOKUP Our Local Quick Printer

SPREADSHEET FUNCTIONS: LOOKUP
FEATURED PROGRAM: SuperCalc³
TEMPLATE FUNCTION: Estimating and Invoicing

BACKGROUNDER

One of the features of spreadsheet programs that really sparked the excitement of the early users, and which has come to be a basic function in many spreadsheet templates, is the LOOKUP function. This is the ability that the program has to be instructed to go to an area of a model in which is stored a formatted "table," and retrieve a value stored there that matches a preset parameter.

To illustrate the function, we are going to use a model that is designed as both an estimator (forecasts the cost of a series of choices) and an invoicer (bills the customer if the estimate is accepted and the work delivered). Our hypothetical operation, the Quick and Clean Print Shop, was chosen because all of us at one time or another have visited such an establishment, and it should be easy to adapt the principles we demonstrate to many other situations.

A spreadsheet LOOKUP table is a matrix in which you can look up an item in the left-hand column, and can find a corresponding value that applies in the right, or adjacent, space. This is much like looking up a phone number—you find the name and the number is right beside it. Spreadsheets generally LOOKUP values instead of names, but expect to find and bring back a corresponding value, stored right beside it.

The table can be inserted in either a vertical or horizontal format but there are two strict rules: the LOOKUP side of the table (left in vertical, or top in horizontal) must have its values in ascending order, and the LOOKUP side and the corresponding "bringback" values must not be separated by space.

The action that a spreadsheet program takes on encountering the LOOKUP instruction is the same among all programs (see the chapter's end for the slight differences in syntax of the command). In SuperCalc³, our featured program for this chapter, the structure is:

LOOKUP(X,G1:G10)

SpreadTalk: The explanation for this formula is "Hey, SuperCalc, go LOOKUP X in the table you will find between G1 and G10, and bring back the value opposite it." The range then in a LOOKUP formula is always the range for the LOOKedUP value, not the bringback values. (This is slightly different in Multiplan. See the section at the chapter's end to understand the differences.)

In this example X can be a number value or the result of a formula. SuperCalc pops off to the table, runs its eye down or across the list, finds X, reads the value opposite, and writes this result in the formula location.

What if it doesn't find it? We thought you'd never ask. The creators of spreadsheets took care of that too. From now on the answer to the claim of a near miss "only in horseshoes," has another option: "only in LOOKUP tables"! The spreadsheet program looks until it finds a match, *or until the value sought has been exceeded*. It then drops back one and delivers the next previous bringback value. Looking for 4.5 in a numerical sequence of 1–10, it will find 5, note that it exceeds 4.5, and drop back and deliver the value opposite 4.

If the number sought is larger than any other in the list, the topmost value is brought back, which is the same rule: when the number is exceeded, bring back the one before. If the number is less than any in the range (for instance, looking up −1 in the numerical 1–10 sequence), then spreadsheets give you N/A for Not Available.

APPLICATION SPREADSHEET

The Invoice and Estimating Template

Let's use this feature for our scenario with Fred and his Quick and Clean Print Shop. The model shown in Figures 4.1 through 4.4 is up and waiting on the computer in his shop all day. Fred does a lot of estimating (much of it on the phone) and often has to produce bids in writing for printing jobs.

It is mostly a cash business but he does have some accounts that have a credit line—as a rule he prepares an invoice for every job, when it is completed,

Let's LOOKUP Our Local Quick Printer

	A	B	C	D	E	F	G	H	I	J	K	L	M	N	O
1	DO NOT DISTURB!			DO NOT DISTURB!				DO NOT DISTURB!						
2			RATE SCHEDULE												
3															
4	NUMBER OF COPIES		75	125	250	350	450	550	650	750	850	950	1000	PAPER	PRICE/1
5	COST		3.00	4.25	6.25	7.50	9.00	10.00	11.00	12.00	13.00	14.00	16.00	TYPE	SHEET!
6	ADDITIONAL 1000'S		12.50											1	.005!
7														2	.006!
8	BINDERY CHARGE		STAPLE	COLLATE	CUT	FOLD	STITCH							3	.007!
9	PER 100		0.23	0.43	0.63	0.83	0.93							4	.011
10	MINIMUM CHARGE		1.00	2.00	3.00	4.00	5.00							5	.015!
11														6	.018!
12	DO NOT DISTURB!			DO NOT DISTURB!				DO NOT DISTURB!							
13	==

Figure 4.1: LOOKUP Tables

```
              A         B         C         D         E
        16 DATA INPUT AREA:
        17 ------------------
        18 NUMBER OF ORIGINALS        :      300
        19 PAPER QUALITY (ENTER 1-6)  :        2
        20 NUMBER OF COPIES OF EACH   :      200
        21 ------------------------
        22            INPUT 1 IF YES
        23            INPUT 0 IF NO
        24
        25            STAPLE   WANTED        1
        26            COLLATE  WANTED        1
        27            CUT      WANTED        1
        28            FOLD     WANTED        1
        29            STITCH   WANTED        1
        30
        31 INVOICE AT A33-G67    ESTIMATE AT I33-O67
```

Figure 4.2:   Data Entry Area

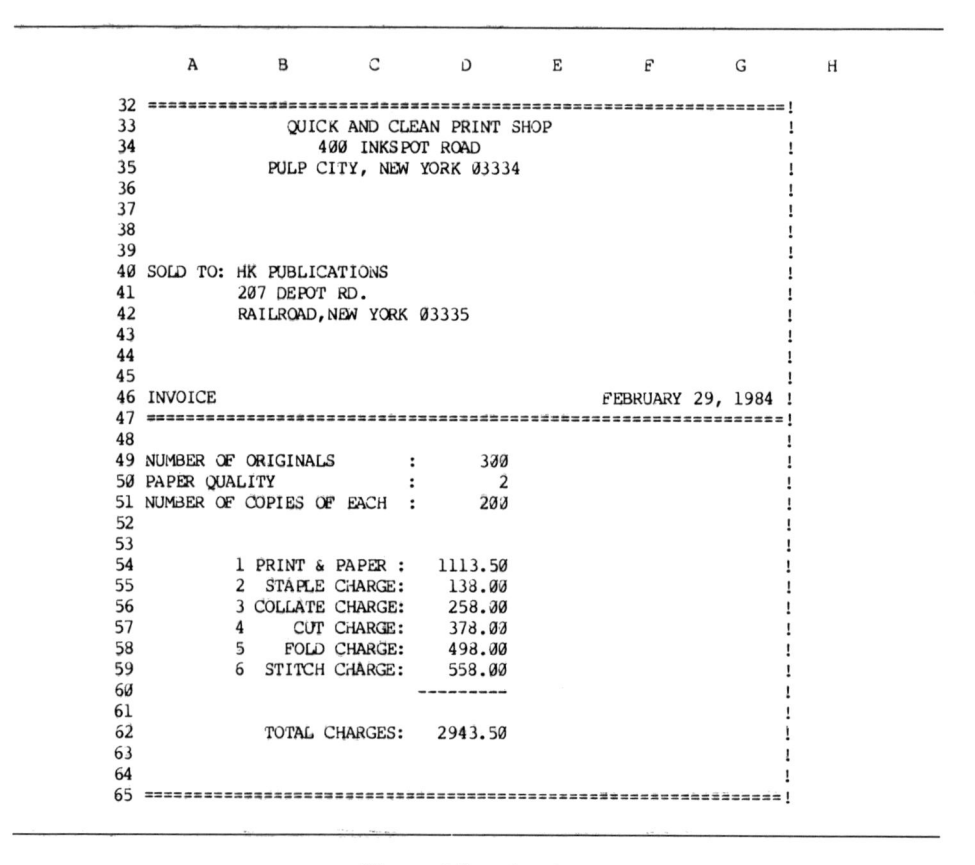

```
           A        B         C        D        E        F        G         H
        32 ================================================================!
        33             QUICK AND CLEAN PRINT SHOP                           !
        34                  400 INKSPOT ROAD                                !
        35              PULP CITY, NEW YORK 03334                           !
        36                                                                  !
        37                                                                  !
        38                                                                  !
        39                                                                  !
        40 SOLD TO: HK PUBLICATIONS                                         !
        41          207 DEPOT RD.                                           !
        42          RAILROAD, NEW YORK 03335                                !
        43                                                                  !
        44                                                                  !
        45                                                                  !
        46 INVOICE                                   FEBRUARY 29, 1984      !
        47 ================================================================!
        48                                                                  !
        49 NUMBER OF ORIGINALS       :    300                               !
        50 PAPER QUALITY             :      2                               !
        51 NUMBER OF COPIES OF EACH  :    200                               !
        52                                                                  !
        53                                                                  !
        54         1  PRINT & PAPER :   1113.50                             !
        55         2  STAPLE CHARGE:     138.00                             !
        56         3  COLLATE CHARGE:    258.00                             !
        57         4     CUT CHARGE:     378.00                             !
        58         5    FOLD CHARGE:     498.00                             !
        59         6  STITCH CHARGE:     558.00                             !
        60                              ---------                           !
        61                                                                  !
        62            TOTAL CHARGES:    2943.50                             !
        63                                                                  !
        64                                                                  !
        65 ================================================================!
```

Figure 4.3:   Invoice

```
                I      J       K       L       M       N
        32      !=====================================================!
        33      !             QUICK AND CLEAN PRINT SHOP              !
        34      !                  400 INKSPOT ROAD                   !
        35      !               PULP CITY, NEW YORK 03334             !
        36      !                                                     !
        37      !                                                     !
        38      !   JOB COST ESTIMATE FOR:                            !
        39      !                                                     !
        40      !                                                     !
        41      !                                                     !
        42      !                                                     !
        43      !=====================================================!
        44      !                                                     !
        45      !   NUMBER OF ORIGINALS         :       300           !
        46      !   NUMBER OF COPIES OF EACH    :       200           !
        47      !   PAPER TYPE (ENTER 1-6)      :         2           !
        48      !                                                     !
        49      !   1 PRINT & PAPER ESTIMATE         1113.50          !
        50      !   2    STAPLE ESTIMATE              138.00          !
        51      !   3 COLLATE ESTIMATE                258.00          !
        52      !   4       CUT ESTIMATE              378.00          !
        53      !   5      FOLD ESTIMATE              498.00          !
        54      !   6    STITCH ESTIMATE              558.00          !
        55      !                                    ---------        !
        56      !                                                     !
        57      !              TOTAL ESTIMATE:       2943.50          !
        58      !                                                     !
        59      !=====================================================!
```

Figure 4.4:   Estimate

so that when the customer collects, or he delivers, he has the invoice ready to be paid or left for later payment.

When booted, the area shown in Figure 4.2 fills the screen, and when the request for an estimate comes in, Fred just plugs in the details, recalculates once and has the numbers ready in a flash to tell the customer. But the SuperCalc[3] program has done a lot in the flash, and we will review it step by step.

Fred gets certain information from the customer for the estimate. He needs to know how many originals are in the job, how many copies of each are required, the paper quality (he has six types available), and which, if any, of a variety of other services will be needed.

He enters the details straight to the keyboard during the conversation, in the places provided. In the services area he just puts a "1" against the selected operations.

The Formulas

The following is the jumbo-sized formula that calculates the cost of printing. It may look a bit intimidating at first but all it is is a simple (IF rather busy) IF statement:

LOOKUP(D18,N6:N11)*(D17*D19+IF(((D17*D19)<1000),
    (LOOKUP((D17*D19),C4:M4)),(((((D17*D19)−1000)/
    1000)*C6)+M5))

SpreadTalk: We will take this in sections. The first part of the formula looks up the paper quality and multiplies the price returned from the LOOKUP by the number of copies. Since Fred has no discount on the number of originals that are handled, only on the total number of copies printed, the formula checks if the originals times the copies required is less than a thousand (the level at which the printing is a flat rate per thousand). That is what is happening in the IF(((D17*D19)<1000), section of the formula.

If it is less than a thousand, the formula calls for a LOOKUP of the total copies in the horizontal table that stretches from C4 to M4, which as you can see in the top part of the model in Figure 4.1, contains the costs for certain breaks of quantity.

(LOOKUP((D17*D19),C4:M4))

If the formula has chosen to execute this LOOKUP, it will find the number in row 4 that eventually is larger than the one looked up, and bring back the associated cost. If on the other hand the number of copies is larger than one thousand, the following segment of the formula goes to work:

(((((D17*D19)−1000)/1000)*C6)+M5))

It first deducts 1000 from the total number of copies, then divides the remainder by 1000. This, of course, gives the number of thousands and part of a thousand, which is then multiplied by C6, the cost of additional thousands. The formula then adds the amount in M5, which pays for the first thousand.

We prefer to use vertical tables (we have used horizontal and vertical in this model) wherever possible, we guess because it is more the way in which one visualizes a table, and it also seems to take up less spreadsheet space.

The SpreadTalk for that formula took a long time to read (never mind to write!) but is in essence quite simple. One of the biggest dangers in entering this type of long formula is the danger of missing a parenthesis. Maybe you are an instinctive algebraic formula visualizer but your authors are not! Many shots are taken at getting it right—we know what we want to do but getting there is none of the fun.

SpreadTip: Our suggestion is to build the formula from the ground up. There will be a kernel in a formula that does the key action. Get that right and then add around it. If you make sure that you always add parentheses in pairs you should avoid trouble. The way to do this is to build each portion of the formula in an empty location. Once you know each segment is doing the right thing, you can add them together using the Edit command, and then put them into the desired location using the Replicate command with No Change references.

Adding the Extras

The formulas for calculating the charges for extras that have been ordered, indicated by the ones Fred adds at the time he gets the job, are all similar. This is the one for figuring the stapling charge:

IF(A24=1,(IF((((D17*D19)/100)*C9)<C10,C10,
(((D17*D19)/100)*C9))),0)

SpreadTalk: If this extra has been ordered, the formula first checks that the item does not qualify for the minimum charge, by finding the number of copies, dividing by 100 and multiplying by the cost per hundred in C9. If it is less than the dollar minimum charge, it inserts the dollar from C10. If it is more than the minimum, however, then the second calculation of the IF comes into play, and the number of copies divided by 100 is multiplied by the per 100 price.

This formula appears on each of the calculation lines in the estimate area and is used only when the column A entry is a "1".

The formula in D61 totals the charges:

SUM(D53:D61)

and now all Fred has to do is recalculate and the invoice or estimate is complete and ready to print out.

The model contains both an invoice section and an estimating section. Both are computed each time Fred does a recalculation, and all he has to do is print out the appropriate section depending on whether he was doing an estimate or totaling up an actual job. The formulas in the estimate section work in the same way that the formulas for the Invoice segment do. Only their locations and some of the labels are different.

A FEW LAST WORDS ON LOOKUP

LOOKUP tables can be either horizontal or vertical, and are often specially constructed and positioned for a purpose within a model. Remember, however, that LOOKUP formulas can use actual working parts of the model too.

For example, perhaps you have a list of numbers down a column— let's say it is a list of part numbers, with their associated prices beside them, in the next column, and these lists are in the main body of your model. If these part numbers are in ascending sequence, even if they are not consecutive, there is no need to create a special table elsewhere to LOOKUP prices. You can use the actual columns in the main model.

You can also use a table to LOOKUP a value and then later use that value that was brought back as the "target" value. In our theoretical Parts and Price List, you would put the first LOOKUP list (Part Number) in column one, the values (Prices) in column two, and the Parts List again in column three. Providing that the values are in ascending order you can use the first Parts list to LOOKUP a Price, then Price can be used to bring back the corresponding Part Number from the second Parts list. This type of LOOKUP is handy when you are doing things such as converting dates to their numeric values and then want to convert them back to their date. We use this utility in other applications in this book.

Some spreadsheet programs allow the movement of text around the matrix as a "textual value" (SuperCalc³ is one of them). This feature can be used in a LOOKUP table, too. Here is an example: your model has a location that produces a number that represents a day of the week, 1 for Sunday, 2 for Monday, and so on. To have the actual day appear, you construct a small table like this:

DAY#	DAYNAME
1	("Sunday")
2	("Monday")
3	("Tuesday")
4	("Wednesday")

and so on. When 2 is looked up, the word "Monday" appears, but without the quotation marks. By the way, this format, the parenthesis quote word quote parenthesis, is the SuperCalc³ format for a textual value, as opposed to a Text or label entry. In order for the LOOKUP to work with text, the text must be a Textual value. Regular labels just won't work.

OtherCalcs

Multiplan

In Multiplan there are several special requirements in using LOOKUP formulas. The formula syntax is different in that the LOOKUP range describes a rectangle—you must include the beginning coordinate of the LOOKUP list and the Ending coordinate of the Values list. For example:

	1	2
1	10	73
2	20	67
3	30	54
4	40	89

Let's LOOKUP Our Local Quick Printer

To LOOKUP a number from the LOOKUP table above, you would type the formula

    LOOKUP(20,R1C1:R4C2)

The result would of course be 67.

You have to describe the rectangular area that describes the table. If this rectangular area is wider than it is long, the LOOKUP will proceed horizontally. If the table is longer than it is wide or is square, the LOOKUP will proceed vertically.

Another important difference in the Multiplan LOOKUP function is that the tables don't have to be arranged with the values in the column adjacent to the LOOKUP list. To LOOKUP values in Column 3, in this table:

	1	2	3
1	10	73	100
2	20	67	200
3	30	54	300
4	40	89	400

you would use the formula

    LOOKUP(20,R1C1:R4C3)

The returned value would be 200 in this case.

Multiplan allows the use of text within formulas, but the text alone cannot be used within a LOOKUP table as in SuperCalc[3].

VisiCalc

In VisiCalc, the LOOKUP tables are used in the same manner as in SuperCalc. The LOOKUP list must be in ascending order, and the values must be in the column or row adjacent to the list. You can only look up values (no text) in a VisiCalc LOOKUP table.

5

There Are Three Sides to Every Question

SPREADSHEET FUNCTIONS: Trigonometric, CHOOSE
FEATURED PROGRAM: VisiCalc
TEMPLATE FUNCTION: Triangle Solver

BACKGROUNDER

Early purchasers of spreadsheet programs, particularly VisiCalc, which was after all the first, were curious about why the authors of the program had included some functions that seemed to have little use for the average business user: the trigonometric functions. No book that claims to be the "Compleat Spreadsheeter" can ignore them, however, so we are going to take a look at them here.

Most all spreadsheet programs have the trig functions, certainly our three featured programs do, so we will use the venerable VisiCalc for our application example, which is a triangle solver.

Apart from an example of how to use most of the trig functions, our model demonstrates a couple of other useful ideas in spreadsheeting. We will show a use of the "windows," the capability for dividing the computer CRT screen into sections, so that different parts of the template may be seen in each. This allows one to change a value or make another modification in one window and instantly see the effect in the other. Very useful for trying to make a budget forecast come out right, for instance!

There Are Three Sides to Every Question

The other idea is the use of windows to hide values, for those spreadsheet programs that do not have a built-in "hide" feature. This allows that the contents of a coordinate will not be revealed on the screen, or in a printout, but you can continue to use the location in formula calculations.

APPLICATION SPREADSHEET

Creating a Triangle Solver

One quickly realizes that there are many ways to solve for the unknowns in a triangle, so we have implemented four different triangle-solving strategies, each involving a different set of trigonometric equations. We will look at the complete model of our triangle solver in a moment (if you cannot wait it can be seen in Figure 5.2).

SpreadTip: In Figure 5.1 we have divided the display screen vertically into two windows. This provides an "entry" window (where information data are entered from the keyboard), and an "answer" window where the calculated angles, sides, area and perimeter are displayed. As with most spreadsheet programs if you arrange your screen the way you want it and then SAVE it, when you reload the template the screen will arrange itself as you intended. This is very useful for directing attention away from parts of the model that you do not

```
              A          B                K
    5    TRIANGLE    SOLVER         5
    6    =====================      6    PRESS !
    7                                7    TWICE TO
    8           ENTER KNOWN          8    CALCULATE
    9           PARTS HERE           9    ALL PARTS
   10                               10
   11                ENTRIES        11        VALUES
   12    --------------------       12    ----------
   13                               13
   14       SIDE A     56.00        14         56.00
   15       SIDE B     79.20        15         79.20
   16       SIDE C                  16         90.62
   17                               17
   18       ANGLE A                 18         37.76
   19       ANGLE B    60.00        19         60.00
   20       ANGLE C                 20         82.24
   21                               21
   22    --------------------       22    ----------
   23       PERIMETER               23        225.82
   24       AREA                    24       2197.30
```

Figure 5.1: Data Entry and Solution Area

wish to highlight, or that are irrelevant to the purpose for which the model is to be used.

In this case we want to enter only the variable data, the "known" data, do a recalculation with the exclamation key, and then read just the answers.

There is a caveat with using this model. The various formulas we use expect to find the variable data (the "known") in specific positions in the input area, depending on what you are solving for. For instance, the known sides and angles will be entered into the positions B14...B16, and B18...B20 respectively.

The Sides. It is necessary that entries for the sides should be made in order, which means that the first known side is entered in B14, the second in B15, etc. If, for example, two sides are known and they are entered in B15 and B16, or B14 and B16, the model will be unable to calculate the answers correctly.

The Angles. The known angles should be input according to the specific instructions that will be found with the explanation of the various formulas and processes that our model uses. Each angle-solving strategy has slightly different requirements, depending on the relationship of the known angles to the known sides.

Once the knowns are input, the model is recalculated twice (!,!), and the answers appear in column K: sides in K14, K15, and K16; angles in K18, K19, and K20; perimeter in K23; and area in K24.

The Hidden Work Area

All the work in this model occurs in Columns D through J which are hidden from view. They are hidden because we do not want anyone to inadvertently wipe out a formula, and it is not necessary to see the formula area to use the model. We can look at how these columns are set up in Figure 5.2. There are four different calculation strategies that are specific to the different combinations of parts that are known.

The calculations are done:

in column E, if one side and any two angles are known
in column F, if two sides and either nonincluded angle is known
in column G, if two sides and the included angle are known
in column H, if three sides are known

The Key Radian Calculation

You can see a small calculation area in Figure 5.2, in column D, in which any of the known angles from Column B, Rows 18...20 are converted into Radians for use in the triangle calculation formulas. The formula that does this is

There Are Three Sides to Every Question

```
          D        E        F        G        H        I        J
  1
  2
  3            SOLUTION METHOD      SOLUTION METHOD
  4            =========================================
  5            !1 SIDE &!2 SIDES  !2 SIDES  !3 SIDES  !
  6            !ANY TWO !(A&B) &  !(A & B)  &!KNOWN   !
  7            !ANGLES  !ANY NON- !INCLUDED !         !
  8            !KNOWN   !INCLUDED !ANGLE    !         !
  9            !        !(ANGLE   !(KNOWN   !         !
 10            !(KNOWN  !CAN BE A !ANGLE =  !         !
 11   RADIANS  ! SIDE=A)!OR B)    !ANGLE C) !         !                ANSWRS
 12   ---------------------------------------------------              ----------
 13
 14                     56.00    56.00    56.00    56.00               56.00
 15                     56.00    79.20    79.20    79.20               79.20
 16                     56.00    90.62    23.20     0.00               90.62
 17
 18    0.00    2.09     0.66     0.00     ERROR                         0.66
 19    1.05    1.05     1.05     0.00     ERROR                         1.05
 20    0.00    2.09     1.44     0.00     ERROR                         1.44
 21
 22
 23                     3.14     0.00
```

Figure 5.2   VisiCalc Solution Matrix

@PI*B18/180

SpreadTalk: Multiply the mathematical constant PI by the known angle divided by 180. This formula is replicated in D18, D19, and D20. If there is no known angle the formula evaluates to zero. The model then uses all known parts to calculate the unknowns for the four methods, which we are going to review one at a time.

Solving Methodologies
Known: One Side and Any Two Angles

In Figure 5.3 we see a triangle with One Side and any Two Angles known. To make use of this part of the template, the known side must be entered as Side A in B14. The angles can be entered into any of the locations, B18...B20. The formulas (seen below) then calculate the unknown angle from B18, B19, or B20 at E18, E19, or E20, wherever it occurs. This calculation uses the rule that the sum of a triangle's angles is PI radians or 180 degrees.

>E14   +B14
>E15   @SIN(E19)*B14/@SIN(E18)

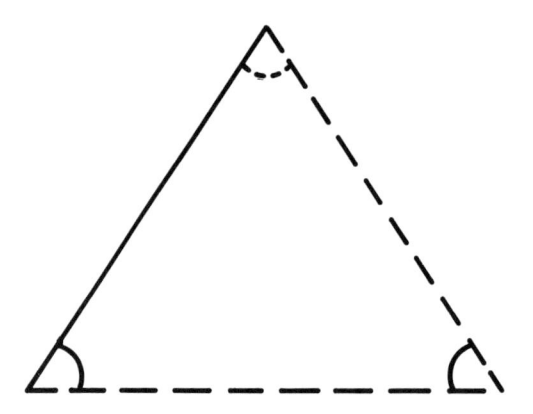

Figure 5.3 The Known Side(s) and Angle(s)

>E16   @SIN(E20)*B14/@SIN(E18)
>E18   @IF(B18=0,@PI−@SUM(D18...D20),D18)
>E19   @IF(B19=0,@PI−@SUM(D18...D20),D19)
>E20   @IF(B20=0,@PI−@SUM(D18...D20),D20)

After the unknown angle is calculated, the formulas at E15 and E16 calculate the length of the unknown sides using the Law of Sines. It is necessary to do two recalculations (! twice) to arrive at the answer, as the formulas in E16 and E17 depend on answers from E18...E20.

Known: Two Sides and Either Nonincluded Angle

As Figure 5.4 shows, the calculations in this area presuppose that the length of two sides of the triangle, and one of the angles is known, BUT the angle is not the angle between the two known sides. The list below contains the formulas which perform this set of calculations.

>F14   +B14
>F15   +B15
>F16   @SQRT((F14*F14)+(F15*F15)−(2*F14*F15*@COS(F20)))
>F18   @IF(D18=0,@ASIN(@SIN(F19)*F14/F15),D18)
>F19   @IF(D19=0,@ASIN(@SIN(F18)*F15/F14),D19)
>F20   @PI−F19−F18

There Are Three Sides to Every Question   41

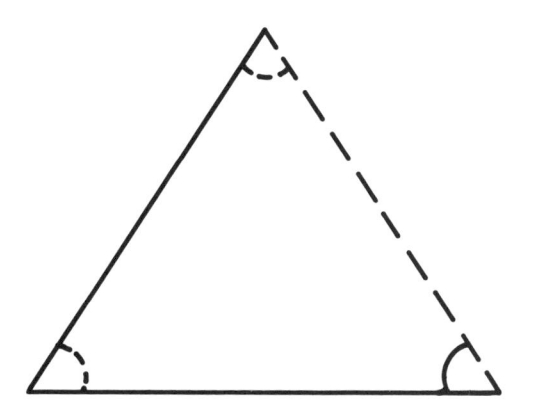

Figure 5.4 The Known Side(s) and Angle(s)

In this case the known sides must be entered as Side A and Side B. The angle will be entered as either Angle A or Angle B. The Law of Sines is used along with an @IF statement in F18 and F19 to calculate the missing A or B angle, and the Sum-of-Angles is used to calculate Angle C at F20. The unknown side will be calculated at F16 using the Law of Cosines.

Known: Two Sides and the Included Angle

Figure 5.5 is an illustration of a triangle with Two Sides and their Included Angle known. In this case the known sides are entered as Sides A and B in B14 and B15, and the known angle is entered at B20 as Angle C. It is very important that the known angle be entered in B20, otherwise the answers will not come out right! The formulas as listed here calculate the unknowns in Column G.

```
>G14     +B14
>G15     +B15
>G16     ;caSQRT(G14*G14+(G15*G15)-(2*G14*G15*@COS(G20)))
>G18     @ASIN(@SIN(G20)*G14/G16)
>G19     @ASIN(@SIN(G20)*G15/G16)
>G20     @PI*B20/180
```

The Law of Cosines is used in the formula at G16 to determine the length of the missing side. The missing angles are then calculated using the Law of Sines at G18 and G19.

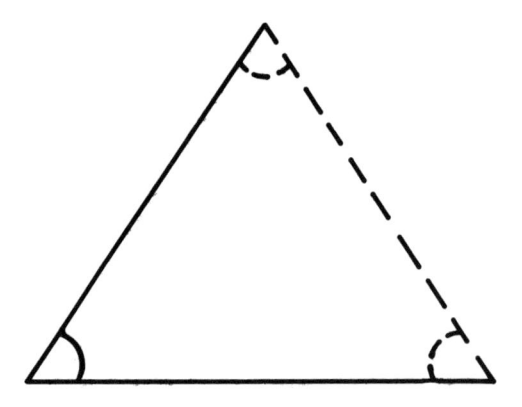

Figure 5.5 The Known Side(s) and Angle(s)

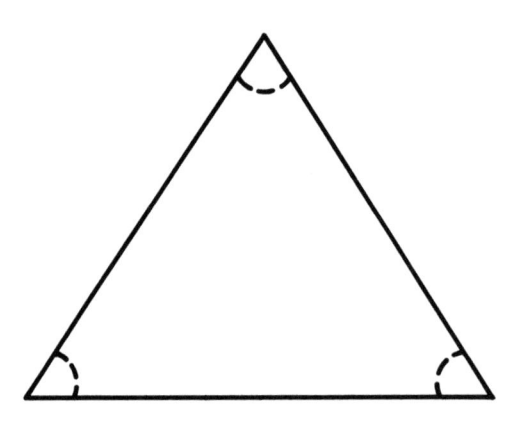

Figure 5.6 The Known Side(s) and Angle(s)

Known: All Three Sides

The last strategy that can be used to solve the triangle is one in which all three sides are known. You see this indicated in Figure 5.6. The formulas for this strategy, which is evaluated in column H, are as follows:

>H14   +B14
>H15   +B15
>H16   +B16
>H18   @ACOS(H14*H14−(H15*H15)−(H16*H16)/(−2*H15*H16))
>H19   @ASIN(@SIN(H18)*H15/H14)
>H20   @PI−H19−H18

The sides are entered in B14, B15, and B16. VisiCalc then uses the Law of Cosines to solve for Angle A at H18. This law could also be used to determine the other two angles, but in this case it is simpler to use the Law of Sines formula at H19 to calculate Angle B and then to use the Sum-of-Angles formula to calculate Angle C because less computation is required.

Choosing the Correct Strategy

How does the spreadsheet program know which strategy to use to solve for the missing parts? The formulas in Column J that begin with @CHOOSE are the ones that pick the correct answer based on the known sides entered in column B.

There is one wrinkle though: by itself @CHOOSE can't distinguish between the second and third methods because they both involve the input of two known sides. To allow VisiCalc to make this distinction, an @IF formula must be included in the @CHOOSE formula. If two sides are entered in column B, the @CHOOSE formula narrows the possibilities down to the "Two Sides and Nonincluded Angle" and "Two Sides Included Angle" strategies, and then the @IF portion of the formula picks the correct one to use. The whole formula looks like this:

@CHOOSE(@COUNT(B14...B16),E14,
@IF(@COUNT(B18...B19)=1,F14,G14),H14

SpreadTalk: Choose the correct answer by counting how many sides are known (input in B14:B16). If one side is known, the correct answer is in column E. If two sides are known, then see whether the known angle is the included angle or a non included angle by counting the number of entries in B18...B19. If it is a non included angle (@COUNT(B18...B19)=1), then the correct answer is in column F. If it is the included angle, then the correct answer is in column G. If the number of known sides is three, the correct answer is in column H.

All of the answers are selected on column J using this neat @CHOOSE formula, adjusted of course relatively. You may ask: if the answers appear in column J, then why is the model set up to place the answers in column K? In the beginning of this chapter we told you that all the angles we calculated were in

Radians and we want to change them back to Degrees, so the formulas in column K, Rows 18–20 do just that. They look like this:

+J20*180/@PI.

The formulas in K14...K16 just transfer the answer chosen for the length of the sides from column J to column K. At K23 the answer for the Perimeter is transferred from J23 where it was calculated using the formula

@SUM(J14...J16)

The final formula in this model is at K24, and that is the Area formula:

+K14*K15*@SIN(J20)/2.

SUMMARY

The mathematicians among you will know that in some cases there are two triangle solutions which will fit a particular set of known sides. In this case, the model does not attempt to find both answers. The template will solve the problem using the "acute angle" formula, rather than the "obtuse angle" method.

Well that's it. If it helps the kids do their homework then that is a blessing. But it may help a businessman who needs to design a new parking lot, see if a piece of furniture will fit somewhere, or who knows, may just give you some fun.

OtherCalcs

Multiplan

In Multiplan this template had to be changed due to the fact that the program does not have the ASIN and ACOS built-in functions. Multiplan does have the ATAN function that will allow you to calculate the ASIN and ACOS values. The formulas that do this are

ASIN(N) = ATAN(N/SQRT(1 − N*N))

and

ACOS(N) = PI()/2 − ATAN(N/SQRT(1 − N*N))

Substitute these formulas into the appropriate VisiCalc formulas where ASIN and ACOS are used and your model will calculate away very happily.

One other change that was made to this template for use in Multiplan was to the formulas that @CHOOSE the correct answer from the solution columns. Multiplan's equivalent to @CHOOSE is the INDEX function. It works similarly to @CHOOSE, but not quite the same.

When we converted the ASIN and ACOS formulas we found it convenient to insert some extra columns for preliminary calculations to make our formulas easier to write and read (See Figure 5.7). Inserting the extra columns caused the computed answer sets to shift slightly. The answers for One Side-Two Angles was still in column 5. The answers for Two Sides-Included Angle were now in column 7. Two Sides-Nonincluded Angle was in column 9, and Three Sides in column 11. This caused the INDEX function to not work the way we wanted it as the columns from which the answers were selected were now out of sequence.

To get around this we wrote another formula to do the selection. The generic formula is:

```
IF(COUNT(KNOWN SIDES) = 1,ANSWER IN COLUMN 5,
       IF(COUNT(ANGLES A&B) = 1,ANSWERS IN COLUMN 7,
           IF(COUNT(KNOWN SIDES) = 3,ANSWERS IN
               COLUMN 11,
                   OTHERWISE ANSWERS IN COLUMN 9)))
```

This formula was put into Column 12 where the answer sets are selected.

Because of the way in which Multiplan does a recalculation it is not necessary to do two recalcs in order to arrive at the answers.

SuperCalc³

As in Multiplan, you will not find the ACOS trigonometric feature in SuperCalc³, although it does have the ATAN function. Make a similar substitution to that suggested earlier for Multiplan.

When we converted the ASIN and ACOS formulas we found it convenient to insert some extra columns for preliminary calculations to make our formulas easier to write and read (See Figure 5.8). Inserting the extra columns caused the computed answer sets to shift slightly. The answers for One Side-Two Angles was still in column E. The answers for Two Sides-Included Angle were now in column G. Two Sides-Nonincluded Angle was in column I, and Three Sides in column K.

A bigger problem than the @ASIN and @ACOS one is the absence of @CHOOSE, which is not so usefully replaced as in Multiplan (with INDEX).

	4	5	6	7	8	9	10	11	12	13
				SOLUTION		METHOD				
		1 SIDE & ANY TWO ANGLES KNOWN		2 SIDES & EITHER NON-IN- CLUDED ANGLE KNOWN		2 SIDES & INCLUDED ANGLE KNOWN		3 SIDES KNOWN		ANSWRS
	RADIANS	(KNOWN SIDE=A)								
14		45.00		45.00		45.00		45.00	2.00	45.00
15		45.00		37.40		37.40		37.40		37.40
16		45.00		82.40		45.92		0.00		45.92
18	0.00	1.97	0.00	0.00	0.90	1.12	#DIV/0!	#DIV/0!		1.12
19	0.00	1.97	0.00	0.00	0.75	0.85	#DIV/0!	#DIV/0!		0.85
20	1.17	1.17		3.14		1.17		#DIV/0!		1.17
23				3.14		3.14				128.32

Figure 5.7 Multiplan Solution Matrix

There Are Three Sides to Every Question

	D	E	F	G	H	I	J	K	L	M
1										
2				SOLUTION		METHOD				
3										
4		1 SIDE &		2 SIDES &		2 SIDES &		3 SIDES		
5		ANY TWO		EITHER		INCLUDED		KNOWN		
6		ANGLES		NON-IN-		ANGLE				
7		KNOWN		CLUDED		KNOWN				
8				ANGLE						
9		(KNOWN		KNOWN						ANSWRS
10		SIDE=A)								
11	RADIANS									
12										
13										
14		45.00		45.00		45.00		45.00	1.00	45.00
15		45.00		37.40		37.40		37.40	2.00	37.40
16		45.00		82.40		45.92		0.00		45.92
17										
18	0.00	1.97	0.00	0.00	0.90	1.12	ERROR	ERROR		1.12
19	0.00	1.97	0.00	0.00	0.75	0.85	ERROR	ERROR		0.85
20	1.17	1.17		3.14		1.17		ERROR		1.17
21										
22				3.14		3.14				128.32
23										

Figure 5.8 SuperCalc³ Solution Matrix

The recommended formula structure to achieve the same effect as @CHOOSE in VisiCalc is quite different:

VisiCalc: @CHOOSE(v,item1,item2,item3,item4,item5,. .
SuperCalc³: (INT(v)*item1,INT(v)*item1,INT(v)*item1,. . .

Because this structure is not easily interpreted we have @CHOSEN (excuse us, we couldn't resist) to change the SuperCalc model somewhat. First, we place the formula:

COUNT(B14:B16)

at L14 in the model. At L15 we place the formula

COUNT(B18:B19)

Now in column M (remember we had to shift our model) we can input the formula:

IF(L14=1,E14,IF(AND(L14=2,L15=1,G14),
 IF(AND(L14=2,L15<>1,I14,K14))

SpreadTalk: If One Side is known, the correct answer is in column E. If Two Sides are known, then see whether the known angle is the Included Angle or a Nonincluded Angle by counting the number of entries in B18:B19. If it is a Nonincluded Angle, (COUNT(B18:B19)=1), then the correct answer is in column G. If it is the Included Angle, then the correct answer is in column I. If the number of Known Sides is three, the correct answer is in column K.

6

Turning a Liability into an Asset

SPREADSHEET FUNCTIONS: Iteration, Forward References, Self Calls, Completion Tests, DELTA(), ITERCNT()
FEATURED PROGRAM: Multiplan
TEMPLATE FUNCTION: Income Statement and Balance Sheet

BACKGROUNDER

There are a couple of features of spreadsheets that sometimes cause annoyance. Sometimes they can cause more than that! They can create error conditions, give misleading information, result in your knowing only half the story, and worse! Fully understood, however, the negative features can be avoided and they can also be put to good use. They are "forward references" (references to a cell which is "ahead," to the right or below, depending on the order of recalculation) and "self calls," (formulas or instructions in a cell that call upon the cell itself).

Let's look at these one at a time, just to remind ourselves of the implications, then we will apply them both in a very useful model: the conditional Income Statement and Balance Sheet.

Forward References

When most spreadsheet programs perform a recalculation, which means running through all the locations in the matrix, updating the formula calculations for which each calls, they do it in one of two "orders": vertically by columns or horizontally by rows. All spreadsheet programs permit the operator to select the order of recalculation.

In the case of a vertical order (columns), the process starts at the top left coordinate in the matrix, runs down the first column, then goes up to the top of the second column and runs down that one. This process continues until all of the columns have been covered.

In a horizontal recalculation, again it starts in the top left corner of the model but this time runs out to the end of the first row, and then returns to the left to start the second row and so on until the model is covered.

In both of these processes, however, if the spreadsheet encounters a reference to a cell or coordinate that has not yet been recalculated in this pass, it picks up the PRESENT value of that cell and uses it—which in many cases might mean an incorrect result. This is the so-called "forward reference" to which we refer. Of course at the end of the pass the forward referenced cell will have been recalculated, and a second (sometimes it takes more than two!) recalculation will make everything correct.

Forward references most often get into models (unless they are intentional) as a result of moving rows and columns around during development and can pass unnoticed. It often takes intensive diagnostics to find them, too! The only clue to an inadvertent forward reference often comes by chance when you notice that a cell does not update when it is expected to. Generally all that can be done when this is discovered is to make certain that enough recalculations are done so that the answer is correct.

Sometimes changing the order of recalculation from vertical to horizontal (or vice versa) is all that is required. If a calculation at the bottom of the first column in a table of figures uses the total of the top row, on the right, then it can be easily seen that in the vertical mode when the process reaches the bottom spot the top right cell has not been done yet. Switch to a horizontal orientation and the top row will have been figured out early enough to be useful.

In some spreadsheet programs such as Multiplan though, the calculation proceeds in what is called "Natural Order." This means that formulas that depend on the calculation done in other formulas are not updated until the formulas depended upon are calculated. If you have many forward references in your model, you will find that you get an ERROR message when you attempt to perform a calculation. Multiplan will beep at you and tell you that "CIRCULAR REFERENCES ARE UNRESOLVED!" All is not lost at this point, however, because Multiplan gives you a means to solve the problem. We will be exploring this solution in our template.

Self Calls—and a Play Period!

Self calls (by this we mean including the cell address that you are writing the formula in in the actual formula) usually occur by mistake, i.e., a typo. The clue

Turning a Liability into an Asset 51

that it is happening is mostly an ERROR legend or a nonsense result. Self calls must be avoided if possible, but there is a useful side effect that can be employed in some circumstances. You will have to think of your own if you don't like ours, but we used it in developing a template to amuse (and educate!) children—a math exerciser game on VisiCalc.

The game kept a running score of correct answers to some math problems that appeared on the screen. It was a very simple matrix that had the questions on the left side of the model, and way off to the right the answers. When the player entered an answer, an asterisk (a "1" with the format set to asterisk) appeared if the answer was correct and nothing appeared if the answer was wrong.

But off to the right also was a diagnostic column that only we knew about. The kids were mystified when we could tell them how many tries it took to get an answer, and we were able to see just where they were having problems.

The matrix (a bit artificial since it appears to have variable column width, which is not a feature of VisiCalc!), with the formulas, looked like that shown in Figure 6.1.

SpreadTalk: The explanation of the TRIES formula is fairly simple. If the ANSWER equals the SOLUTION, add zero to the total that is already in M, otherwise add one.

We set the recalculation feature from automatic to manual, so that after every attempt at an answer, the player had to do a recalculation to know if the answer was right. The end of a typical session might look like that shown in Figure 6.2.

This indicates that the player has had a lot of tries at getting the third problem right, and that addition of larger numbers needs a bit of practice.

Incidentally this game worked only for a while and we have to blame VisiCalc. A hoped-for result of playing this game on the computer, besides get-

---

The Formulas, in their cells.

A	B	C	N	M
QUESTION	ANSWER	RIGHT	SOLUTIONS	TRIES
2 X 4		@IF(B=M,1,0)	(2*4)	@IF(B=M,M+0,M+1)
10 X 14		@IF(B=M,1,0)	(10*14)	@IF(B=M,M+0,M+1)
146 + 382		@IF(B=M,1,0)	(146+382)	@IF(B=M,M+0,M+1)
TOTAL CORRECT:		@SUM(COLUMN)	TOTAL TRIES:	@SUM(column)

Figure 6.1:   The Children's Game

	A	B	C	N	M
	QUESTION	ANSWER	RIGHT	SOLUTIONS	TRIES
	2 X 4	4	*	4	1
	10 X 14	140	*	140	2
	146 + 382	528	*	528	6
	TOTAL CORRECT:		3	TOTAL TRIES:	9

Figure 6.2: A Typical Game

ting them drilled in math, was that they would get interested in computing, and in VisiCalc. It worked very well in getting them interested in VisiCalc, and one of the kids soon figured out what we had done and rigged it so that they always got the right answer!

So you can see that sometimes it is desirable to have a cell call upon itself. However, if you are getting very odd numbers for a simple sum or other formula, check first to see if the formula is calling on itself.

APPLICATION SPREADSHEET

A Chicken and Egg Proposition

Our hypothesis in the following example matrix is that a small company has an arrangement with the bank that allows a floating credit line. From time to time the company treasurer must demonstrate to the bank that the business is sound enough to support the credit line.

This is a chicken and egg proposition, however, in the circumstances surrounding the supporting financial statement. A company's Balance Sheet is driven by the Income Statement. But an important component, line item if you like, of an Income Statement is the one called "Interest Expense." The Interest Expense cannot be calculated without knowing what the Notes Payable Liability is. And the Notes Payable is a factor related to the credit arrangement this company has with the bank!

This dilemma can be solved using repeated recalculations in most spreadsheets and some forward references, causing the Income Statement and Balance Sheet to "converge" with each recalculation. The complete balance sheet with supporting variable and assumption information can be see in Figure 6.3. Mul-

Turning a Liability into an Asset 53

```
            1          2          3          4         5        6        7        8        9
 1 INCOME STATEMENT AND BALANCE SHEET
 2    WITH INTEREST EXPENSE AND NOTES
 3    PAYABLE UNKNOWN
 4
 5
 6
 7
 8 NOTES/ASSMPTS.     INCOME STATEMENT (PROFIT&LOSS) & BALANCE SHEET
 9
10                     INCOME STATEMENT
11                     ----------------
12                                        Q1       Q2       Q3       Q4      TOTAL
13                                      -------  -------  -------  -------  -------
14 PERIODIC: ACTUAL   SALES              100000   120000   125000   200000   545000
15 % SALES   0.55     COST OF GOODS SOLD  55000    66000    68750   110000   299750
16                                      -------------------------------------------
17                    GROSS PROFIT        45000    54000    56250    90000   245250
18                                      -------------------------------------------
19                    OPERATING EXPENSES
20                    ------------------
21 % SALES   0.45     GEN & ADMIN         20250    24300    25313    40500   110363
22 % SALES   0.15     SELLING              6750     8100     8438    13500    36788
23 % SALES   0.10     RESEARCH & DEVEL.    4500     5400     5625     9000    24525
24                                      -------------------------------------------
25                    TOTAL OPER EXPENSE  31500    37800    39375    63000   171675
26                                      -------------------------------------------
27                    OPERATING INCOME    13500    16200    16875    27000    73575
28 INTEREST INCOME    OTHER INCOME            0        0        0        0        0
29                    INTEREST             1731     3935     4486    12752    22903
30                                      -------------------------------------------
31                    NET INC BEFORE TAX  11769    12265    12389    14248    50672
32 TAX RATE 0.32      INCOME TAXES         3766     3925     3965     4560    16215
33                                      -------------------------------------------
34                    NET INCOME           8003     8340     8425     9689    34457
35                                      ===========================================
36
37                    BALANCE SHEET
38                    -------------
39                    ASSETS              1/1      3/31     6/30     9/30    12/31
40                                       ----     ----     ----     ----    -----
41
42            2.50    CURRENT            225500   250000   300000   312500   500000
43 PERIODIC: ACTUAL   FIXED               45000    45000    45000    45000    45000
44 PERIODIC: ACTUAL   OTHER               10000    10000    10000    10000    10000
45                                      -------------------------------------------
46                    TOTAL ASSETS       280500   305000   355000   367500   555000
47                                      ===========================================
48
49                    LIABILITIES
50                    -----------
51 % COGS/IT 0.50     CURRENT             47500    29383    34962    36357    57280
52 INT RATE:20        NOTES PAYABLE           0    34614    78697    89718   255031
53                                      -------------------------------------------
54 EQUITY=            STOCKHOLDERS'
55 CAP STCK:200000    EQUITY             233000   241003   241340   241425   242689
56 RET EARN:33000                        -------------------------------------------
57 + INC YTD ROW 27
58                    TOTAL LIABILITIES  280500   305000   355000   367500   555000
59                                      ===========================================
60                                                 Q1       Q2       Q3       Q4
61
62                          COMPUTE INTEREST:     1731     3935     4486    12752
63                                                                           TRUE
```

Figure 6.3: Income Statement and Balance Sheet

tiplan however, has some difficulties with forward references as we mentioned before. It also has a unique and rather good method of resolving the forward reference problem.

Multiplan's solution is the ability to select an Iteration Option in the Options Command. The iteration option keeps Multiplan calculating away until all of the forward references formulas have been solved. No more CIRCULAR REFERENCES UNRESOLVED messages!

We will discuss this option more fully later on, but for now it is sufficient to know that the option exists and is in some cases preferable to doing multiple manual recalculations (mainly your fingers don't get tired, and you always know you are looking at the final answer!).

The Formulas

First, the assumptions and other necessary values are entered, and we (in our omnipotent position) have placed these in columns A and B, to drive key formulas throughout. Based on historical data, we have entered these crucial assumptions in the following locations (NOTE: most of the expense calculations are driven by the sales figures and a related percentage assumption.).

R15C2:	COGS Expense (% Sales)
R21C2:	General and Administrative Operating Expenses (% Sales)
R22C2:	Selling Expenses (% Sales)
R23C2:	R & D Expenses (% Sales)
R32C2:	Corporate Tax Rate
R42C2:	Current Assets (% Sales)
R51C2:	Current Liabilities (% COGS)
R52C2:	Interest Rate Paid on Bank Loan
R55C2:	Capital Stock ($)
R56C2:	Retained Earnings ($)

Next we entered those numbers that we could forecast (guesstimate) and which we knew from the books:

Row 14:	Estimated Sales for each quarter (columns 5:8)
Row 42:	Current Assets (column 5)
Row 43:	Fixed Assets (columns 5:8)
Row 44:	Other Assets (columns 5:8)
Row 51:	Current Liabilities (column 5)

The formulas for the various locations in the matrix will be found in the figure. We have chosen this method for showing the formulas in this chapter since most of them are obvious. There are, however, certain key ones that we will look at in depth. Since we are using a forward reference system if you are

Turning a Liability into an Asset

using this model in VisiCalc, there will be ERROR messages all over the place when you boot the model—this will perhaps worry you as you enter the formulas and get this result. Worry not—all will be cleared up in time! In Multiplan these ERRORs will only appear when you set up the model. After you have calculated the model and saved it no ERRORs will appear because the saved model will be recalculated upon loading, and use of the iteration option will take care of any future ERROR problems.

To just run through to the end result quickly (reassurance if you like that the VisiCalc ERRORs—and first time Multiplan ERRORS will indeed disappear!):

When the template is all set up, we enter the Options command. Type O, tab to Iteration Option, hit Y and then hit RETURN. Don't worry yet about a completion test, that will come later if we need it.

Now a recalculation is made. The first recalc or iteration clears the ERROR condition from several different locations:

Other Income (row 28)
Net Income Before Taxes (row 31)
Income Taxes (row 32)
Current Liabilities (row 51)
Stockholders' Equity (row 55)

But Notes Payable (row 52) still displays an ERROR. The value zero from a "work location" (which is a calculation that is required as a step towards another in the main model). The value currently in Compute Interest (row 62) has been passed up to Other Income Expense (row 28) in the Income Statement position.

Another round of iteration done. This second recalculation now computes Notes Payable (row 52) and an accompanying periodic Interest Expense (row 29).

Another iteration happens and passes Computed Interest from row 62 to row 29 (Interest—Income Statement). Corresponding values are changed on the Balance Sheet and a new Notes Payable and Compute Interest value is obtained.

Subsequent iterations cause the value to converge until there is no discernible change in the displayed values.

SpreadTip: If you are using VisiCalc for this model you should set the format to integer. By showing all our values in integer format, the cessation of change will occur earlier than if you set the format to dollars, and certainly earlier than if you have chosen several decimal places! And since you are manually recalculating until there is no discernible change, this will save you some time.

Note that Multiplan may need to make three to six iteration passes of recalculation depending on the magnitude of the values and the interest rate (but you only have to hit ! once for all of this to happen).

The Forward Reference Formulas

Let's take a look at the chain of formulas that resolve our "chicken and egg" unknowns.

The formula for Other Interest Income is in R28C5:

@IF((R[+34]C[+1]<=0),(-1*R[+34]C[+1]),0)

and is copied into R28C6:R28C8.

SpreadTalk: Row 28 displays Other Interest Income, if it exists. If Compute Interest calculated at R62C6 is negative, this formula converts it to a positive value and shows it as "earned interest" in the Other Income category. If the value in R62C6 is less than zero (which means a negative) or equal to zero, convert the negative value to positive and write it here. If it is not negative then use zero here.

The INTEREST PAYMENT formula is in R29C5:

@IF(@ISERROR(NTPYBLE),0,@IF((R[+33]C[+1]>0),R[+33]C[+1],0))

SpreadTalk: If the Notes Payable is in an ERROR condition, a zero is displayed. If it is not, and Compute Interest Expense (R62C6:9) is a positive value, then that positive value is displayed. Otherwise, zero is displayed.

SpreadTip: Multiplan allows you to assign names to cells or groups of cells. This often makes formulas more readable and understandable. In this case we have assigned the Name NTPYBLE to the row containing Notes Payable (row 52). When we Copy the formula for computed interest across the row, we can use the Name NTPYBLE and the formula will use the note payable amount that is in the same column as the formula being considered. This only works when the referenced formulas are in the same column relative to the column where the formula is being evaluated. We cannot name the COMPUTE INTEREST row of formulas (row 62) and put that name in the Interest Payment formula. This is because the Compute Interest formulas are offset by one column.

For the NOTES PAYABLE (really Available Credit) line in R52C5 the formula would be:

TOTASSETS - CURRENT - EQUITY

SpreadTalk: This formula shows the credit line available. It subtracts Current Liabilities and Equity from Total Assets. This is the "balancing" equation on the Balance Sheet.

The TOTAL LIABILITIES formula is written in R58C5 as:

Turning a Liability into an Asset

TOTASSETS

SpreadTalk: Total Liabilities is set to equal Total Assets. While this might seem like rigging the books a bit (isn't that what one does when one keeps two sets of books?), this is a "post" around which the converging values swing. In making the factors that contribute to the Total Liabilities meet this total, we get the convergence effect desired.

The formula for COMPUTE INTEREST in R62C6 would be:

@IF(@ISERROR(NTPYBLE),0,((R52C5+NTPYBLE)*((INTRTE/100/4))

To compute periodic interest, this formula creates a scratch pad area used to drive the Interest Expense cells on the Income Statement portion of the template.

SpreadTalk: If Notes Payable (R52C6 named NTPYBLE) is in an ERROR condition, display zero. On the other hand, if Notes Payable contains a value, add starting Notes Payable to first quarter Notes Payable then multiply this by one-quarter of the interest rate (the interest rate percentage is created "on the fly" by dividing the Interest Rate variable (B52) by 100, then by four for the number of forecast periods). Note that because we were using a Notes Payable value from the preceding column (R52C5) we could not use the assigned name NTPYBLE for this cell reference. We could use it to add the NTPYBLE amount from column 6, though.

The formula for the Second Quarter COMPUTE INTEREST is in G62:

@IF(@ISERROR(NTPYBLE),0,(NTPYBLE*((INTRTE/100/4))

The SpreadTalk is similar, except that this formula operates only on the current period's NTPYBLE values. This formula is replicated into R62C8 and R62C9.

The Values Converge

Once the values converge, our company treasurer can print out the Income Statement and Balance Sheet, run down to the friendly neighborhood banker, and easily get him/her to agree to continue the line of credit.

The Completion Test

One option when using the Iteration method of recalculating in Multiplan is to set a completion test value somewhere in the spreadsheet. This will cause the iteration to stop when the conditions in the completion test formula are TRUE. In this model it is not necessary to use the completion test, because it does not take long for the values to converge. If you want to shorten the time it takes for these values to converge, however, you can use a built-in function of Multiplan to test when the changes in the Compute Interest portion of the model are less than a certain value—say $1.00.

To do this, we move to cell R63C9 (the cell underneath the last cell of the model). We enter the formula DELTA()<1. This formula evaluates to TRUE when the change between the new computed value in cell R62C9 and the last value computed for R62C9 is less than 1. When this formula is TRUE, the iteration stops. In order for the iteration to use this formula as a test you have to enter the Options command, and tab to Completion Test At: and enter R63C9. Now when you recalculate the model, Multiplan keeps checking the status of this formula. As soon as it encounters a TRUE condition, iteration stops.

Another of Multiplan's built-in functions that you can use to limit the number of iterations performed is ITERCNT(). This formula counts the number of iterations done. You can use it in the completion test by writing a formula such as ITERCNT()=12. This will evaluate to TRUE when 12 iterations have been completed. If you have given the location of this formula as the location of the Completion Test, iteration will stop when 12 iterations have been completed.

SUMMARY

There are many times in spreadsheets when you may want to use forward references to arrive at a value. If you are using Multiplan, the iteration option is the only way that you have of recalculating the model. You can use the completion test option to control the number of iterations performed so that less time is taken up in the recalc process. In VisiCalc or other spreadsheets that do not have such an option, you have to force manual recalculations until the value you are interested in does not change.

Using self-calls in a model is always done with caution and much forethought. This feature is best used to count the number of times you have performed a recalc, as in our math tester example

OtherCalcs

VisiCalc

In VisiCalc, the forward references will be solved only by using multiple forced recalcs. You must keep watching the values in the Compute Interest cells to see when they stop changing. This will happen sooner if you have the format set to Integer than if the format is set to $. When you have entered the known data into the model and are ready to calculate the answer, move the cursor down to I62

Turning a Liability into an Asset 59

(where the Compute Interest formulas are visible). Now hit ! and keep forcing recalcs until the values in the Compute Interest row stop changing.

SuperCalc³

In SuperCalc³ (and other SuperCalc versions), the forward references will be solved only by using multiple forced recalcs. You must keep watching the values in the Compute Interest cells to see when they stop changing. This will happen sooner if you have the format set to Integer than if the format is set to $. When you have entered the known data into the model and are ready to calculate the answer, move the cursor down to I62 (where the Compute Interest formulas are visible). Now hit ! and keep forcing recalcs until the values in the Compute Interest row stop changing.

If you are working with SuperCalc³, you have the option to use completion tests and iteration in order to complete the calculations. These options are accessed by pressing /Global IterS then selecting Delta to solve using the completion test as in our Multiplan discussion, or a number from 1 to 99 to have a specific number of recalculations performed.

7

"The Penalties for Early Withdrawal Are..."

SPREADSHEET FUNCTIONS: IF, Hiding Cell Contents, Using the Variable Matrix Method to What-If
FEATURED PROGRAM: SuperCalc³
TEMPLATE FUNCTION: IRA Analysis

BACKGROUNDER

As we warned (or perhaps "promised" is a better word!) in our introduction, there is a lot of "what-iffing" done in this book, primarily because that is what spreadsheets do so well. Gone are the days of the eraser, when most work done on ruled paper was smudged and worn from the continual changes and modifications necessary from changed ideas or circumstances (not to speak of the penalties of trying to do mental arithmetic at the end of a long day!).

This chapter will be full of tips and hints on better use of the functions and capabilities of your spreadsheet program. We'll use the asterisks to good effect, we'll provide a very flexible method of quickly printing reports that must have data changed between printings, and we will have one or two good formatting suggestions as we go along.

These models do something that we all should do—they let you evaluate the benefits of placing savings in an IRA account versus a regular savings account. One of the major drawbacks under the rules for IRA accounts is the penalty assessed, if for any reason you decide to withdraw the funds. This model determines the effect of that penalty so that you see the risk involved with this aspect of an IRA investment—and you may be surprised to find that is *not* a big deal (we think the banks emphasize it so they get to play with your money longer!).

The benefits of an IRA are fairly obvious to us all. We must hasten to add that we are not espousing one investment vehicle over another, you make up your own mind (or let an advisor do it for you!). We are *not* giving tax advice either—please treat any comments that follow in this area as opinion (and likely to be fairly ill-informed at that!).

Many companies, large and small, help with establishing IRAs. They will arrange to have the money directly deposited from the employees' pay, which guarantees that the money gets into the account and not spent. The deposits, or contributions, are taken from pre-tax earnings, which reduce overall tax liability. The drawback we mentioned earlier seems to put some people off the whole idea: the penalty if the money must be withdrawn early. This attitude is particularly prevalent amongst the younger people (among whom one of your authors is not!)—they feel that they might need the money earlier than age 60, to pay for a house, or other major expenditures that might occur.

We had an excited letter from a member of InterCalc, the International Spreadsheet Users' Group (see Introduction), in which the writer said that the article on the subject and the model we had recently published had revealed that the IRA was not a bad idea at all—the penalty was really not that significant, and if the withdrawal was put off for just a few early years, the cost versus the necessity for the withdrawal might be an easy decision. How this conclusion was arrived at we shall shortly see. . .

APPLICATION SPREADSHEET

The Input Area

We are going to review this model top down, starting with the Input Area, since most of the interesting spreadsheeting techniques are at the top. Then we will look at the formulas that make up the actual IRA analysis.

There are two types of input the model can take: fixed data, that since it refers to personal information about the person for whom the analysis is being made is also labelled "PRIVATE DATA," and variable data, on which "what-ifs" can be done.

SpreadTip: In Figure 7.1 you can see the private data entry area. When you have a matrix that contains information that you do not wish a casual passer-by to see on your CRT screen, it is a good idea to make that part of the model "isolatable." This we have done by placing it in an area that, once it has been

```
                        A         B         C

         1  I.R.A. INVESTMENT ANALYZER
         2
         3  FIXED DATA  (PRIVATE)
         4  ----------------------------
         5  CURRENT AGE:              ******
         6  CURRENT TX BRACKET        ******
         7  RETIREMENT AGE:           ******
         8  ----------------------------
         9
        10
        11  PRINT FROM E9...L63 FOR REP
```

Figure 7.1:   Private Data in VisiCalc

completed, moves off the screen to the left and does not have to be looked at again, and thus won't be inadvertently seen by passers-by.

We have further hidden this data by using the /Hide format in the locations in which it sits (the keystrokes are: /F,C5:C7,H) so that the amount or values entered appear as blank cells (Note that the figure is a VisiCalc figure, we didn't think that showing the SuperCalc[3] example would be very interesting—just a bunch of blank looking cells!). In SuperCalc you also have the option of hiding data in an invisible column. All you do is set the column width for the column you wish to hide to 0. You can still enter data, but no one can see it on the screen.

The Variable Switch

Sometimes while doing "what-if" exercises with a model, one wants to first look at options, then print them out, one by one. In our case, in Figure 7.2, in rows 5 and 6 we have two variables we are using, the amount of the annual deposit to the IRA and the projected interest rate.

In cases like this or when there are several variables you would like to review, we have a useful technique you can use, which we call the Variable Switch. Without it you must go into the model and change the variables, making sure that the right combination of changes has been made, then print, then go back and revise each location one more time before printing once more. If you have, say, six variables, and want to try many of the different combinations, then this can be done only with a pencil and paper, checking them off as you go. Not any more! The Variable Switch will take care of it.

Across the top of our model, in Figure 7.2, you will see there are six options. Each represents a deposit amount and an interest rate, and several combinations have been entered. Note that the first option has an asterisk beneath it, and that the figures in that option are repeated in the right hand column,

"The Penalties for Early Withdrawal Are. . ." 63

called IN USE. That is no coincidence, since the IN USE values were "switched" on by the asterisk.

The formula in the IN USE column is a long nested IF statement:

IF(F7 = 1,F5,IF(G7 = 1,G5,IF(H7 = 1,H5,IF(I7 = 1,I5,
    IF(J7 = 1,J5,IF(K7 = 1,K5,0))))))

SpreadTalk: If F1 equals 1, write in the value at F5, if not solve the next expression. If G1 equals 1, write G5, if not. . . and so it goes. The formula on each line of the options matrix uses the same switch but brings over the relative value.

It must be obvious that the model calls the variables in the IN USE column to where ever it needs them. Now it is much easier to sit and plan sets of various combinations, especially since they are in a neat row to be compared and checked, just "switch'em in" and print.

We find this method particularly useful when preparing outlooks for meetings. Inevitably at the last minute someone will have the bright idea of plugging in "just one more set of options" and we can do it for them in a flash and have a printout of the variation on the theme ready in time.

The only limit to the number of option sets that can be used is the character capacity of a cell in your particular spreadsheet. And there is another hidden benefit.

SpreadTip: For diagnostics in your model, include an option set that is all zeros. By selecting it, switching it on, you can probably find all the places in the model that call the variables—a useful aid if you want to go in and fix something. If your spreadsheet has the ISERROR convention, or the NA possibility, then for sure you can find them, as when a spreadsheet calls a location with this entry, it will not calculate but transfers the ERROR or NA to the calling location.

But let's get back to the IRA. . .

	D	E	F	G	H	I	J	K	L
1									
2			OPTION	OPTION	OPTION	OPTION	OPTION	OPTION	
3		VARIABLE DATA	1	2	3	4	5	6	IN USE
4		---	---	---	---	---	---	---	---
5		YEARLY DEPOSIT	1500	1500	1750	1750	2000	2000	1500
6		PROJ INT RATE	8	10	8	10	8	10	8
7		SWITCH	*						
8		---	---	---	---	---	---	---	---

Figure 7.2: Variable Switch Data

Completing the Input

Once the private data are in, and the option sets of variables have been selected and inserted (you can use all six but it's not necessary), then all that needs to be done is enter the name of the "analysee" (if that's a word!) in H11, then enter the date in the format shown, with the year as value, not text.(This is important, as the year part of the date is used in the model.) One recalculation and you are ready to print: follow the printing instructions on the left for a report.

The Formulas in the Model

The complete report area for this model is shown in Figure 7.3. The first formula is in L16, in the report heading, which calculates the actual year of retirement. It is

$$(C7 + L9 - L14)$$

SpreadTalk: Add the retirement age to the date and subtract from the current age, which of course works out to be the year date of retirement.

There are other formulas in the report heading that call-down values from the input area, but we are not going to detail them here since they are fairly obvious. If you must know what they are see the Key Formula listing in the Appendix.

In the body of the report we are going to look only at the first row, row 23, since all the formulas are replicated down the column. Take care when doing this, however, since the Adjust and No Adjust relationships are very intermixed.

SpreadTip: When replicating series of formulas there is a danger of inserting an incorrect relationship requirement, especially if you are a SuperCalc whiz. You may inadvertently press Return instead of A, for Ask, at the end of a replicate command sequence and find all of the references relative although they weren't supposed to be. The error may not be noticed for some time, and there is a way to at least minimize the chance of this happening. Always hit A for Ask at the end of a replication command sequence, unless you are absolutely positive that all of the references should be adjusted.

When Asked whether to Adjust or No Adjust, remember that nine times out of ten if the reference is to a cell on the same row or in the same column, it is going to be relative. If the reference shares neither row number nor column letter with the reference cell, then there is probably going to be no change. We will look at this in a bit more depth in a formula in the report area, when we get to it.

In the meantime the formula at the top of the first column, YEAR, is a call down of the year entry in the date, which as you can see is given a cell to itself at L9, in the report heading. The second formula down that column is:

"The Penalties for Early Withdrawal Are. . ." 65

```
            E       F         G        H        I         J       K         L
    9 ANALYSIS                                        DATE:        6/12     1984
   10 ---------------------------                     ---------------------------
   11     PREPARED FOR:SUSAN BELLMAN
   12
   13 ASSUMED ANNUAL GROWTH RATE:           8%       ANNUAL DEPOSIT   $     1500
   14 MARGINAL INCOME TAX RATE:            30%       CURRENT AGE      :       30
   15
   16 FIRST DEPOSIT FOR:       1984                   RETIREMENT YEAR :     2013
   17
   18 $$$$$$$$$$$$$$$$$$$$$$$$$$$$$$$$$$$$$$$$$$$$$$$$$$$$$$$$$$$$$$$$$$$$$$$$
   19                 I.  R.  A.      N O N - I R A    SAVINGS            EARLY
   20              ANNUAL  YEAR END   ANNUAL YEAR END   USING           WITHDRAWL
   21      YEAR    DEPOSIT   VALUE    DEPOSIT  VALUE   I R A    AGE      PENALTY
   22      ====    ===== $  ====== $  ===== $ ====== $ ====== $ =====    ===== $
   23      1984     1500     1620     1050     1109     511     30       -137
   24      1985     1500     3370     1050     2280    1090     31       -258
   25      1986     1500     5259     1050     3516    1743     32       -361
   26      1987     1500     7300     1050     4822    2478     33       -442
   27      1988     1500     9504     1050     6201    3303     34       -498
   28
   29      1989     1500    11884     1050     7657    4227     35       -526
   30      1990     1500    14455     1050     9194    5261     36       -521
   31      1991     1500    17231     1050    10818    6413     37       -479
   32      1992     1500    20230     1050    12533    7697     38       -395
   33      1993     1500    23468     1050    14343    9125     39       -262
   34
   35      1994     1500    26966     1050    16255   10710     40        -76
   36      1995     1500    30743     1050    18274   12469     41        171
   37      1996     1500    34822     1050    20406   14416     42        487
   38      1997     1500    39228     1050    22658   16570     43        879
   39      1998     1500    43986     1050    25036   18951     44       1356
   40
   41      1999     1500    49125     1050    27547   21579     45       1929
   42      2000     1500    54675     1050    30198   24477     46       2607
   43      2001     1500    60669     1050    32998   27672     47       3404
   44      2002     1500    67143     1050    35954   31138     48       4331
   45      2003     1500    74134     1050    39077   35058     49       5404
   46
   47      2004     1500    81685     1050    42374   39311     50       6637
   48      2005     1500    89840     1050    45856   43984     51       8048
   49      2006     1500    98647     1050    49532   49115     52       9656
   50      2007     1500   108159     1050    53415   54744     53      11480
   51      2008     1500   118432     1050    57515   60917     54      13544
   52
   53      2009     1500   129526     1050    61845   67682     55      15871
   54      2010     1500   141508     1050    66417   75092     56      18488
   55      2011     1500   154449     1050    71245   83204     57      21425
   56      2012     1500   168425     1050    76343   92082     58      24712
   57      2013     1500   183519     1050    81727  101792     59      28384
   58
   59        0        0        0        0        0       0       0          0
```

Figure 7.3:   IRA Analysis Report

IF(OR(E23 = L16,E23 = 0),0,E23 + 1))

replicated down, thus producing a sequence of years for 30 years (in our model).

SpreadTalk: If the previous year equals the retirement year, or if the previous year equals zero, write a zero here, otherwise add one to the previous year. Written this way the formula turns off the year calculation when the retirement year is reached. This makes the printed report a little neater as there aren't any extra years hanging around unnecessarily.

The next formula is at F23:

IF(E23=0,0,L5)

SpreadTalk: If the year is equal to zero, write zero, otherwise insert the annual deposit figure. This neatly cuts off the contributions further down the column, when the person finally retires and stops depositing money!

The replication commands for relativity in this case illustrates the earlier tip we gave you perfectly: when you have ASKed, the program asks you to tell it the instructions for each of the components, the first one being E23. This is in the same column and likely to be Adjusted (and so it is). The next one, L5, shares neither row nor column with the current cell and is likely to be No Adjust—and it is. Check this supposition with the next few formulas...

At G23, the formula

IF(F23>0,((F23+G22)*(1+(H13/100))),0)

is entered.

SpreadTalk: This formula looked to see if there was a deposit amount in column f. If there was, that amount was multiplied by the interest rate, otherwise a zero was entered.

One of the analyses that this model is doing is comparing the benefits of regular savings account with an IRA. Any money deposited to a regular savings account would be after taxes, whereas IRA deductions are either made by an employer before taxes, or are allowed as a deduction from income at 1040 time, before calculating taxes. Either way, this means that if the same amount of money from salary was to be deposited to a regular savings account, it must first have the taxes on the amount deducted. In H23, this adjusted deposit amount is calculated using the formula:

(F23*(1−(C6/100)))

or the after-tax rate times the deposit amount.

The year-end value of the non-IRA deposit is determined at I23. This formula is:

IF(H23=0,0,(I22+H23)*(1+((H13/100)*(1−(C6/100)))))

SpreadTip (before we SpreadTalk the formula!): In some templates the formula which starts a column is not quite the same as that which will appear in the second row of the column, and subsequent rows. This applies certainly to columns that are accumulating, or using the preceding row total to perform a calculation. In the first column there is no preceding row to work on, so there will be instructions that are in the second row but not in the first. This means that you must devise two formulas, right? Wrong—it's not necessary.

If the preceding row (above the top row of formulas) is blank, or filled with a text label, or a row of dashes (probably the most frequent circumstance), then it can be safely referenced. It will evaluate as zero and therefore will not affect the result of most calculations. The prime exception is a formula that requires a division by the preceding value—a division by zero is mathematically unacceptable, and an ERROR condition will result.

In the case of the formula under discussion in I23, we can do this safely. Let's compare the formulas we would enter in I23 and I24 if we do not do it, and SpreadTalk our way through them.

    I23:   (H23*(1+((H13/100)*(1−(C6/100)))
    I24:   IF(H23=0,0,(I22+H23)*(1+((H13/100)*(1−(C6/100))))

SpreadTalk: In I23 the instructions are to multiply the non-IRA deposit by the result of multiplying the interest rate (converted to a percentage) and the current tax bracket (as a reciprocal percentage). There is no mention of the previous row entry as the total amount of the investment at this point is only the first year's deposit plus interest.

In the next row, 24, the formula has an additional component. We have to add the previous year's total so that it too earns its interest. The parenthetical statement (I22+H23) does this. So you can see that if we put this whole formula in the first location it would work the same—we would be in effect adding in a column heading which the program evaluates as zero, but the math would work out just fine.

By the way, to complete the SpreadTalk, the IF statement at the beginning just checks to see that the IRA program is still in effect, and the person has not yet retired. It does this by seeing if an amount appears in column H. If the person is in Florida or Palm Springs by this time, then a zero is entered!

The calculated savings using IRA is simply the difference between the two year-end amounts, or

    (G23−I23)

The age column is a little more complicated than one might expect. One could just bring down the current age, then add one to it all the way down the column. But it's different for two reasons: we wanted to be consistent and have all entries stop at retirement, and the penalty for early withdrawal applies only to those before the age 59.5, regardless of actual retirement age. The first formula in K23 brings down the age from L14.

There is a longer formula in the second row and on down:

IF(F24>0,IF(K23<=C7,K23+1,0),0)

SpreadTalk: Cut off the age entry first if there is no deposit made, and also if the age gets to be more than the retirement age. This pair of formulas in column K is one case in which there has to be a separate formula after the start value of the column has been established.

The last column, L, is the one where the effect of an early withdrawal is shown. The formula at L23 is:

IF(K23<59.5,+G23−(+G23*(C6/100)+(.1*G23))−I23,0)

SpreadTalk: The model is calculating the difference between the two accounts if an early withdrawal occurs, and it is penalized and taxed. If a withdrawal occurs before age 59.5, the amount currently in the IRA account is taxed, and assessed a 10 percent penalty. This formula assesses that penalty and the taxes, and compares this to the regular account year-end value.

This model can be difficult to read with all those numbers so close together. To make it more visually pleasing we have inserted a blank line between the numbers every five years.

SpreadTip: Do this type of report formatting at the very end of your spreadsheet session! The program will adjust all the formulas that need it. But if you make the model "pretty" with blank lines and columns before you have finished with the model, the replication process will require you to either do it in bits, or go in afterwards and delete all the values that appeared in the intended white space. Indeed if you have already inserted the lines, thinking you were finished, and have to change a formula it is often quicker to go back, erase the blank lines, do the replication and then re-insert them (it certainly reduces the chance of error).

SUMMARY

This model can be set up to calculate as many years as needed, just by replicating the formulas into more rows. All that has to be done to use this model to make projections for another person's situation, is to change the data in the input area, add the name, recalculate, and print out the one page report.

OtherCalcs

Multiplan

Since Multiplan has no format to hide the contents of a cell, it is necessary to format the cells in the Personal Data area to * (F C R5C3:R7C3 Tab Tab * Return). This will "hide" the entries behind a row of asterisks.

When setting up formulas in Multiplan it is important to assess whether a variable will be an absolute number in the formula, that is, that cell reference will not change for each formula, or if the cell will be a relative variable in the formula. You must determine this before you start using the Copy command or you will find some very strange things happening.

Any cell that will not be changing in relation to copies of the formula must be entered as a specific cell address, such as R21C3. Any cell reference that you want to have changed when the formula is copied you have to write as a relative reference, R[−X]C[+Y]. For example, the SuperCalc formula for age used in the text above:

IF(F24>0,IF(K23<=C7,K23+1,0),0)

could be written:

IF(R24C6>0,IF(R23C11<=R7C3,R23C11+1,0),0)

If the formula is copied into the other cells in the column, you would not get the correct results for this template as Multiplan reads the cell references as absolutes and thus copies these exact cell addresses into the other formulas. You don't want to always be evaluating the contents of R24C6 or R23C11 in this example.

To correct this problem let's try writing the formula as a Relative reference:

IF(RC[−5]>0,IF(R[−1]C<=R[−14]C[−8],R[−1]C+1,0),0)

This formula, copied into the other cells in the column, will produce a lot of strange numbers because the reference to the retirement age will not be right when it is copied. The retirement age is in R7C3. It is 14 rows above and 8 columns to the left of the formula in R24C11. The formula resulting in R25C11 from the copying operation is also checking for a number in the cell 14 rows above and 8 columns to the left of it. There is no number there (R8C3) so the formula is useless.

To write this formula correctly, you have to mix the references using some relative and one absolute. You can see from the examples used here why you have to make this decision first. Multiplan does not automatically adjust the formulas for you.

The correct formula for age would be:

IF(RC[−5]>0,IF(R[−1]C<=R7C3,R[−1]C+1,0),0)

Now when the formula is copied the retirement age will always be found, and the previous year's age and deposit will always be correct.

One problem with the way that Multiplan does these references is that when a formula contains a lot of relative cells, the formula can be very long. You may even find that sometimes the formula is too long to fit in the cell. When this happens your only recourse (other than building a series of formulas that will take up too much room in the model, make it unwieldy, and confuse everything) is to use the Name command in Multiplan to shorten the formulas. Using the Name command will also solve some of the problems with having to decide if a cell reference has to be absolute or relative.

For example, in our age formula we will use names to define the retirement age and the annual deposit amounts. First we place the cursor on cell R7C3 and hit N, type RETAGE, hit TAB, hit RETURN. Now we move to R23C6. Hit N, type DEP, hit Tab, type R23C6:R57C6, hit RETURN. Now when we write the formula at R24C11 it looks like:

IF(DEP>0,IF(R[−1]C<=RETAGE,R[−1]C+1,0),0)

You can only use the Name in a relative manner, such as DEP, if the reference is to a cell in the same row as the formula (or in the same column if the formulas are replicated across a row instead of down a column). Naming the Account Deposit works in this case because the reference is in the same row. We could not name the age column and use it in the formula as the references are to cells one row up from the current cell.

VisiCalc

Since VisiCalc has no format that allows you to hide the contents of a cell, it is necessary to format the cells in the Personal Data area to * (/F*). This will "hide" the entries behind a row of asterisks as seen in Figure 7.1.

The /Replicating instructions for VisiCalc follow the SuperCalc[3] pattern except that you don't have to Ask. VisiCalc always prompts you for the Relative and No Change responses.

SpreadTip: When replicating series of formulas there is a danger of inserting an incorrect relationship requirement. The error may not be noticed for some time, and there is a way to at least minimize the chance of this happening. Nine times out of ten if the reference is to a cell on the same row or in the same column, it is going to be Relative. If the reference shares neither row number nor column letter with the reference cell, then it is probably going to be No Change.

8

Investment Property—to Buy or Not to Buy...

SPREADSHEET FUNCTIONS: NPV, MAX
FEATURED PROGRAM: VisiCalc
TEMPLATE FUNCTION: RentalCash Flow

BACKGROUNDER

Relatively few of us have cause to use NPV, or NET Present Value, in a matrix. To those of you who respond "use it all the time," our apologies. The arrival of spreadsheets was a godsend for these authors, since math had never been one of our strong points, and esoteric math was, and remains, a completely closed subject.

What little ability we may have once had has all gone, victim of the ease with which one can calculate in a spreadsheet program, and the ease with which one can build formulas that produce the correct result. Lurking behind the coordinates that contain results of many of our templates are some pretty inelegant formulas, we suspect—but if they work, so what! We know also that we probably spend much more time than a mathematician would in creating spreadsheets, since we have to talk to ourselves in a kind of SpreadTalk in order to get things to come out right.

There are several different tricks of the trade in this model, and it also provides a useful model for outlooking investments in income real estate. It calculates the projected income, estimated taxes, cash flow, and return on investment a rental income property. The model is designed to accept variable data for up to four properties and apply the same principles of evaluation to each with a single keystroke.

APPLICATION SPREADSHEET

The following model resulted from using a spreadsheet program which did not have the NPV function. It belonged to a friend who was planning an investment in real estate, in apartment buildings, and wished to examine a couple of different opportunities.

Variations on the Variable Switch

To start with, we will look at a variation of the Multiple Variable Switch, that we introduced in the last chapter, relating to the IRA analysis model. You will recall that by inserting a "1" in a location, the variables in the column above it were used throughout the model as variables.

Look at the top of our Discounted Cash Flow Rental model in Figure 8.1. There you will see in the first rows the list of variables that we wish to apply to each property being evaluated. There are four pieces of property and the column for each is headed appropriately. Finally, on the right side, there is a column called PROPERTY UNDER REVIEW, with a figure underneath. In this switchable matrix we use the actual property identifier number for pulling over the values from the right column. When you want to change the property that is reported upon, the number is inserted here and the necessary recalculations done. In the same way as before the formula, which is

@IF(G4=C4,C6,@IF(G4=D4,D6,@IF(G4=E4,E6,@IF(G4=F4,F6,0))))

checks to see if the column applies, and if it does carries over the figures.

SpreadTalk: If number in the switch location matches the number at the head of the column, bring over the value on this row from that column.

This method is a little more "polished" than the previous one, in that the switch digit is incorporated into the matrix and has a value in itself, as opposed to just a spare "1" hanging around, apparently in space. As you can see if you look at the illustration, we even bring that figure down and use it to head up the report area, in H17, just in case it is to be printed out.

A Few Other Variables

The format for the reporting area has a few variables in it too, but we did not bother to put them up in the selector area as they tend to apply to every property being evaluated. For instance the inflation rate, which is used extensively in the

Investment Property—to Buy or Not to Buy... 73

```
                A        B         C         D         E         F         G         H
 1 DISCOUNTED CASH FLOW RENTAL CALCULATION                              PROPERTY
 2                                                                      UNDER
 3                        PROPERTY  PROPERTY  PROPERTY  PROPERTY        REVIEW
 4 ASSUMPTIONS:              1         2         3         4            4<--SWITCH
 5 ------------------
 6      DISCOUNT RATE:     10.00     10.00     10.00     10.00          10.00
 7 ANNUAL RENTAL INC:      30000     38000     42000     104000         104000
 8          TAX RATE:         35        35        35        35              35
 9 ACQUISITION COST:$      120000    145000    187000    1210000        1210000
10 SALVAGE VALUE $          25000     30500     45000     260000         260000
11 MAINTENANCE               5000      6500      7250     18000          18000
12 OTHER EXPENSES            1000      2500      3200     10000          10000
13 ---------------------------------------------------------------------------
14
15 PROJECTED INFLATION RATE:                     4         5         3         6
16
17                                             PROJECTION FOR PROPERTY #   4
18 ---------------------------------------------------------------------------
19 YEAR:                    1934      1935      1936      1937      1938      1939
20 NUMBER OF YEARS:            0         1         2         3         4         5
21 ------------------
22 RENTAL INCOME                     104000    108160    113568    116975    123994
23 MAINTENANCE                        18000     18720     19656     20246     21460
24 OTHER EXPENSES                     10000     10400     10920     11248     11922
25 SALVAGE VALUE                                                               260000
26 DEPRECIATION (STRAIGHT)            190000    190000    190000    190000    190000
27
28 INCOME BEFORE TAX                 -114000   -110960   -107008   -104518    -99389
29 TAXES                              39900     38836     37453     36581     34786
30 NET INCOME                        -153900   -149796   -144461   -141100   -134176
31 ---------------------------------------------------------------------------
32 CASH FLOW                          36100     40204     45539     48900     55824
33 ---------------------------------------------------------------------------
34 DISCOUNTED CASH FLOW/YEAR          32818     33226     34214     33400     34663
35 ACCUMULATED DISCOUNTED C.F.        32818     66045    100259    133659    168321
36 PAYBACK                          -1177182  -1111137  -1010878   -877220   -708899
37 TOTAL DISCOUNTED CASH FLOW        168321
38 NET PRESENT VALUE                -1041679
39 ===========================================================================
40 @NPV=         -1041679
```

Figure 8.1: Investment Model

formulas below, is on row 15. It represents a best guess as to what the inflation rate will be over the forthcoming five-year period.

The year dates are entered with future saving of keystrokes in mind—only the first one is a hard number, the rest across merely add one to the preceding column. Beneath it we used the same method for numbering the years, which we will need discounting purposes, but this time placed a zero for the start of the investment period, and then added one to develop the year numbers for the entire investment period.

The Investment Evaluator

We are going to review each row from top to bottom. Most of the rows have a different formula in the first investment year from the second, so we will review them in pairs. Unless we note otherwise you can assume that the second formula is replicated across the remainder of the years, all relative.

The first location, the RENTAL INCOME row, has in columns D and E the following formulas:

    D22:   +G7
    E22:   +D22*(1+(E15/100))

The first is a bring-down of the figure the seller quoted for the annual income, from the UNDER REVIEW location, and the second works using the first—as you can see it increases the income in succeeding years by the inflation rate.
The MAINTENANCE EXPENSE and the OTHER EXPENSES are similarly handled, with their formulas being:

    D23:   (G11)
    E23:   +D23*(1+(E15/100)
    D24:   (G12)
    E24:   +D24*(1+(E15/100))

The next item is the SALVAGE VALUE (visions of a pile of apartment house rubble!). This is the accepted term for the residual value the property has at the end of the period being reviewed, and is the price one could get for it. This value can be calculated in any number of ways. In our model we have simply entered a value that was calculated elsewhere. If you have your own methods for computing this value, by all means insert them here! In our model, however, it is brought in from the variable area (G10) and used at the end of the period.

In deciding to use the straight line method for DEPRECIATION on row 26, we confess to copping out—put it down to formula fatigue! This method allows the write-off an equal amount of the investment each year down to the salvage value. The formula is easy:

    (+G9−(@MAX(D25...H25)))/@MAX(D20...H20)

and replicates right across without any mental gymnastics. Of course you can add whatever depreciation method you heart (or that of your tax advisor) desires!

    SpreadTalk: Take the Acquisition Cost and subtract from it the maximum value found in row 26 (there is only one value there, the salvage value, and this formula will find it no matter what year it may occur in). Then divide the resulting number by the project life in years (which is the Maximum year number in row 20).

In case you wish to use this model for other investments that may be longer than the one under consideration at present, the formula is constructed to allow for longer or shorter investments.

The formula for INCOME BEFORE TAX is the same, relatively, across the columns:

(D22 + D26) − @SUM(D23...D25)

SpreadTalk: Take the RENTAL INCOME figure from this year, add the salvage value (which only occurs in the last year), and subtracts the total of the expenses between rows 23 and 25.

Row 28 is for TAXES (inevitable as death we hear). Simply multiply the tax rate (decimalized) times the income figure :

−(G8/100)*D28

and NET INCOME will be the result of subtracting this from the INCOME figure,

(D28 − D29)

CASH FLOW is a factor of adding depreciation and net income, with the formula

(D25 + D30)

And then we get into the interesting stuff!

Discounted Cash Flow

We want to take a look at what the cash flows are when they are discounted back to today. We want to look at them individually by year, and also in total. The mathematical formula for discounted cash flow is

$$\text{Cash flow} \times \frac{1}{(1 + i)^t}$$

where i = interest rate or inflation rate (as a decimal) and t = time.

This is one of those areas where our mathematical weakness caused us a lot of problems, but we finally got it right. The spreadsheet equivalent of this equation, as fitted into the model is:

(D32)*(1/(1 + (G6/100))^D20)

SpreadTalk: Add the decimalized percentage rate to one. Raise this to the power of the elapsed years from row 20, and then divide one by the result. Finally, multiply the cash flow by the result.

The next line, the ACCUMULATED DISCOUNTED CASH FLOW is a simple running SUM.

SpreadTip: This is something to remember if you haven't noticed it for yourself. The most frequent uses for the @SUM function is the summing of columns to get totals, and then cross-footing the columns. For the latter, you generally enter the @SUM formula in the leftmost column, then /Replicate it across the other columns. During the replication sequence, you almost without thinking rap twice smartly on the "R" key, so often in fact that it becomes a reflex action. You can create a cumulative (or running) total if you make the first range coordinate No Change, and the second Relative. The starting location for the SUM does not change, but the end of the range keeps extending out one at a time.

The formulas across our five columns look like this:

@SUM(D34...D34)
@SUM(D34...E34)
@SUM(D34...F34)
@SUM(D34...G34)
@SUM(D34...H34)

The first one looks a bit odd but it has the desired effect!

The PAYBACK entries are simply to show when the investment pays off and becomes profitable. We put a simple formula in row 36 to show when the projected investment begins to turn a profit: using the formula

$-G9+D35$

in the first column and

$+D36+E35$

thereafter (relatively). All this does, in the first column, is subtract the total cash flow figure from the acquisition cost, then after that reduces the previous year's figure by the current year's cash flow. Naturally when the figure turns positive, the project has turned profitable.

The NET PRESENT VALUE entry shown is just a bring-over from the fifth year accumulated discounted cash flow. We did this just so that the last calculation, NET PRESENT VALUE, could be done beneath it—just a convenience, nothing magic about the location in which it is done. The last formula in D38 is:

$+D37-G9$

which is, of course, the acquisition cost minus the discounted cash flow total.

Investment Property—to Buy or Not to Buy...

Since, as we said earlier, we had done this model on a non-NPV spreadsheet program, we punched it into the computer in VisiCalc for the purposes of this chapter. We have used the standard VisiCalc @NPV formula on the last line (row 40), just to check it out.

The formula construction is

@NPV(G6/100,D32...H32)−G9

SpreadTalk: Calculate the Net Present Value using the percentage discount rate, on the range that includes all of the year's cash flows, then subtract the acquisition cost.

As you can see it works fine, and for those of you that do not have NPV—well, you do now!

OtherCalcs

Multiplan

All of the formulas shown here will work just the same in Multiplan. Remember, though, that in Multiplan, built-in functions are not preceded by the @ symbol. When using the Cumulative summing tip, remember to write the first variable as an absolute reference BEFORE doing the copying.

SuperCalc[3]

Similarly, all formulas will work in SuperCalc[3], remembering that the @ symbol is not used.

9
Here's Looking at You, Kid!

SPREADSHEET FUNCTIONS: LOOKUP, ISNA, ABS, ERROR
FEATURED PROGRAM: All
TEMPLATE FUNCTION: Price List

BACKGROUNDER

As we said in the introduction to this book, this is not intended as a tutorial for the completely uninitiated in the spreadsheet world. But we have been teaching the use of spreadsheet programs since the very first one, VisiCalc, appeared on the scene in 1979. We have taught high school kids (regular and underachievers), individuals and groups of business people, classes in adult education, and so on.

This has given us a very good idea of those aspects of spreadsheet programs that give people trouble, so if we seem to dwell on a particular function or feature (and become a bit pedantic in our delivery!), it is because we feel it may be helpful. If you are not one of those having trouble with the feature under discussion (and can bear to miss this "deathless prose"!), just skip the chapter and move on.

The subject here is once again the LOOKUP feature of spreadsheets. All spreadsheets worth the name have it, and since it is so useful, we feel that emphasis is worthwhile so that it can be used to maximum effect, and once again, apologies if you feel we are repetitious.

Here's Looking at You, Kid!   79

    While we are showing a LOOKUP function we will also be showing you some very useful systems for error checking—having the model automatically validate some of the data entered by the operator, and not permitting incorrect data to be processed.

The LOOKUP Function

As we have mentioned before, the LOOKUP function seems simple enough: it allows you to find an entry (value) in a table in the spreadsheet, and bring back a corresponding value that has been assigned to it.

    In some spreadsheet programs, including Multiplan and SuperCalc³, you can actually bring back text (or "textual values," as they are called) which gives endless possibilities— like a legend that appears and says "Told you to enter a digit greater than twelve, dummy!" instead of the familiar ERROR message. This is covered in Chapter 4.

    We will use as an example of LOOKUP tables for a price list, looking up the product numbers and bringing back the price, to illustrate the subject. This application is readily adaptable to all sorts of other uses, and is probably understood by all.

    Two major components go into the construction of a LOOKUP table. It consists of two "lists," the COMPARISON LIST and the RESULT LIST. There are two ways in which a LOOKUP table can be arranged: in a columnar format (a vertical table) or a row format (a horizontal table). Take a look at Figure 9.1.

```
Vertical Lookup Table

                A       B       C       D
    1                           Part No. Price
    2  Lookup-->        3         1       0.20
    3  Result-->       .45        2       3.10
    4                              3       0.45
    5                              4       0.62
    6                              5       0.84
    7                              6       1.10
    8                              7       0.10
    9                              8       0.67

Horizontal Lookup Table

            A       B       C       D       E       F       G       H       I       J       K       L
    2  Lookup      3       Part #  1       2       3       4       5       6       7       8
    3  Result>    .45      Price   0.20    3.10    0.45    0.62    0.84    1.10    0.10    0.67
```

    Figure 9.1:   Vertical and Horizontal LOOKUP examples

There are really only two rules about LOOKUP tables:

Rule 1: The COMPARISON LIST (the one to the left and above) must have its values in ascending order. Notice that the Part Numbers are arranged smallest first. This is important as the LOOKUP function will not work if they are descending, or mixed.

Rule 2: The COMPARISON LIST and the RESULT LIST in VisiCalc and in SuperCalc must be adjacent, in the column or row directly next to each other. Again notice that the Prices which correspond to the Part Numbers are listed in an ADJACENT column.

In Multiplan these columns and rows do not have to be actually adjacent, but the LOOKUP COMPARISON list must be located to the left of or above the RESULT list.

In these little examples we have an actual "working" model. A part number entered in "LOOKUP" produces the "Result." The formula that is in the "result" cell, for each of the programs, is:

VisiCalc: @LOOKUP(B2,C2...C9)
SuperCalc: LOOKUP(B2,C2:C9)
Multiplan: LOOKUP(R2C2,R2C3:R9C4)

The SpreadTalk in VisiCalc and SuperCalc[3] says to take the value in cell B2 and compare it to the values in the range C2...C9, and return the corresponding price.

The SpreadTalk in Multiplan is different: to LOOKUP a value in a column not adjacent to the Comparison list, if we had the RESULTS list in column 7 for example, the formula would be changed to read:

LOOKUP(R2C2,R2C3:R9C7)

If the Results list was in column E instead of in column D, the formulas for VisiCalc and SuperCalc would not work.

All seems simple enough so far, but it is important to understand what the programs are doing when they LOOKUP (and they all do the same thing!). When the program searches the LOOKUP comparison value list *it is not just looking for an exact match to the value you are interested in!* It searches the list for the first value that *exceeds* the input value, and then moves back one step and returns the Result assigned to the value in the list immediately before it. This handles an exact match just fine, but also enables you to find other acceptable values, too.

Here's Looking at You, Kid!

In our example, the programs search for the first value that exceeds 3, our input product number. This number is 4 in our list. They then take one step back to 3 and return the corresponding $.45. However, please note that if you were to input the numbers 3.5, 3.001, or 3.9999999999 (which do not equal any of the product numbers in our list) the same result, $.45, would be returned.

Now we can appreciate why the list must be in ascending order.

There are a couple of other useful features in the LOOKUP function we will look at, then we will get on with our example. If the value you are looking for is less than the first (lowest) value in your Comparison List, your program will return the legend NA (not available). For example, in Figure 9.1 if you input the number .5 at B2 (in either of the tables, vertical or horizontal) the value returned at B3 would be NA.

If, however, the value you are looking for is greater than the last value in your Comparison List, your program will return the value corresponding to the last entry in the LOOKUP Value list (exceeded, then stepped back one, see?). For example, if you entered the value 10 in Figure 9.1, you would get back the value $.67 at B3.

GUIDELINES FOR LOOKUPS

1. The LOOKUP Values list must be arranged in ascending order (lowest value to highest value).
2. In VisiCalc and SuperCalc the Result list must be in a column or row adjacent to the LOOKUP Values list.
3. In Multiplan, the Result list does not have to be adjacent to the LOOKUP Comparison list, but it must be to the right or below it. The range specified in the LOOKUP table range is described by the FIRST value of the COMPARISON List and the LAST value in the RESULT list.
4. The LOOKUP function searches the Comparison List for the first value that is GREATER than the search value, and returns the Result value which is placed opposite the immediately preceding value.
5. In Multiplan, the program determines whether the LOOKUP is horizontal or vertical based on the shape of the table. If the table as defined by the first and last values in the LOOKUP range is wider than it is high, the LOOKUP will proceed horizontally. If the LOOKUP table is square or taller than it is wide, the LOOKUP will be done vertically.

Now to our example.

APPLICATION SPREADSHEET

Entering the Data

Figures 9.2 through 9.5 show the various parts of a fairly straightforward model of an order cost estimator. The column letters will indicate to you how they are positioned in the overall model. It has a data entry area, in which an operator would enter the various items that were ordered and the quantity of each required.

SpreadTip: It may be a holdover from the days when VisiCalc was the only program available and there was no such thing as "protected cells" (as found now in SuperCalc³ and Multiplan) but we have a personal thing about data entry areas. It is all too easy to clobber a formula if an unwary person starts bashing the keys. If a model is to be used by strangers (and by that we do not necessarily mean people who drop in off the street, but anyone who was not intimately involved with the creation of the model, or is aware of spreadsheeting in general), then we like to clearly mark those areas that are for data entry and those areas that should be avoided.

Of course, if your spreadsheet program has a /Protect or Lock feature (by which you can "seal" a cell against being written over or into) or /Hide (by which you can also conceal the presence of a formula or entry from CRT display), then this precaution is unnecessary.

In this model then we have included a data entry area shown in Figure 9.2. The operator enters the part numbers in column C and the quantities of each desired in column D. One recalc creates a formatted cost proposal for the customer, who in this example is Ms. Smith.

This model is using the LOOKUP feature in the classic way—a straight look down the table of stock numbers that brings back the prices opposite each. There are a couple of "niceties" in this simple model, however. We have included several error-trapping formulas that guard against incorrect entries of stock numbers or quantities.

The First ERROR Trap

First in Figure 9.3 you see two columns labeled Step 1 and Step 2. Here the program is checking to be sure that the correct stock numbers were entered. Column A contains the formula

@LOOKUP(C9,N7...N18)

SpreadTalk: LOOKUP the entered stock number from column C in the LOOKUP table in column N.

Here's Looking at You, Kid!

```
             C           D         E        F
      1!---------------!
      2! DATA ENTRY    !
      3!    AREA       !    ORDER COST
      4!               !    ESTIMATION
      5!    ENTER      !
      6! STOCK QUANTTY !
      7!      #        !
      8----------------
      9     2010        11     MOVE TO K1 TO
     10     5442         1     SEE RESULTS
     11     3145         6     AND TO PRINT
     12     6751         4
     13     1101         5
     14        0         0
     15        0         0
     16        0         0
     17        0         0
     18        0         0
     19        0         0
     20        0         0
```

Figure 9.2: Data Entry Area

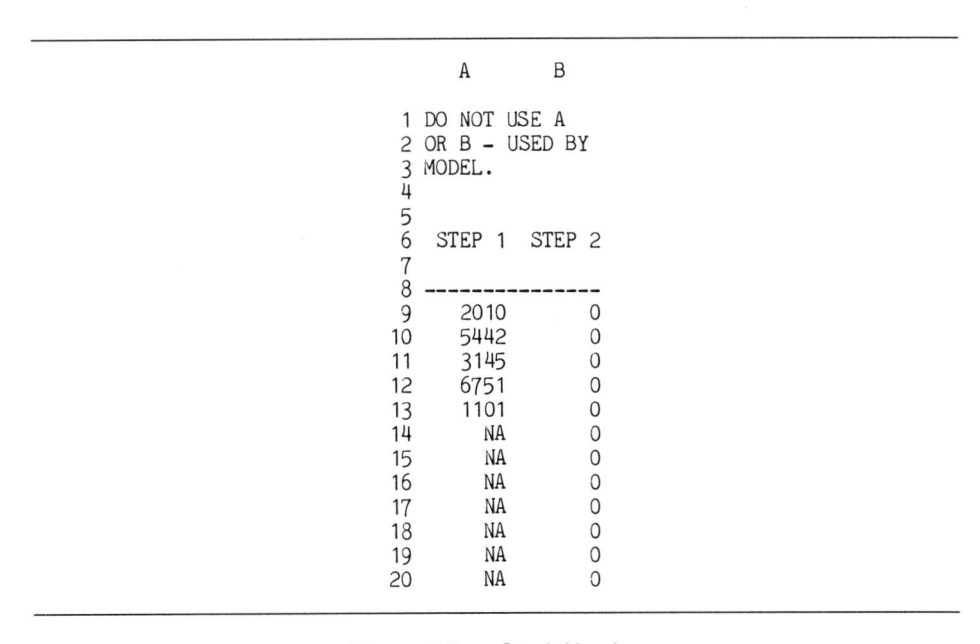

```
                   A         B
      1  DO NOT USE A
      2  OR B - USED BY
      3  MODEL.
      4
      5
      6    STEP 1    STEP 2
      7
      8  ----------------
      9     2010        0
     10     5442        0
     11     3145        0
     12     6751        0
     13     1101        0
     14       NA        0
     15       NA        0
     16       NA        0
     17       NA        0
     18       NA        0
     19       NA        0
     20       NA        0
```

Figure 9.3: Stock Number

If the number is only one or two units off, 1245 instead of 1246 for example, the correct stock number will be returned. A strange stock number will appear if there are too many digits are transposed, or a gross error has been made. If no stock number has been entered, an NA will result.

In column B the formula:

@IF(@ISNA(A9),0,(C9 − A9))

determines the difference between between the entered stock number and the Looked-up one.

SpreadTalk: If the number in column A is NA, then write a zero, otherwise enter the difference between the entered stock number and the LOOKedUP stock number. The first part of this formula that writes the zero if an NA is present, prevents the totals in the results section (Figure 9.3) from containing NAs (remember that formulas that reference cells containing NA or ERROR carry the NA or ERROR forward).

With the data input and a recalc performed, the information is written into the results area Shown in Figure 9.4. If there has been a gross error in the entry of a stock number, the formula in column H will catch it. This formula is:

@IF(B9 = 0,C9,(C9* − @ABS(B9)))

```
              G      H       I      J       K      L
    1                PRINT FROM G3 TO L23
    2
    3                -----------------------------
    4         !            PROPOSAL FOR MS.SMITH        !
    5         !                                         !
    6         !       ITEM    PRICE    QTY    TOTAL     !
    7         !               EACH                      !
    8         !     ---------------------------         !
    9         !       2010   114.89    11   1263.79     !
   10         !       5442    62.50     1     62.50     !
   11         !       3145    73.62     6    441.72     !
   12         !       6751    35.10     4    140.40     !
   13         !       1101    14.37     5     71.87     !
   14         !          0       NA     0      0.00     !
   15         !          0       NA     0      0.00     !
   16         !          0       NA     0      0.00     !
   17         !          0       NA     0      0.00     !
   18         !          0       NA     0      0.00     !
   19         !          0       NA     0      0.00     !
   20         !          0       NA     0      0.00     !
   21         !                                --------  !
   22         !                        TOTAL $ 1980.28   !
   23                -----------------------------
```

Figure 9.4:   Results Area

Here's Looking at You, Kid!

SpreadTalk: If the difference between the entered stock number and the value LOOKedUP is zero, then enter the stock number from C9. If the difference is anything other than zero, multiply the stock number in C9 by the negative of the absolute value of the difference. This ensures that the stock number is negative which will trigger an ERROR message in Column K. We will see how this occurs a little further on.

Pricing the Goods and the Second ERROR Trap

In column I, the price for each of the stock items is determined by the formula

@LOOKUP(H9,O7...O18)

SpreadTalk: Look up the stock number in the list in O7...O18 (and of course bring back the price from column P). Notice here that if there is a zero in column H, the price returned will be NA, because 0 is less than any stock number entered in our LOOKUP Table.

A Little Extra About a Little Less . . .

We have thrown in another idea here, useful if you have discounts, or any other conditional numbers in a LOOKUP table. The formula is in column P which determines the price for the items. We have built in quantity discounts, which are automatically applied without operator intervention. In the extreme right-hand column of the LOOKUP table, the one in Figure 9.5 that is labeled DISC PRICE, we have the following formula:

+M7*@IF(@AND(D9>=1,D9<=5),1,
    @IF(@AND(D9>=6,B10<=10),.9,@IF(B10>10,.8,@ERROR)

SpreadTalk: Multiply the regular price from M7 by the result of what follows. If the amount ordered is greater than or equal to 1 AND less than or equal to five (on which there is no discount) use 1; if it is between 6 and 10 then use .90 (a 10 percent discount); if it is over 11, then use .80 (which is a 20 percent discount), if none of these conditions are true enter an ERROR. This last segment of the formula prevents negative entries from being evaluated, indicating a mistake in the entering of the order amount.

Column J in Figure 9.3 brings over the quantity from the entry area using a simple cell call such as (D9).

	M	N	O	P
1				
2		LOOKUP TABLES		
3				
4		STOCK	STOCK	DISC
5	PRICE	#	#	PRICE
6				
7	15.97	1101	1101	14.37
8	114.89	2010	2010	114.89
9	81.80	3145	3145	73.62
10	66.87	4222	4222	66.87
11	62.50	5442	5442	62.50
12	39.00	6751	6751	35.10
13	10.00	7998	7998	9.00
14	44.50	8005	8005	40.05
15	76.12	9000	9000	68.51
16	10.00	9567	9567	9.00
17	20.00	10101	10101	18.00
18	26.00	13456	13456	23.40

Figure 9.5: LOOKUP Tables

The Third ERROR Trap

Column K finishes the proposal by calculating the price. Here is where we use the error-flagging device mentioned in the SpreadTalk about formulas in column H. The formula in column K reads:

@IF(H9<0,@ERROR,@IF(@AND(H9=0,@ISNA(I9)),0,(I9*J9)))

SpreadTalk: If the contents of column H are less than zero (occurring because we made a mistake entering a stock number), write ERROR in this column. If column H equals zero AND column J is NA, enter a zero because we have not ordered anything. Otherwise, multiply the calculated price from column I by the quantity in column J.

SUMMARY

In this simple model we have relieved the operator of tedious mathematical work on a calculator: if he or she can type we are in business! Even if the user is not a good typist, the built-in error catching devices will indicate any mistakes! The error trapping devices are good utilities to use in any program where someone is entering a lot of values and there are chances for wrong or transposed digits.

This was a simple application, which if you were entering it yourself could have been done quite quickly—we have shown you several error trapping ideas which will, we are sure, give you ideas for your own models that require operator entry of data.

OtherCalcs

In this chapter we have explained most of the differences between the programs LOOKUP functions within the chapters. Therefore, here we will simply show you a list of the detailed formulas as they would appear in each program (the model formulas are listed in VisiCalc syntax in the chapter).

Multiplan

```
LOOKUP(R9C3,R7C14:R18C15)
IF(ISNA(R9C1),0,(R9C3 − R9C1))
IF(R9C2 = 0,R9C3,(R9C3* − ABS(R9C2)))
LOOKUP(R9C8,R7C15:R18C16)
 + M7*IF(AND(R9C4> = 1,R9C4< = 5),1,
         IF(AND(R9C4> = 6,R10C2< = 10),.9,IF(R10C2>10,.8,ERROR)
IF(R9C8<0,ERROR,IF(AND(R9C8 = 0,ISNA(R9C9)),0,(R9C9*R9C10)))
```

SuperCalc³

```
LOOKUP(C9,N7:N18)
IF(ISNA(A9),0,(C9 − A9))
IF(B9 = 0,C9,(C9* − ABS(B9)))
LOOKUP(H9,O7:O18)
 + M7*IF(AND(D9> = 1,D9< = 5),1,
         IF(AND(D9> = 6,B10< = 10),.9,IF(B10>10,.8,ERROR)
IF(H9<0,ERROR,IF(AND(H9 = 0,ISNA(I9)),0,(I9*J9)))
```

10

Parcels, Unite!

SPREADSHEET FUNCTIONS: CHOOSE, Nested LOOKUP
FEATURED PROGRAM: VisiCalc
TEMPLATE FUNCTION: Calculating the United Parcel Service Charges

BACKGROUNDER

Some people using spreadsheets have problems with the concept of "nesting." By the judicious use of parentheses it is possible to have a formula that works itself into frenzy checking all kinds of possibilities! This chapter is going to explore this concept, in the form of a nested LOOKUP table. Other chapters in this book will use nested IFs, ANDs, and others.

Shipping the Goods

There are many different services that deliver packages, some with the speed of light, others in a more pedestrian way. We are going to put the LOOKUP function of spreadsheets through a real exercising with the next template. We have chosen to illustrate it with the United Parcel Service standard overland freight system, since that is probably the most complex. Adaptation of the model to any other freight service will be easy, as they are almost all less complicated.

There is also another feature of freight services that makes this model particularly useful. If you do not have an account with them or a regular standard pickup, you have to call them for a special visit. The clerks on the other end of the phone have a litany of questions they ask about each package to be picked

Parcels, Unite!   89

up—and if there are several, the questions have to be answered for each one. The reason for this is to calculate for you the total cost of each package so you can have a check ready when the delivery service truck comes.

The freight clerk on the phone uses a standard sheet of rates and a calculator to tell callers their charges. In using this template you will probably be more advanced than the freight company's own system—and save much time (which will be very useful if you charge freight to the customer and add the charge to an invoice that must go each package). By the way, the charges in our illustrations may be out of date by the time you read this but the principle will be the same.

APPLICATION SPREADSHEET

United Parcel's System

There are three charts that are required to figure out the charges for UPS. The first is the Zone Chart, a sample of which is shown in Figure 10.1. In this, one looks up the destination Zip Code and finds the UPS Zone code, a single digit. Then there is the Blue Label Air Zone Chart (Figure 10.2)—all the states served are given a letter code, and the exception areas (no service) are listed.

Finally there's the Rate Chart—this has two sections called Common Carrier (Zones 1–8) and Blue Label Air (Zones A–E, or 9–12), shown in Figure 10.3. Under each are all the pound weights up to 50 lbs (maximum for UPS), and if you look across to the UPS ZONE column you can find the actual cost for that package, Common Carrier for regular delivery and Blue Label for air shipment.

There are a few other options. You can specify C.O.D. ($1.50 extra), ask for an address correction ($1.50), get acknowledgment of delivery ($0.26), and buy insurance on a $0.25 per $100 basis.

One last point—each of the UPS Zones will have a unique set of rate charts and Zip Code lists—they may be absolutely similar or relatable but the rates in this model cover only one area in the Northeast. When you key all this in be sure to get your local UPS charts and use the correct values.

Take a look at Figure 10.4. When the model is loaded, on an Apple, for instance, the area in Figure 10.4 comes up—and that's all you need. On the Apple, of course, unless you have an eighty column card installed, there is the necessity to move back and forth to enter data. If you are going to key this model into your machine, you may choose to shorten the Labels that indicate the information required to get it all on one screen.

As the legend at the top of Figure 10.4 indicates, the only entries required are those in column L. First a one is entered to indicate if the shipment is Blue Label, zero if not. Then the actual complete Zip Code for the destination is entered, then the exact weight of the package—taking the next highest pound which is the way UPS does it.

Down a few rows to row 62 and the little questionnaire: ones are entered

	A	B		A	B		A	B
1	CONVERSION	TABLE	(ROW #)	(ZIP)	(ZONE)	(ROW #)	(ZIP)	(ZONE)
2	ZIP	ZONE						
3	.01	2	51	.294	5	99	.586	
4	.019	3	52	.295	4	100	.594	8
5	.02	2	53	.296	5	101	.6	5
6	.026	3	54	.297	4	102	.64	6
7	.027	2	55	.298	5	103	.65	5
8	.032	3	56	.3	5	104	.653	6
9	.034	2	57	.325	6	105	.654	5
10	.035	3	58	.326	5	106	.656	6
11	.036	2	59	.33	6	107	.677	7
12	.037	3	60	.338	5	108	.68	6
13	.044	4	61	.339	6	109	.693	7
14	.045	3	62	.35	5	110	.7	6
15	.046	4	63	.365	6	111	.723	5
16	.048	3	64	.367	5	112	.725	6
17	.051	2	65	.369	6	113	.739	7
18	.054	3	66	.37	5	114	.74	6
19	.06	2	67	.376	4	115	.763	7
20	.1	2	68	.377	5	116	.773	6
21	.129	3	69	.387	6	117	.774	7
22	.133	2	70	.388	5	118	.776	6
23	.136	3	71	.39	6	119	.778	7
24	.137	2	72	.397	5	120	.798	8
25	.14	3	73	.4	5	121	.8	7
26	.15	4	74	.403	4	122	.813	8
27	.155	3	75	.407	5	123	.814	7
28	.156	4	76	.41	4	124	.815	8
29	.157	3	77	.42	5	125	.816	7
30	.161	4	78	.43	4	126	.821	8
31	.162	3	79	.46	5	127	.822	7
32	.164	4	80	.467	4	128	.829	8
33	.166	3	81	.469	5	129	.875	7
34	.175	2	82	.47	4	130	.878	8
35	.176	2	83	.471	5	131	.881	7
36	.177	3	84	.473	4	132	.89	8
37	.178	2	85	.474	5	133	.9	8
38	.199	3	86	.48	4	134	.97	8
39	.2	3	87	.49	5	135	.988	8
40	.219	2	88	.492	4	136	.994	8
41	.22	3	89	.493	5			
42	.228	4	90	.5	6			
43	.229	3	91	.504	5			
44	.233	4	92	.505	6			
45	.254	3	93	.506	5			
46	.255	4	94	.508	6			
47	.267	3	95	.52	5			
48	.268	4	96	.56	6			
49	.289	5	97	.577	7			
50	.293	4	98	.58	6			

Figure 10.1: The Zone Chart (In Columns A and B Only)

for those that apply, and if insurance is required the actual value of the shipment is entered. Unless this is a C.O.D. shipment that is all there is to it—a Recalculation is performed (!) and the correct rates appear for direct entry into the UPS form. Notice that only the applicable entry appears opposite the freight charges legend—with a zero for those that do not apply. If the staff wants to see how much more it would cost to send the package Blue Label, they can do an "estimate" of each way just by changing that first zero at the top to a one.

If the package is C.O.D. then the invoice amount to be collected is entered

Parcels, Unite!

	C	D	E
1		BLUE LABEL STATES	
2			
3	PR/VI	.009	NA
4	MA	.027	NA
5	RI	.029	NA
6	NH	.038	NA
7	ME	.049	NA
8	VT	.059	NA
9	CT	.069	NA
10	NJ	.089	NA
11	NY	.149	NA
12	DE	.199	NA
13	DC	.205	NA
14	MD	.219	NA
15	VA	.246	NA
16	WV	.268	NA
17	NC	.289	NA
18	SC	.299	NA
19	GA	.319	9
20	FL	.34	9
21	AL	.369	9
22	TN	.385	9
23	MS	.397	9
24	KY	.427	9
25	OH	.458	13
26	IN	.479	9
27	MI	.499	9
28	IA	.528	9
29	WI	.549	9
30	MN	.567	9
31	SD	.577	9
32	ND	.588	9
33	MT	.599	10
34	IL	.629	9
35	MO	.658	9
36	KS	.679	9
37	NE	.693	9
38	LA	.714	9
39	AR	.729	10
40	OK	.749	9
41	TX	.799	9
42	CO	.816	9
43	WY	.831	10
44	ID	.838	10
45	UT	.847	10
46	AR	.865	10
47	NM	.884	9
48	NV	.898	10
49	CA	.966	10
50	HI	.968	14
51	AG/GUAM	.969	NA
52	OR	.979	10
53	WA	.994	10
54	AK	.995	15

Figure 10.2: Blue Label Chart

at O72, and that will then do the addition for the special C.O.D. label that UPS requires.

The LOOKUPs

This model is really very simple, but it uses a feature of spreadsheets that you may not have used much—nested LOOKUPs. Let us just step through what is

	F	G	H	I	J	K	L	M	N	O
1	LBS	ZONE 2	LBS	ZONE 3	LBS	ZONE 4	LBS	ZONE 5	LBS	ZONE 6
2	1	1.25	1	1.28	1	1.32	1	1.36	1	1.42
3	2	1.34	2	1.4	2	1.47	2	1.55	2	1.67
4	3	1.43	3	1.52	3	1.63	3	1.75	3	1.92
5	4	1.52	4	1.64	4	1.78	4	1.94	4	2.18
6	5	1.61	5	1.75	5	1.93	5	2.14	5	2.43
7	6	1.7	6	1.87	6	2.09	6	2.33	6	2.68
8	7	1.79	7	1.99	7	2.24	7	2.53	7	2.94
9	8	1.88	8	2.11	8	2.4	8	2.72	8	3.19
10	9	1.97	9	2.23	9	2.55	9	2.92	9	3.44
11	10	2.05	10	2.34	10	2.7	10	3.11	10	3.69
12	11	2.14	11	2.46	11	2.85	11	3.31	11	3.95
13	12	2.23	12	2.58	12	3.01	12	3.5	12	4.2
14	13	2.32	13	2.7	13	3.17	13	3.7	13	4.45
15	14	2.41	14	2.82	14	3.32	14	3.89	14	4.71
16	15	2.5	15	2.93	15	3.47	15	4.09	15	4.96
17	16	2.59	16	3.05	16	3.63	16	4.28	16	5.21
18	17	2.68	17	3.17	17	3.78	17	4.48	17	5.47
19	18	2.77	18	3.29	18	3.94	18	4.67	18	5.72
20	19	2.86	19	3.41	19	4.09	19	4.87	19	5.97
21	20	2.94	20	3.52	20	4.24	20	5.06	20	6.22
22	21	3.03	21	3.64	21	4.4	21	5.26	21	6.48
23	22	3.12	22	3.76	22	4.55	22	5.45	22	6.73
24	23	3.21	23	3.88	23	4.71	23	5.65	23	6.98
25	24	3.3	24	4	24	4.86	24	5.84	24	7.24
26	25	3.39	25	4.11	25	5.01	25	6.04	25	7.49
27	26	3.48	26	4.23	26	5.17	26	6.23	26	7.74
28	27	3.57	27	4.35	27	5.32	27	6.43	27	8
29	28	3.66	28	4.47	28	5.48	28	6.62	28	8.25
30	29	3.75	29	4.59	29	5.63	29	6.82	29	8.5
31	30	3.83	30	4.7	30	5.78	30	7.01	30	8.75
32	31	3.92	31	4.82	31	5.94	31	7.21	31	9.01
33	32	4.01	32	4.94	32	6.09	32	7.4	32	9.26
34	33	4.1	33	5.06	33	6.25	33	7.6	33	9.51
35	34	4.19	34	5.18	34	6.4	34	7.79	34	9.77
36	35	4.28	35	5.29	35	6.55	35	7.99	35	10.02
37	36	4.37	36	5.41	36	6.71	36	8.18	36	10.27
38	37	4.46	37	5.53	37	6.86	37	8.38	37	10.53
39	38	4.55	38	5.65	38	7.02	38	8.57	38	10.78
40	39	4.64	39	5.77	39	7.17	39	8.77	39	11.03
41	40	4.72	40	5.88	40	7.32	40	8.96	40	11.28
42	41	4.81	41	6	41	7.48	41	9.16	41	11.54
43	42	4.9	42	6.12	42	7.63	42	9.35	42	11.79
44	43	4.99	43	6.24	43	7.79	43	9.55	43	12.04
45	44	5.08	44	6.36	44	7.94	44	9.74	44	12.3
46	45	5.17	45	6.47	45	8.09	45	9.94	45	12.55
47	46	5.26	46	6.59	46	8.25	46	10.13	46	12.8
48	47	5.35	47	6.71	47	8.4	47	10.33	47	13.06
49	48	5.44	48	6.83	48	8.56	48	10.52	48	13.31
50	49	5.53	49	6.95	49	8.71	49	10.72	49	13.56
51	50	5.61	50	7.06	50	8.86	50	10.91	50	13.81

Figure 10.3: Common Carrier LOOKUP Tables (part 1 of 2)

happening so that everything is clear. The work is being done in the small work area in the model.

When the Recalculation starts, the formula in S54 takes a look at the Zip Code previously entered and converts it to a format that we can use. A problem with Zip Codes is that they can start with zero, as in 06907, and spreadsheets have trouble with this. The formula, in VisiCalc, is

Parcels, Unite!

	P	Q	R	S	T	U	V	X	Y	Z	AA	AB
	LBS	ZONE 7	LBS	ZONE 8	ZONE A&B(9)		ZONE C(10)		ZONE D(11)		ZONE E(12)	
1												
2	1	1.48	1	1.55	1	2.77	1	2.9	1	4.53	1	4.6
3	2	1.79	2	1.93	2	3.74	2	4	2	5.71	2	5.73
4	3	2.11	3	2.32	3	4.71	3	5.11	3	6.89	3	6.86
5	4	2.42	4	2.7	4	5.68	4	6.21	4	8.07	4	7.99
6	5	2.74	5	3.09	5	6.65	5	7.31	5	9.25	5	9.12
7	6	3.05	6	3.47	6	7.62	6	8.42	6	10.43	6	10.25
8	7	3.37	7	3.86	7	8.59	7	9.52	7	11.61	7	11.38
9	8	3.68	8	4.24	8	9.56	8	10.63	8	12.79	8	12.51
10	9	4	9	4.63	9	10.53	9	11.73	9	13.97	9	13.64
11	10	4.31	10	5.01	10	11.5	10	12.83	10	15.15	10	14.77
12	11	4.63	11	5.4	11	12.48	11	13.94	11	16.33	11	15.9
13	12	4.94	12	5.78	12	13.45	12	15.04	12	17.51	12	17.03
14	13	5.26	13	6.17	13	14.42	13	16.15	13	18.69	13	18.16
15	14	5.57	14	6.55	14	15.39	14	17.25	14	19.87	14	19.29
16	15	5.89	15	6.94	15	16.36	15	18.35	15	21.05	15	20.42
17	16	6.2	16	7.32	16	17.33	16	19.46	16	22.23	16	21.55
18	17	6.52	17	7.71	17	18.3	17	20.56	17	23.41	17	22.68
19	18	6.83	18	8.09	18	19.27	18	21.67	18	24.59	18	23.81
20	19	7.15	19	8.48	19	20.24	19	22.77	19	25.77	19	24.94
21	20	7.46	20	8.86	20	21.21	20	23.87	20	26.95	20	26.07
22	21	7.78	21	9.25	21	22.19	21	24.98	21	28.13	21	27.2
23	22	8.09	22	9.63	22	23.16	22	26.08	22	29.31	22	28.33
24	23	8.41	23	10.02	23	24.13	23	27.19	23	30.49	23	29.46
25	24	8.72	24	10.4	24	25.1	24	28.29	24	31.67	24	30.59
26	25	9.04	25	10.79	25	26.07	25	29.39	25	32.85	25	31.72
27	26	9.35	26	11.17	26	27.04	26	30.5	26	34.03	26	32.85
28	27	9.67	27	11.56	27	28.01	27	31.6	27	35.21	27	33.98
29	28	9.98	28	11.94	28	28.98	28	32.71	28	36.39	28	35.11
30	29	10.3	29	12.33	29	29.95	29	33.81	29	37.57	29	36.24
31	30	10.61	30	12.71	30	30.92	30	34.91	30	38.75	30	37.37
32	31	10.93	31	13.1	31	31.9	31	36.02	31	39.93	31	38.5
33	32	11.24	32	13.48	32	32.87	32	37.12	32	41.11	32	39.63
34	33	11.56	33	13.87	33	33.94	33	38.23	33	42.29	33	40.76
35	34	11.87	34	14.25	34	34.81	34	39.33	34	43.47	34	41.89
36	35	12.19	35	14.64	35	35.78	35	40.43	35	44.65	35	43.02
37	36	12.5	36	15.02	36	36.75	36	41.54	36	45.83	36	44.15
38	37	12.82	37	15.41	37	37.72	37	42.64	37	47.01	37	45.28
39	38	13.13	38	15.79	38	38.69	38	43.75	38	48.19	38	46.41
40	39	13.45	39	16.18	39	39.66	39	44.85	39	49.37	39	47.54
41	40	13.76	40	16.56	40	40.63	40	45.95	40	50.55	40	48.67
42	41	14.08	41	16.95	41	41.61	41	47.06	41	51.73	41	49.8
43	42	14.39	42	17.33	42	42.58	42	48.16	42	52.91	42	50.93
44	43	14.71	43	17.72	43	43.55	43	49.27	43	54.09	43	52.06
45	44	15.02	44	18.1	44	44.52	44	50.37	44	55.27	44	53.19
46	45	15.34	45	18.49	45	45.49	45	51.47	45	56.45	45	54.32
47	46	15.65	46	18.87	46	46.46	46	52.58	46	57.63	46	55.45
48	47	15.97	47	19.26	47	47.43	47	53.68	47	58.81	47	56.58
49	48	16.28	48	19.64	48	48.4	48	54.79	48	59.99	48	57.71
50	49	16.6	49	20.03	49	49.37	49	55.89	49	61.17	49	58.84
51	50	16.91	50	20.4	50	50.34	50	56.99	50	62.35	50	59.97

Figure 10.3: Common Carrier LOOKUP Tables (part 2 of 2)

@INT(L57/100)/1000

This does a simple division to move the digits to the right of a decimal point and drop the last two that we do not need. Therefore 06903 becomes .069, while 10583 becomes .105.

Now the formula in V54 takes over:

94   Parcels, Unite!

```
     H     I    J    K    L         M       N       O       P              Q        R      S      T      U      V       W

53                                                                                                ***********************
54  YOU INSERT INFORMATION IN COL. L                                                              * WORK AREA - DO NOT DISTURB.    *
55  VISICALC DOES THE REST !                              IF ASTERISKS APPEAR HERE                *ADJ ZIP   .995       LOOKUP   15 *
56                                                        THIS STATE HAS NON-BLUE                 ***********************
57  ENTER ONE IF BLUE LABEL 0 IF NOT         1            LABEL AREAS - CHECK RATE                *   UPS PRICE:      0      0    0 *
58  ENTER COMPLETE 6 DIGIT ZIP CODE>     99511            CHART BEFORE SHIPPING !                 *    BL PRICE:      0      0 33.98 *
59  ENTER EXACT WEIGHT OF PACKAGE-->        27                ->{{{ ****** }}}<-                  ***********************
60
61  ENTER ONE FOR EACH CHARGE THAT APPLIES, ZERO IF NOT APPLICABLE.
62                                                               AMOUNT
63  IS PACKAGE SENT COD ?......                1       ........    1.50
64  IS ADDRESS CORRECTION REQUIRED ?           0       ........    0.00
65  WANT DELIVERY ACKNOWLEDGMENT ?             0       ........    0.00
66  IF INSURANCE REQUIRED, INSERT TOTAL
67      VALUE OF PACKAGE HERE.....     4000            ........    9.75 [NA HERE
68  CHARGES FOR        27 LBS TO UPS ZONE               ........    0.00{ MEANS
69  BLUE LABEL          0 LBS TO BL ZONE                ........   33.98{  NON-BL
70                                                                 _____  AREA]
71             TOTAL SHIPPING CHARGES THIS PACKAGE............    45.23
72    IF THIS PACKAGE IS COD - ENTER INVOICE AMOUNT.....          22.55
73  ****  MAKE OUT UPS COD LABEL TO COLLECT THIS AMOUNT..          0.00
```

Figure 10.4:   Entry and Results Area

Parcels, Unite!

@IF(L56<>1,@LOOKUP(S54,A2...A137),
@LOOKUP(S54,D3...D54))

SpreadTalk: If the Blue Label indicator is turned off with a zero, then S54 is found in the long table that stretches from A3 down to A137 (displayed in Figure 10.1). This contains the reformatted three digit Zip Codes and opposite each the zone in which UPS has placed them. If the Blue Label indicator is on, then it looks up the Zip Code in the table in column D instead.

While UPS assigns a letter code to Blue Label Zones, this model has it converted to a number so that the spreadsheet can use it (a label would be no good!). The state names listed in column C are there just for convenience, but note that each state that does not have Blue Label service has an entry—@NA. This is so that an attempt to send a package Blue Label to one of these states will produce an NA entry, thus flagging to the operator that they cannot do it.

In addition there are some states that have only partial service, in which case UPS indicates on the chart the Zip Codes NOT serviced. Asterisks appear in O58, as a warning that the state selected has such areas, and that the rate card should be manually checked, the formula being simply

@IF(@OR(V54=13,V54=14,V54=15),6,0) [set asterisk]

VisiCalc merely looks at the zone to see if it is one of the zones to be watched for.

The LOOKUPs Nest

The next step is to look up the rates—and a limitation of spreadsheets (particularly VisiCalc) made this a three-step process. There is a limit to the number of characters that can be in a formula, therefore the full range of LOOKUPs could not be done in one shot. The formula in T56 is:

@IF(@AND(L56<>1,V54<=4),@CHOOSE(V54,0,
@LOOKUP(L58,F2...F52),@LOOKUP(L58,H2...H52),
@LOOKUP(L58,J2...J52)),0)

and here are the first nested LOOKUPs, in an CHOOSE function.

SpreadTalk: First the formula checks that the package is indeed for regular UPS (does not equal 1) AND also that it is in the first group of zones, less than or equal to 4. If it fails these two tests then a zero results (that lonely zero at the end of the formula!). If it passes the test then the long CHOOSE bit comes into play—it takes the zone value and uses it to choose one of the lists across the top in which to look up the weight (which is the value in L58).

By the way, notice the important zero as the first element in the CHOOSE statement—since UPS zones start at two there will never be a one, but we must give the CHOOSE statement a first element to "pass over" in its search for element two, thus the zero.

Similar formulas in U56 and V56 pick up where this one left off —in U56:

@IF(@AND(L56<>1,V54>=5,V54<=7),@CHOOSE(V54−4,
@LOOKUP(L58,L2...L52),@LOOKUP(L58,N2...N52),
@LOOKUP(L58,P2...P52)),0)

and in V56

@IF(@AND(L56<>1,V54=8),@LOOKUP(L58,R2...R52),0)

By these three entries (T56, U56, and V56) we cover the zones 2 through 8. The Blue Label zones on the next row are treated the same way, just changing the greater than/less than value to cover zones 9,10,11, and 12, using the LOOKUP lists in the correct columns. The amount brought back into one of these locations is going to be a dollar value, the UPS rate for the pounds shipped.

Except for a little arithmetic in the display area that is all there is to it. For the first three questions in the little questionnaire, the formulas are simple:

>O62   @IF(L62=1,1.5,0) (Insert $1.50 if C.O.D.)
>O63   @IF(L63=1,1.5,0) (Insert $1.50 for address correction)
>O64   @IF(L64=1,.26,0) (Insert 26 cents if receipt required)

The insurance rate is a bit complicated. UPS charges $.25 per hundred for each hundred (or part) after the first. So for instance, a $350 package value costs $.50—nothing for the first hundred, $.25 for the second and $.25 for the part of the next. Telling VisiCalc all about this is a bit of typing! The formula in O66 is:

.25*(@INT(L66−100/100)+
@IF(L66−100/100<>@INT(L66−100/100),1,0))

The next two lines of the display area bring over the applicable pound freight rates from the work area. For regular rates,

>O67:   @IF(L56<>1,@SUM(T56...V56),0,)

For Blue Label

>O68:   @IF(L56=1,@SUM(T57...V57),0,)

Parcels, Unite!

and these are obvious too—there can only be one rate in the T to V locations so a sum of them is going to work fine. Notice that this is where the NA will come up if a try is made to ship Blue Label to an inapplicable area.

This could finish it, except that a C.O.D. shipment might be planned. If a one was entered above, then this model reminds with a row of asterisks at the bottom left that the invoice amount should be entered in O72, so that the correct amount to be collected can be calculated for the UPS C.O.D. label.

Keying In All Those Rates

This looks like an awesome job, and since accuracy is important, it must indeed be handled carefully. We do have a couple of tips to make this easier (since we had to do it ourselves!): note that there is a relationship between the rates down the columns, irregular but there nonetheless. When it is figured out for each column it is a case of replicating mostly, but then an all-important read-and-check process.

OtherCalcs

SuperCalc³

This model will work as shown in the chapter with the exception, that there is no CHOOSE function in SuperCalc³, so the nested Lookup Formulas must be changed somewhat. The formula from T56 that reads:

```
@IF(@AND(L56<>1,V54<=4),@CHOOSE(V54,0,
        @LOOKUP(L58,F2...F52),@LOOKUP(L58,H2...H52),
        @LOOKUP(L58,J2...J52)),0)
```

would be changed in SuperCalc³ to:

```
IF(V54=2,LOOKUP(L58,F2:F52),
    IF(V54=3,LOOKUP(L58,H2:H52),
        IF(V54=4,LOOKUP(L58,H2:J52),0)))
```

The formulas in U56 and V56 would be changed similarly.

Multiplan

You could build this model just as shown in Multiplan, except that you would need to change the CHOOSE formulas as illustrated in the SuperCalc³ segment. You could however, eliminate many of the columns in the model, as Multiplan allows you to make multiple lookups from a table having only one search list.

This would be done for the tables shown in Figure 10.3. Here you could eliminate all but the first column of the lbs., and only the list the rates that differ. To illustrate this concept, suppose that you enter the lbs. list in column 6. Then in column 7 you enter the rates for Zone 2, in column 8 the rates for Zone 3, in column 9, the rates for Zone 4, etc. Now you could write the formula for R56C20 (T56 as shown earlier) as:

IF(R54C22 = 2,LOOKUP(R58C12,R2C6:R52C7),
    IF(R54C22 = 3,LOOKUP(R58C12,R2C6:R52C8),
        IF(R54C22 = 4,LOOKUP(R58C12,R2C6:R52C9),0)))

The formulas in R56C21 and R56C22 would be changed similarly.

11
Will I Ever Stop Paying?

SPREADSHEET FUNCTIONS: IF, SUM, ERROR
FEATURED PROGRAM: VisiCalc
TEMPLATE FUNCTION: Loan Amortization Calculator

BACKGROUNDER

Neither a borrower nor a lender be... That old adage certainly does not hold up these days—seems the only way to get by is to be in debt. But who are we, mere authors, to philosophize!

Ever taken out a mortgage? One of the exhibits that the bank supplies you with at the closing is a long sheet or sheets that list the actual dates of payments you will make for the next thirty years (or however long you signed up for). It breaks each payment into the amount of the principal that has been repaid, and the amount of interest in that payment. Each monthly payment is the same amount, just the proportions differ.

The bank probably (but don't depend on it!) produces that printout from their large mainframe computer. Now with this utility you can make the same examination for your own loans, compare the options on lengthening the period, shop around for banks with different interest rates, and so on.

There are a couple of interesting gimmicks in this model, including a neat trap for people who do not read the directions.

APPLICATION SPREADSHEET

This template determines the amount of each monthly payment on a planned loan. It also presents the amounts of interest and principal which make up each payment, and provides a yearly summary of each for tax purposes.

The Input Area

This model requires only three bits of information to do its thing: the amount to be borrowed, the interest rate, and the length of the term of the loan, expressed in years.

Look at the top of Figure 11.1. The place to put these variables is clearly indicated. Once they are entered, the requested recalc is done and the column of figures starts to appear.

```
            A           B           C          D          E          F          G
  1                           AMORTIZATION SCHEDULE
  2                           EQUAL MONTHLY PAYMENTS
  3    ================================================================================
  4    PRINCIPAL AMOUNT               10000.00  <-ENTER
  5    INTEREST RATE                        14  <-THESE
  6    NUMBER OF YEARS TO PAY                2  <-AMOUNTS
  7    AMOUNT OF MONTHLY PYMT           480.13     THEN
  8                                              ! RE-CALC
  9              MAX YRS=10:ERROR IF>10
 10    ================================================================================
 11         PAYMENT   REMAINING   INTEREST   PRINCIPAL CUMULATIVE  TOT YEARS  TOT YEARS
 12         NUMBER    PRINCIPAL      PAID        PAID    PAYMENT   INTEREST   PRINCIPAL
 13    --------------------------------------------------------------------------------
 14              1    10000.00     116.67      363.46     480.13
 15              2     9636.54     112.43      367.70     960.26
 16              3     9263.84     108.14      371.99    1440.39
 17              4     8896.84     103.80      376.33    1920.52
 18              5     8520.51      99.41      380.72    2400.64
 19              6     8139.79      94.96      385.16    2880.77
 20              7     7754.62      90.47      389.66    3360.90
 21              8     7364.96      85.92      394.20    3841.03
 22              9     6970.76      81.33      398.80    4321.16
 23             10     6571.96      76.67      403.46    4801.29
 24             11     6168.50      71.97      408.16    5281.42
 25             12     5760.34      67.20      412.92    5761.55    1108.96    4652.59
 26             13     5347.41      62.39      417.74    6241.67
 27             14     4929.67      57.51      422.62    6721.80
 28             15     4507.06      52.58      427.55    7201.93
 29             16     4079.51      47.59      432.53    7682.06
 30             17     3646.97      42.55      437.58    8162.19
 31             18     3209.39      37.44      442.69    8642.32
 32             19     2766.71      32.28      447.85    9122.45
 33             20     2318.86      27.05      453.08    9602.58
 34             21     1865.78      21.77      458.36   10082.71
 35             22     1407.42      16.42      463.71   10562.83
 36             23      943.71      11.01      469.12   11042.96
 37             24      474.59       5.54      474.59   11523.09     414.13    5347.41
 38              0        0.00       0.00        0.00       0.00
 39              0        0.00       0.00        0.00       0.00
 40              0        0.00       0.00        0.00       0.00

 MODEL CONTINUES TO ROW 123
```

Figure 11.1: Amortization Model

The Monthly Payment Amount

After the recalc, the first figure to appear is an important one in evaluating a loan: how much money has to come out of your budget each month. And this formula, in C7, is a doozy!

$$(C4*((C5/100)/12))/(1-((1+((C5/100)/12))^\wedge(-C6*12)))$$

We will have to SpreadTalk our way through this one in small chunks! This formula is the standard financial formula for determining payments. In generic terms this formula reads:

$$\text{Payment} = P*i/(1-((1+i)^\wedge -n))$$

where

P	=	principal
i	=	interest rate
n	=	number of payments

In English this is: the Payment equals the Principal times the interest rate divided by the result of (1 − (1/(1 + interest rate)) raised to the negative power of the number of loan payments.

C4 in our spreadsheet formula is the Principal. The next portion of the formula (C5/100)/12 is the interest rate on a monthly basis. The number of payments over the life of the loan is the number of years of the loan times twelve months. The formula is

$$C6*12$$

Of course, by playing with the years, one can converge on the monthly payment one can afford (then you have to find a bank that will play the game, too!)

You Gotta Read the Directions!

Before the report area, above the dotted line, there is a warning that the model only handles loans up to ten years—and we have a trap for those who ignore this. You will find this useful in any model that you prepare for others to use, if there is a critical entry that can make a nonsense of the action the model is supposed to perform. Two formulas do the trick, and one of them, if the trap is not sprung, goes about the business of preparing the report.

The first formula to react to a figure of larger than ten years, after the recalc command, is the apparently blank space to the left of the warning, A9, which is:

@IF(C6>10,7,0) set /F*

SpreadTalk: If the amount in C6 is greater than 10, print seven asterisks.

At the same time as these asterisks appear, in B4 there appears the word ERROR, and the word gets repeated down the column. Most spreadsheet programs react this way to finding an ERROR, repeating the word everywhere that calls on the location in which the first error appears.

SpreadTip: This ERROR flagging is a useful diagnostic device, and purposely entering ISERROR in a location quickly finds all the other locations that are calling it.

The formula that does the trick in B14 is

@IF(C6>10,@ERROR,C4)

SpreadTalk: If C6 is greater than 10, label this location as an error, otherwise bring down the amount in C4, which is the principal amount. Since this is the first entry we need for this row and column to start the action in the rest of the model, any value greater than ten is going to make the rest of it impossible to use, thus really calling attention to the mistake!

Numbering the Payments

Just so that you do not think we forgot the entry in the top of the PAYMENT NUMBER column is the number 1... it doesn't need a formula, since it will always be the first payment, even if there's only one! But while we are talking about this column we can do the formula in the second row of it, A15, since once this is replicated down the column (for 120 rows) we won't have to = come back to it.

It looks as if a straight "add one to the preceding row" would do, right? Sure it would, but we are polished performers on the keyboard in this department, so we have added a "frill."

The formula is

@IF(@OR(A14+1>(C6*12),A14=0),0,A14+1)

SpreadTalk: If the result of adding one to the preceding column is greater than the result of multiplying the "years to pay" entry by 12, OR the preceding payment number equals zero, then write zero, otherwise do the addition. We did

Will I Ever Stop Paying?

this to cut off the numbering of payments when the last one is reached, instead of having the numbers run on past the end of the report area.

Calculating the Outstanding Balance

Naturally, as you pay off the loan each month the amount outstanding, the remaining principal is reducing. With longer-term loans, since the interest rate is constant on the outstanding balance, the amount of principal you pay down is quite small.

The formula in B15, the one after the error trapping signal formula, is

@IF((B14<.005),0,(B14 − D14)

Ignore for a moment the IF .005 value there, we'll discuss it in a moment as it occurs in several formulas in this model. When it is stripped out the formula is simple: deduct from the last principal balance the amount of principal paid (B14 − D14).

For Those Interested in the Interest

In column C, we are figuring what proportion of the standard monthly payment is in fact interest. The formula in C14 is

(C4*((C5/100)/12))

SpreadTalk: Multiply the principal by one-twelfth of the interest rate (decimalized). The next entry in this column, on C15, varies as one might expect, to use the steadily reducing balance figure from column B instead of the originally entered figure from above:

(B15*((C5/100)/12))

Principally About Principal

In column D we figure the principal. The formula is

@IF(C14<.005,0,(C7 − C14))

Once again this should be a simple subtraction of the interest proportion in this monthly payment from the monthly payment amount in C7, but again we have put in the half a cent in an IF statement we used before , and it is time to explain it, as promised.

The problem illustrates the absolute honesty of a spreadsheet program. If one simply enters here the subtraction (C7 − C14) and replicates down the column, a peculiar thing happens down at the bottom.

We have adjusted the model slightly to illustrate this, reducing the payback period to two years, just to get the problem to develop a bit earlier—it happens around the time that the loan is nearly paid off.

PAYMENT NUMBER	REMAINING PRINCIPAL	INTEREST PAID	PRINCIPAL PAID	CUMULATIVE PAYMENT
20	2318.86	27.05	453.08	9602.58
21	1865.78	21.77	458.36	10082.71
22	1407.42	16.42	463.71	10562.83
23	943.71	11.01	469.12	11042.96
24	474.59	5.54	474.59	11523.09
0	0.00	0.00	480.13	12003.22
0	−480.13	−5.60	485.73	12483.35
0	−965.86	−11.27	491.40	12963.48
0	−1457.26	−17.00	497.13	13443.61
0	−1954.39	−22.80	502.93	13923.74

As you can see, things go fine down to the 24th payment, and eventually the REMAINING PRINCIPAL gets to zero, as does the INTEREST PAID—apparently! But the PRINCIPAL PAID goes on increasing and does not go to zero!

Spreadsheet programs work in up to sixteen decimal places. Since the column C (INTEREST PAID) formula is a multiplication by the result of a division, you can understand that at some point it may still be generating a result even though the figures it is dealing with will have dropped below a dollar, or even below a cent.

We converted the model to /GFG (Global Format General), to show the "numbers behind the numbers:"

PAYMENT NUMBER	REMAINING PRINCIPAL	INTEREST PAID	PRINCIPAL PAID	CUMULATIVE PAYMENT
20	2318.85670	27.0533281	453.075501	9602.57659
21	1865.78119	21.7674473	458.361382	10082.7054
22	1407.41981	16.4198978	463.708932	10562.8342
23	943.710880	11.0099603	469.118869	11042.9631
24	474.592011	5.53690680	474.591923	11523.0919
0	.0000885	0.00	480.128828	12003.2207
0	−480.12874	−5.6015020	485.730331	12483.3496
0	−965.85907	−11.268356	491.397185	12963.4784
0	−1457.2563	−17.001323	497.130152	13443.6072
0	−1954.3864	−22.801175	502.930004	13923.7361

The month following the last payment still shows a balance of .0000885 of a cent, and the model dutifully goes on working down this balance but since the monthly amount paid does not change, the numbers turn negative (meaning of course that you are building up a positive balance at the bank!). While starting a savings account may be a good idea, no bank wants to pay you 14 percent on it!

So to correct this precise precision, we have all the formulas check if the amount in the balance column has become less than one-half cent with the addition of the CHECK FOR A LITTLE BIT formula:

SpreadTalk: IF C14 is less than .005, do whatever, otherwise enter 0. Now we get the effect we want, which can be seen in our main illustration, that the model "turns off" when you and the bank agree that you have done all you can.

The Tax Forecaster Columns

The two right-and columns are useful if you want to outlook the amounts that you will have as an "Interest Paid" tax deduction over the life of the loan. They are SUM formulas adding up the preceding twelve months, and are of course based in our illustration on a neat situation that the first payment is in a January. You will have to place the first one in your model at the first December that will occur, then replicate down in the right places each twelve months.

If you do this kind of calculation regularly, you will have your model saved to disk as LOANBLANK, or some such name, so that you always have an original with no data entered.

Handling Loans Longer than Ten Years

If the loans you will be dealing with tend to run longer than ten years, you will need to prepare a special blank version of this model that takes out our ERROR trapping feature at the top of column B. You will use this new model just as has been outlined in this chapter, and the procedure is simple:

1. Go to A9 and /B to erase the Error trapping formula.
2. Go to B14 and write the formula +C4.
3. Enter the principal, interest rate, and the TOTAL NUMBER OF YEARS FOR THE LOAN.
4. Calculate the model.
5. Save the model to disk as LOANTEN (or other meaningful name).
6. Go back up to the top and enter the principal amount from B133 in the data entry area as a new PRINCIPAL AMOUNT figure.

7. Adjust the YEARS TO PAY suitably.
8. Make the MONTHLY PAYMENT NUMBER hard.
9. Change the PAYMENT NUMBER figure in A14 to 121 (1st month, 11th year).
10. Recalculate.

Repeat if the loan is longer than twenty years. Remember not to try and use one of these "succeeding years" models as an original, because you have "damaged" it by changing the MONTHLY PAYMENT amount to a hard value.

OtherCalcs

Multiplan

In Multiplan you can compute loans longer than ten years using the eXternal file linking command. To do this you want to have a blank loan template set up with the error mechanism turned off. Note the location of the last principal amount on your first 10 year template. Also note the location of the monthly payment figure (R7C3). Call up your next ten year template. Place the cursor at the location for principal. Now hit X, type the name of the first ten-year file, hit Tab, then type the location of the principal that you noted. Hit Tab twice, then Y for yes. Now hit Return. Input the years remaining. Move the cursor to the monthly payment cell, and hit X. Type the name of the first ten year template, hit Tab, type the location of the monthly payment amount. Hit Tab twice, then Y for yes. The next ten years (or however many remain) will be calculated. Every time you make a change to the first ten year template, the second one will update itself automatically when you load it.

You can also use the ROUND(n,digits) function in Multiplan to turn off the calculations after the loan is paid out. This might be simpler than our CHECK FOR A LITTLE BIT formula.

IF(R14C3<.005,0,(R7C3 − R14C3))

would become

ROUND(R7C3 − R14C3,2)

Now all of your figures will be rounded out to two decimal places, and any amount less than .005 should show up as a zero.

If you don't like to look at all of those zeros in the model after the loan payout is complete, Multiplan will allow you to put a blank space in for the zero.

Will I Ever Stop Paying?

This way there will be no numbers showing after the loan term has ended. To do this, write the CHECK FOR A LITTLE BIT formula this way:

IF(R14C3<.005, " " ,(R7C3 − R14C3))

or the ROUND formula this way:

IF(ROUND(R7C3 − R14C3,2) = 0," ",ROUND(R7C3 − R14C3))

Make sure that you put a blank space between the two quotes or the formula won't work.

SuperCalc³

There is a built-in PMT function in SuperCalc³ which is written PMT(Principal, Interest, Term) The formula as written in our spreadsheet would be:

PMT(C4,(C5/100)/12,C6*12)

Here one must put the interest and terms figures on a monthly basis.

If you don't like the look of all those zeros on your template after the loan payout is complete, SuperCalc³ will allow you to put a blank space in for the zero. This way there will be no numbers showing after the loan term has ended. As an example of how to do this, write the CHECK FOR A LITTLE BIT formula this way:

IF(C14<.005,(" "),(C7 − C14))

This is using the SuperCalc³ textual values feature. Note that the correct syntax for a textual value of a blank space is (" ").

12

Making It Come Out Even

SPREADSHEET FUNCTIONS: Math Operators
FEATURED PROGRAM: Multiplan
TEMPLATE FUNCTION: Break-even Analysis

BACKGROUNDER

One of the most frequent tasks a business planner has is evaluating the chances of a project or activity breaking even— another way to put it is the "risk evaluation" of a project. Whether this is done on a computer or not, or merely by using good judgment (after all many of us are doing such analyses instinctively, in our heads, all the time!), the process is fairly logical.

This template is designed to help you evaluate the risks involved in various production strategies. It determines the break-even point and safety margins for high, low, and intermediate production volumes. Businesspeople involved in manufacturing will find it useful, but it can be adapted to other purposes in which the variables are used in similar ways.

APPLICATION SPREADSHEET

Break-even Analysis

We are going to base our example on an unidentified industry, but the key issue being explored is simple. There is a set of options that exist in all industries

Making It Come Out Even

where the cost of goods is under the control of the planner. The planning considerations can be summed up as follows:

EITHER: go with high volume, lower price
OR: go with low volume, higher price

In the record publishing industry, for instance, this might translate to either producing a large number of records, getting them distributed widely and pricing them at a "popular" price, or producing a small number of records, pricing them high, and targeting them at the hard core buyers. The same options exist for automobiles, candy, toys, or anything—all that changes is probably the magnitude of the dollar production costs or the unit sales.

This marketing quandary appeals to the spreadsheet user, because the programs make it very easy to play the "What If. . ." game involved in this decision. We have designed a template that allows you to plug in the various projected unit selling prices and quantity of units produced, expected sales, plus the estimated direct and fixed expenses for different production level possibilities. The template contains some equations that will calculate the break-even points and safety margins for the four levels of production we have chosen to test. You will be able to modify it to suit your application. The template can be seen in Figure 12.1. It is arbitrarily set to accommodate four levels of production, Low, Low-Mid, High-Mid, and High.

The first input into the model is the Total No. Produced and the four different amounts for the four levels are entered into the cells in row 6. The next information to be entered at Row 7 is the Projected Sales Percent for the number of records produced (probably derived from historical sales and production data). This number is entered as a decimal (.55 for example) but formatted in Multiplan to display as a percent. This is done by hitting F(ormat), C(ells), entering the range to be formatted, Tab, Tab, %, Tab, 2.

Next entered are the projected prices per unit for the product, either based on historical data, or on industry standard prices for each production level, at row 9.

The next set of entries are the cost per unit of production for Labor, Materials, and Supplies, labor costs in row 14, materials in row 15, and finally, supplies in row 16.

We have entered an item called Fixed Costs in row 22, and these are shown as standard regardless of the quantity of records pressed. Fixed costs are just that, fixed. They usually are an allocation of overhead to the division, and could be computed in the spreadsheet, though to make this model more general, we chose just to enter the hard numbers here.

Once all the entries are made, with a press of the recalculation key, the formulas which are in the model calculate the Break-even Points and Safety Margins for each of the levels of production. You can then evaluate the risks associated with each production scheme and make decisions.

```
              1         2         3         4         5         6
     1  BREAK-EVEN MARKETING ANALYSIS
     2                                        LOW       HIGH
     3                              LOW       MID       MID       HIGH
     4  PRODUCTION LEVEL:           RANGE     RANGE     RANGE     RANGE
     5                              -----     -----     -----     -----
     6  TOT. NO. PRODUCED           50000     100000    150000    250000
     7  EXPECTED SALES %            55.00%    65.00%    75.00%    85.00%
     8  PROJECTED SALES             27500     65000     112500    212500
     9  UNIT SALES PRICE            5.84      3.76      3.50      2.75
    10  ------------------------------------------------------------
    11  EXPECTED REVENUES           160600    244400    393750    584375
    12
    13  PRODUCTION COSTS
    14    LABOR (PER UNIT)          $1.46     $1.02     $0.98     $0.79
    15    MATERIALS/UNIT            $0.34     $0.32     $0.30     $0.28
    16    SUPPLIES/UNIT             $1.50     $1.10     $0.75     $0.73
    17                              -----------------------------------
    18  COST PER UNIT               $3.30     $2.44     $2.03     $1.80
    19
    20
    21  VARIABLE COSTS              165000    244000    304500    450000
    22  FIXED COSTS                 21780     21780     21780     21780
    23                              -----------------------------------
    24  TOTAL COSTS                 186780    265780    326280    471780
    25
    26
    27
    28  BREAK-EVEN ($)              -794970   13307580  96088     94718
    29  BREAK-EVEN (PCS)            -136125   3539250   27454     34443
    30
    31  SAFETY MARGIN (%)           595.00    -5345.00  75.60     83.79
    32  ============================================================
```

Figure 12.1: Break-even Analysis in Multiplan

The Simpler Formulas

Let's look now at the formulas that perform these calculations. Note that we have named all of the variables in Multiplan using the Name command, so that the formulas were easier to write. By doing so we can also avoid having to discuss which column these formulas are in, and in addition, the Copy instructions become very simple. Once all of the variables have been assigned names, any formula written in column 3 using those names can be Copied across a row using the simple C(opy) R(ight) 3 Return instruction.

The first calculation occurs in row 11: the Projected Unit Sales calculation, using the formula

SLES%*PRDCTN

SpreadTalk: Multiply the Number of Records Produced times the Expected Unit Sales Percent. Since all of the formulas in this discussion were written using Named variables we will not use any more SpreadTalk unless the formula

Making It Come Out Even

is very complex. Once this number is determined, the model can calculate the Projected Sales Revenues in row 11. The formula for this operation is

(SALES*PRICE)

The next formula in the model calculates the Cost per Piece, by adding up the individual Labor, Material, and Supply costs. In row 18 it is

(LABOR+MATRL+SUPLY)

The Variable costs in row 21 are calculated based on the number of units produced and the per unit cost to produce them which was calculated in row 18. The formula reads:

(PRDCTN*COST)

The Total Costs of Production are determined at Row 24 with the formula:

(VARCST+FIXCST)

The Break-even Formulas

Once these intermediate formulas are evaluated, the model can use the Break-even and Safety Margin formulas to finish the calculations. The Break-even point is determined in two ways, the Dollar Break-even Point and the Number of Pieces necessary to break even.

The Dollar Break-even in row 28 is calculated as follows: the Fixed Costs are divided by the result of the Sales Revenue minus the Variable Costs, divided by the Sales Revenue. The formula looks like this

(FIXCST)/((REV − VARCST)/REV)

and is the same for all levels of production.

The Pieces Break-even is the Break-even Dollar amount divided by the Expected Price, or

(BRKEVN$/PRICE)

The Safety Margin, which is the percent chance that the expected results will be achieved, is determined using the formula

((REV − BRKEVN$)/REV)*100

SpreadTalk: Take the Sales Revenue minus the Break-even Dollars, and divide by the Sales Revenue. Then multiply by 100 to make it a into the familiar format for a percent.

SUMMARY

Evaluating the Result

How does one evaluate the results of this model? If you look at the Safety Margin in Figure 12.1, you will see a somewhat strange result. In the Low Range the safety margin is 595.00 percent! Does this mean there is a 600 percent chance that this range will be successful? No, this number is positive only because the break-even dollar amount is a negative that is being subtracted making a positive number. If in the Safety Margin row there are variables above 100 percent or less than 0, these numbers indicate a very high probability that the range under consideration will never be successful without some change in the variables. If on the other hand the number is positive and approaches 100 percent, this means that there is a high likelihood of success. In our example, the best scenario is the High Range where the chances for success are 83.79 percent.

OtherCalcs

VisiCalc

In VisiCalc there is no naming facility, but if you follow the above discussion, you should be able to construct the necessary formulas without too much trouble. If you are really stuck, the VisiCalc formulas appear in the appendix. There is no % format in VisiCalc, so you will have to be content with the $ or two decimal place format, shown in Figure 12.2.

SuperCalc[3]

There is no ability in SuperCalc[3] to assign names to cells, but the formulas are straightforward enough that you should have no trouble. If you need some hints, refer to the VisiCalc formulas shown in the formula list in the Appendix.

Making It Come Out Even   113

```
              A        B         C          D          E          F
                                                       LOW       HIGH
 1  BREAK-EVEN MARKETING ANALYSIS
 2                                          LOW        MID
 3                                LOW       MID        MID       HIGH
 4  PRODUCTION LEVEL:             RANGE     RANGE      RANGE     RANGE
 5                                -----     -----      -----     -----
 6  TOT. NO. PRODUCED             50000     100000     150000    250000
 7  EXPECTED SALES %              0.55      0.65       0.75      0.85
 8  PROJECTED SALES               27500     65000      112500    212500
 9  UNIT SALES PRICE              5.84      3.76       3.50      2.75
10                                ------------------------------------
11  EXPECTED REVENUES             160600    244400     393750    584375
12
13  PRODUCTION COSTS
14     LABOR (PER UNIT)           1.46      1.02       0.98      0.79
15     MATERIALS/UNIT             0.34      0.32       0.30      0.28
16     SUPPLIES/UNIT              1.50      1.10       0.75      0.73
17                                ------------------------------------
18  COST PER UNIT                 3.30      2.44       2.03      1.80
19
20
21  VARIABLE COSTS                165000    244000     304500    450000
22  FIXED COSTS                   21780     21780      21780     21780
23                                ------------------------------------
24  TOTAL COSTS                   186780    265780     326280    471780
25
26
27
28  BREAK-EVEN ($)                -794970   13307580   96088     94718
29  BREAK-EVEN (PCS)              -136125   3539250    27454     34443
30
31  SAFETY MARGIN (%)             595.00    -5345.00   75.60     83.79
32  ================================================================
```

Figure 12.2:   Break-even Analysis in SuperCalc[3] and VisiCalc

Making a Score

13

SPREADSHEET FUNCTIONS: SUM, IF, ISERROR, AVERAGE
FEATURED PROGRAM: VisiCalc
TEMPLATE FUNCTION: Weighted Scoring, Multiparameter Subjective Analysis

BACKGROUNDER

All businesspeople make decisions every day. Many of these decisions are subjective, and based on general experiences—they would be hard put to explain just *how* they arrived at the decision, since the mind works with speed and precision. Everything will have been weighed and balanced based on experience and only later, perhaps, can people reconstruct the thought process.

This model is designed to take the guesswork out of at least some of the decisions that must be made, especially those in the area of selecting from a set of fixed alternatives, and to display the results of some of the evaluation techniques that some of us may use instinctively. It can be used, for instance, by anyone responsible for selection of vendors, equipment, or other contract items that are put up for bid, whose selection depends on subjective factors other than cost.

The model was developed for evaluation of the weighted scores in a multiparameter subjective analysis. The model is in five parts:

1. Raw Score Entry and Weighted Criterion
2. Individual Weighting of Evaluation Items
3. Weights by Category
4. Sensitivity Weighting by Category
5. Range and Comparison of Results

Making a Score   115

APPLICATION SPREADSHEET

Our example is based on a hypothetical situation: the selection of a new data base management (DBM) system for a computer. All of the available systems and vendors must be reviewed and a recommendation made. Our assumption is that there are five systems under consideration and we must select the best one to meet our mythical company's needs.

The first task is, of course, to determine the most important criteria to be included in the evaluation, and rank these criteria according to their importance to the evaluation. We then plug them into a spreadsheet model, to help keep track of the items to be evaluated, and to score each vendor and rank them for their perceived capability to supply the desired services.

The Technical Criterion labels are entered into rows 5 through 50, columns A through F as they appear in Figure 13.1. At this early development stage none of the "white space" or underlines were included—there is a lot to be done before we clean the model up and prepare it for presentation.

The assigned weights for each category and subcategory were then entered in column G, and for multiplication purposes we entered them as decimal values, with the format set to dollars. The subcategory weights are a percent of the total weight for the category, so in column H at the end of each subcategory list, we have entered the following formula:

@IF(@SUM(G14...G18)<>1,@ERROR,1)

SpreadTalk: If the total of the weights assigned in this category do not equal one, print the word ERROR; otherwise enter 1, to confirm it is right. This gives us an automatic check while we are deciding the various weights for the factors. We are in fact making them add up to 100 percent (or 1 in this case).

```
         A    B    C    D    E    F    G    H          24  B.3  ACCESS METHODS           0.10
 1  WEIGHTED PARAMETER SCORING MODEL                    25  B.4  PHYSICAL STORAGE         0.25
 2  ================================                    26  B.5  OPERATIONAL INTERFACE    0.10
 3                                                      27  B.6  ARCHIVING & RESTORATION  0.05
 4                                                      28  B.7  PRIVACY/SECURITY/INTEGRITY 0.15
 5  TABLE 1: ORIGINAL SCORES AND WEIGHTS                29  B.8  ADJUNCT SERVICES & UTIL. 0.10  1.00
 6  ----------------------------------                  30
 7                                                      31  C.   EASE OF INSTALLATION     0.12
 8  TECHNICAL CRITERION             WEIGHTS             32  ------------------------------------
 9  ---------------------------------------             33  C.1  INSTALLATION             0.35
10                                                      34  C.2  IMPLEMENTATION           0.40
11                                                      35  C.3  USE BY TECHNICAL PERSON. 0.25  1.00
12  A.   END USER EASE              0.32                36
13  ---------------------------------------             37  D.   VENDOR SUPPORT           0.05
14  A.1  KNOWLEDGE REQUIRED         0.10                38  ------------------------------------
15  A.2  QUERY HANDLING             0.30                39  D.1  TRAINING                 0.35
16  A.3  REPORT WRITING             0.20                40  D.2  DOCUMENTATION            0.15
17  A.4  UPDATING CAPABILTIES       0.25                41  D.3  VENDOR POSITION          0.25
18  A.5  EXTERNAL FILE CONSTR.      0.15  1.00          42  D.4  VENDOR ASSISTANCE        0.25  1.00
19                                                      43
20  B.   SYSTEM CHAR. & FEATURES    0.35                44  E.   DATA BASE ALTERATION     0.16
21  ---------------------------------------             45  ------------------------------------
22  B.1  DATA DEFINITION & REPRE.   0.15                46  E.1  CHANGE IMPLEMENTATION    0.40
23  B.2  DATA STRUCTURE SUPPORT     0.10                47  E.2  GROWTH IMPLEMENTATION    0.60  1.00
```

Figure 13.1:   Parameters and Weights

The next item of business is to design a space for the input of the vendor scores. As we said earlier, this model can be used for the evaluation of virtually any kind of research project that involves scoring the results of questionnaires. In this hypothetical project, each vendor was to be given a list of the Technical Criteria, and invited to present information on each factor. As a result of their input their database management system would be ranked on a scale of one to ten for each item on the list.

As the information becomes available, the resulting scores are entered into the matrix on the right (see Figure 13.2), our vendors being represented by mythical companies called GROSS, RICH, MRG, EJW, and TASK.

	J	K	L	M	N
7	RESULTS OF				
8	VENDOR QUESTIONNAIRE				
9	----	----	----	----	----
10	GROSS	RICH	MRG	EJW	TASK
11	----	----	----	----	----
12					
13					
14	8.60	8.40	7.80	7.20	7.00
15	6.20	9.20	9.00	7.20	5.80
16	9.20	5.80	7.20	6.80	6.00
17	8.60	4.80	7.20	8.00	6.40
18	6.80	7.60	6.80	6.80	3.60
19					
20					
21					
22	8.60	5.80	8.20	8.80	6.20
23	8.60	5.60	9.00	9.40	5.80
24	7.80	7.60	8.20	7.60	8.20
25	8.60	7.40	8.20	7.80	7.40
26	7.00	7.40	7.20	7.80	8.80
27	5.60	7.60	9.40	8.20	7.60
28	8.20	8.60	8.00	8.80	7.40
29	9.00	5.80	7.80	8.00	8.00
30					
31					
32					
33	7.60	7.80	7.00	7.60	8.20
34	7.20	7.00	5.80	7.60	8.20
35	7.00	6.80	6.20	7.00	8.40
36					
37					
38					
39	9.00	7.40	7.80	8.80	7.80
40	8.00	7.00	7.80	8.60	7.80
41	8.00	5.80	7.40	7.40	7.40
42	7.80	5.40	7.40	9.00	8.20
43					
44					
45					
46	8.80	9.00	9.00	6.20	4.80
47	8.40	9.20	9.00	5.60	4.80
48					
49					
50	================================				

Figure 13.2: Vendor Results

Making a Score 117

Once the input section of the model is completed, the data are available for the evaluation part of the model, which in our template is positioned below the input area. This is a large model, as you can see if you check the last illustration—the "winner" shows up in row 147!

Weighting the Raw Scores

The first order of business is to reduce the vendor scores for each subcategory by the weight given to the item in column G. This involves developing a table in which each of the vendor scores is multiplied by the weight. This takes place in an area of the model we have called TABLE 2: Scores Weighted by Subcategory Weights, which starts at H51. Notice that we have included an index of the tables in the model at the top left of this area, so that when one has to move around the model it can be done with "jumps" or "GOTO's," which is generally quicker than using the cursor movement keys.

In order to make the formulas easy to replicate, we have placed the results for each vendor in the same column as their scores on the rows above. First we enter the table title beginning at H51, and then in column H we label the criteria.

In J57 appears the formula:

(G14*J14)

This is first replicated across the row, with the first value as no change and the second relative, thus using the same weighting factor for each of the criteria on each of the scores in the same column. Now we copy this set of formulas into all of the other cells in the table.

Two SpreadTips: We have said it elsewhere but we want to repeat this tip. When replicating a large solid block of formulas, such as we are now doing, do them all at once. Ignore for a moment the subtotal rows and the white space. All these can be inserted afterward by inserting extra rows. Your spreadsheet program will adjust the cell names in all the formulas to make them come out right.

The second tip is relative to reproducing a chunk of a model in another area. Since your spreadsheet program will replicate text labels as well as values, use it to copy the "form" of your model into the new location. In this way you will be sure of getting the two areas identical for the purpose of passing data back and forth—the relationship will be the same in each.

In combining these two tips there is something important to remember. *Do not clean up* the top area with pretty white space or dotted lines until everything is done, otherwise when you develop the solid block of formulas in the lower area, the locations will not be relative to one another.

The SubTotal formulas in rows 63, 74, 80, 87 and 92 are just a summing of the subcategory weighted scores, @SUM(J57...J61) for instance, and with the

118   Making a Score

completion of these Subtotal formulas Table 2 is finished, as you can see it in Figure 13.3.

Producing the Category Scores

The next job the model has to do is to reduce the subcategory scores to an overall score for each category. TABLE 3: Scores Weighted by Category Weights is shown in Figure 13.4.

We are going to multiply the total weight for each category, which had been assigned in Table 1, by the subcategory Subtotals from Table 2. We place the category labels in columns A through E, starting at row 101. Then to make the

```
         A     B     C     D     E     F     G     H     I     J     K     L     M     N
51
52    INDEX OF RESULT TABLES                   TABLE 2: SCORES WEIGHTED
53                                                   BY SUBCATEGORY WEIGHTS
54    TABLE 2 WEIGHTED SUBCATEGORY SCORES      -------------------------------------------
55         TO VIEW GOTO M54                    CRITERIA  GROSS  RICH   MRG   EJW   TASK
56    TABLE 3 WEIGHTED CATEGORY SCORES         -------------------------------------------
57         TO VIEW GOTO M110                   A.1       0.86   0.84   0.78  0.72  0.70
58    TABLE 4 SCORES WITH SENSITIVITY FACTORS  A.2       1.86   2.76   2.70  2.16  1.74
59         TO VIEW GOTO M127                   A.3       1.84   1.16   1.44  1.36  1.20
60    TABLE 5 RESULTS COMPARISON               A.4       2.15   1.20   1.80  2.00  1.60
61         TO VIEW GOTO A149                   A.5       1.02   1.14   1.02  1.02  0.54
62
63                                             SUB-TOTAL 7.73   7.10   7.74  0.78  5.78
64
65                                             B.1       1.29   0.87   1.23  1.32  0.93
66                                             B.2       0.86   0.56   0.90  0.94  0.58
67                                             B.3       0.78   0.76   0.82  0.76  0.82
68                                             B.4       2.15   1.85   2.05  1.95  1.85
69                                             B.5       0.70   0.74   0.72  0.78  0.88
70                                             B.6       0.28   0.38   0.47  0.41  0.38
71                                             B.7       1.23   1.29   1.20  1.32  1.11
72                                             B.8       0.90   0.58   0.78  0.80  0.80
73
74                                             SUB-TOTAL 8.19   7.03   8.17  8.28  7.35
75
76                                             C.1       2.66   2.73   2.45  2.66  2.87
77                                             C.2       2.88   2.80   2.32  3.04  3.28
78                                             C.3       1.75   1.70   1.55  1.75  2.10
79
80                                             SUB-TOTAL 7.29   7.23   6.32  7.45  8.25
81
82                                             D.1       3.15   2.59   2.73  3.08  2.73
83                                             D.2       1.20   1.05   1.17  1.29  1.17
84                                             D.3       2.00   1.45   1.85  1.85  1.85
85                                             D.4       1.95   1.35   1.85  2.25  2.05
86
87                                             SUB-TOTAL 8.30   6.44   7.60  8.47  7.80
88
89                                             E.1       3.52   3.60   3.60  2.48  1.92
90                                             E.2       5.04   5.52   5.40  3.36  2.88
91
92                                             SUB-TOTAL 8.56   9.12   9.00  5.84  4.80
93
94    =============================================================================
```

Figure 13.3:   Scores Weighted by Subcategory

Making a Score   119

```
            A     B       C       D       E     F     G     H      I     J       K      L      M      N      O      P      Q      R
 95
 96
 97                                                        TABLE 3:      SCORES WEIGHTED BY
 98                                                                      CATEGORY WEIGHTS
 99                                                        --------------------------------------------          AVER-  STANDARD
100                                                        WEIGHT     GROSS  RICH   MRG    EJW    TASK           AGE    DEV
101    A.   END USER EASE                                   0.32       2.47  2.27   2.48   0.25   1.85           1.86   0.84
102    B.   SYSTEM CHAR. & FEATURES                         0.35       2.87  2.46   2.86   2.90   2.57           2.73   0.18
103    C.   EASE OF INSTALLATION                            0.12       0.87  0.87   0.76   0.89   0.99           0.88   0.07
104    D.   VENDOR SUPPORT                                  0.05       0.42  0.32   0.38   0.42   0.39           0.39   0.04
105    E.   DATA BASE ALTERATION                            0.16       1.37  1.46   1.44   0.93   0.77           1.19   0.29
106                                                        -----      ---------------------------------
107                                                         1.00       8.00  7.38   7.91   5.40   6.57
108
109    ===========================================================================================================================
```

Figure 13.4:   Scores Weighted by Category Weights

table easy to understand, and also to make the replication easier, we bring down the total category weights from Table 1 into column H, beside each category label, using the simple formula (+ Category Weight Location), such as

(+G12)

for the End User Ease category.

The formulas for the weighted scores are then easy to construct. In J101 we have the formula

(J63*H101)

which is of course the Gross Company's subtotal score for END USER EASE from Table 2 multiplied by the category weight we brought down. The formula is replicated across the row, and then into the rest of the table, using the other relative subtotal scores.

In Table 3, we want to have the means to be able to compare the scores, so we have built two tables next to the scores, for the Average and Standard Deviation for each category. The formula for the Average Score is:

@AVERAGE(J101...N101)

and is copied into each row from P101...P105 and at P107. The formula for the

Standard Deviation is a bit more complex:

@SQRT((((J102^2)+(K101^2)+(L101^2)+(M101^2)+(N101^2))−
(@SUM(J101...N101)^2/@COUNT(J101...N101)))/
(@COUNT(J101...N101)−1))

Mathematicians will recognize that this is a spreadsheet representation of the more familiar construction:

$$s = \text{square root of } \frac{\text{sum of (items)}^2 \text{ minus } \frac{(\text{sum of items})^2}{\text{\# of items}}}{\text{\# of items}^{-1}}$$

Finally in Table 3, the total scores, the sums of the various categories, are added at the bottom under each company with a simple SUM formula of the list above.

Adding Sensitivity

In many evaluation studies it may be that some of the categories of criteria may be much more important than the weights actually shown. We have inserted one more table in the model, seen in Figure 13.5, in which a sensitivity factor is applied to the scores. This factor expresses the financial impact rather than the user impact, of each of the categories. We have assigned the weights for sensi-

```
         A    B    C    D    E    F       G        H     I     J     K     L     M     N    O      P      Q       R
110
111
112                                      TABLE 4: ALTERNATIVE TOTAL
113                                      USING SENSITIVITY FACTORS
114      ------------------------------------------------------------
115                                   SENSITIVITY                                         AVER-  STANDARD
116                                   FACTOR  WEIGHT   GROSS  RICH  MRG   EJW   TASK      AGE    DEV
117                                   ------------------------------------------------------------
118  A.  END USER EASE                 1.00   0.32     2.47   2.27  2.48  0.25  1.85      1.86   0.84
119  B.  SYSTEM CHAR. & FEATURES       0.70   0.25     2.01   1.72  2.00  2.03  1.80      1.91   0.13
120  C.  EASE OF INSTALLATION          1.20   0.14     1.05   1.04  0.91  1.07  1.19      1.05   0.09
121  D.  VENDOR SUPPORT                2.00   0.10     0.83   0.64  0.76  0.85  0.78      0.77   0.07
122  E.  DATA BASE ALTERATION          1.00   0.16     1.37   1.46  1.44  0.93  0.77      1.19   0.29
123                                   ------------------------------------------------------------
124                                   ERROR  1.00     7.73   7.14  7.59  5.13  6.39      6.80   0.95
125
126      ============================================================
```

Figure 13.5: Scores Weighted with Sensitivity Factors

Making a Score

tivity as they related to the importance to our hypothetical company in terms of overall system use rather than solely upon the technical merits of the products being evaluated.

This Alternative Total Table, Table 4, begins at H112. The sensitivity factors that you see were entered starting in G118. These factors were then applied to the individual Category weights at H118...H122. The formula for this is

(G118*H103)

and it is replicated into the range H119...H122. The formulas for the weighted scores by category for each vendor are similar to the formulas in Table 3, in that they multiply the adjusted weight times the Subtotal score for each category from Table 2. An example of the formula is the one at K118, which is

(H118*K63)

Once again we have added the Average Score and the Standard Deviation, inserted by replicating the formulas from Table 3 into the same relative locations next to Table 4. In G124 and H124 we have formulas that allow a tolerance of plus or minus 5 percent for the Total of the Sensitivity Factor and Total Weight. This is similar to the formulas in the other tables that checked to make sure that the weights did not exceed 1, but here the totals for the two could be no greater than 1.05 and no less than .95. The formula at G124 is written:

@IF(@OR(@SUM(G118...G122)>1.05,
@SUM(G118...G122)<.95,@ERROR,1)

and is the same only relative at H124.

The last formulas compute the Total Alternative Score by adding up the columns.

SUMMARY

And the Winner is . . .

One could be satisfied with the model as it stands, but there is one more step that can be inserted—the indication of the winner. We have prepared one more section that compares the scores and shows which vendor was rated the best, just for those who do not wish to wade through the entire model. Our last segment appears in Figure 13.6.

We have simply transferred the scores from Table 3 and Table 4 to rows 135 and 138. We have decided that an average score of both systems are needed, so we add the two scores (weighted with and without sensitivity) from each ven-

```
         A       B       C       D       E       F       G       H       I       J
127
128                     TABLE 5: RANGE AND COMPARISON
129                             OF RESULTS
130
131
132                                                     GROSS   RICH    MRG     EJW     TASK
133                                                     ----------------------------------------
134     OVERALL SCORE WITHOUT
135             SENSITIVITY                             8.00    7.38    7.91    5.40    6.57
136
137     OVERALL SCORE WITH
138             SENSITIVITY                             7.73    7.14    7.59    5.13    6.39
139
140                     AVERAGE                         7.86    7.26    7.75    5.27    6.48
141
142
143
144                                                     GROSS   RICH    MRG     EJW     TASK
145                                                     ----------------------------------------
146     HIGH SCORE DETERMINES                           *****
147             BID WINNER
```

Figure 13.6: The Results Table

dor together and divided them by 2, which of course is an average (you can also use the AVERAGE feature of your spreadsheet but it will probably be a bit more typing!).

Just to get a bit fancy and make it perfectly clear to anyone who reads it who won the evaluation, we have listed the vendors again in row 144, and written the following formula into F146:

@IF(F140=@MAX(F140...J140),5,0)

We placed the * format (/F*) in the cell, and replicated it across the row from G146...J146.

Let's hear it for vendor Gross!

OtherCalcs

Multiplan

The principles of this model will work identically in Multiplan. The model may be too large to fit into your machine's memory, though, if you have only 64K. This means that the model will have to be split into two or more files depending on the memory capacity of your machine. Because there are many natural points in this model at which it can be divided, this should not be a difficult task.

For example, suppose we want to split the model into separate files with one file containing the initial weights and vendor results and Table 2, and one file containing the rest of the model. We will want to link these models, so that any changes to the first file will be carried through to the second file.

The numbers that have to be linked between the two files would be the Category Weight totals used in Table 3 and the Subtotals of the vendor weighted scores from Table 2. These items would be brought into the second model by using the eXternal Linking Command in Multiplan. The easiest way to do this is to set up the first file, and then use the Name command to name the Category Weight totals in column 7, rows 12, 20, 31, 37, and 44. Then name the subtotal rows in Table 2. Save the file. Clear the screen, and use the eXternal Linking command to bring in the Named variables from the first file into the top of the new model. Once they have been brought into the second file, they can be used in the same manner to compute the scores in Tables 3 and 4 and to find the winner in Table 5.

The formula for Standard Deviation in Multiplan uses the sample standard deviation equation, so that our formulas for the Standard Deviations would be reduced to the much simpler:

STDEV(RC[−7]:RC[−3])

Another formula that would have to be changed in the Multiplan version of this model would be the one that totals the sensitivity factors in Table 4. This formula would be:

IF(OR(SUM(R118:122C7)>1.05,
        SUM(R118:122C7)<.95,ERROR,1)

SuperCalc³

This model could be set up exactly the same as the VisiCalc model. SuperCalc³ also has no built-in Standard Deviation function. To arrive at the standard deviation the formula would appear as follows:

SQRT((((J101^2)+(K101^2)+(L101^2)+(M101^2)+
        (N101^2))−(SUM(J101:N101)^2)/COUNT(J101:N101)))/
        (COUNT(J101:N101)−1))

Another modification you may wish to make is to replace the *****'s which show the winner, with a message made up of textual values.

14

Where Did All the Money Go?

SPREADSHEET FUNCTIONS: SUM, DIF—Data Save/Load
FEATURED PROGRAM: VisiCalc
TEMPLATE FUNCTION: Household Expense Register

BACKGROUNDER

The inventors and writers of VisiCalc, Dan Bricklin and Bob Frankston, did something else for the world besides developing a microcomputer activity, spreadsheeting, that would all by itself be the prime reason for meteoric growth by Apple, and give a whole bunch of other software writers something to do in trying to top their invention. They developed the Data Interchange Format or DIF. This was a method of formatting in a text file on disk the information from a column-and-row structured matrix so that it could be read by another program that supported the convention.

So now the data created by a VisiCalc model can be used elsewhere, for instance in a BASIC program. A side benefit of the DIF procedure is that data can be moved between models within VisiCalc, thus permitting the consolidation of data. The data are not location dependent, as they are with a regular model, and be taken out of one model in, say, the top left corner, and brought back into another in the bottom right.

The DIF format has fast become an industry standard and even though other spreadsheet programs have their own special formats, most of the developers of the other programs took care to see the their program also read the DIF files from VisiCalc.

The DIF Process

In VisiCalc the DIF files are created by a process called DATA SAVE. They are reloaded into a VisiCalc matrix by the DATA LOAD command sequence. Let's say you have a model in your computer and want to DIF it out [yes, it can truly be called an industry standard when the acronym can be used as a verb, as an adjective (a DIFfed file), or as an adverb (the file is DIFfable!)]. If you type / S and then #, the words

DATA   SAVE   LOAD

are offered for choice.

Answer with S for SAVE and once again things become familiar—a filename is requested. Once given (and if it exists you get asked if there is to be an overwrite) a new option appears, in this context—you are asked for the bottom right location. The DATA SAVE function saves only that area of the matrix that you want, rather than all of it as with a regular SAVE.

Now another unfamiliar question: R C OR ENTER—which means "save it by row or by column?" The DIF procedure allows you to reverse or twist a model, and you can do it now or later. If you have a vertically oriented table of data and want it to be horizontal, you tell it to save it by row: the data from the first column will be saved as if they had been done as the top row. (At LOAD time you could also have the file reversed.)

So what happens? First thing is that the DIF procedure saves values only, not formulas. There's a clue in the "#" symbol kicking off this process—because the DIF procedure effectively applies the # command to each cell as it saves it, the result of a formula is saved to full precision. Labels are saved okay but all formatting information is lost—the familiar repeating label, using the minus sign for a row of dashes, has gone and when you restore the file you just get the single minus instead of a row. Format left and right are also gone, although spaces are inserted so that the labels appear to have been formatted.

Bringing the file back is mostly a repeat of the SAVE procedure, except that there is no need to specify a lower right coordinate, the whole file comes back. Unlike a regular file load in VisiCalc, in which the file always come back into the area from which it was saved, a DIF file is not location dependent.

The process is invoked with the cursor in the cell that will form the top left of the retrieved data, the location in which you wish to have the retrieved data appear. If the empty cells it is to occupy have been preformatted, the incoming data will adopt the format found there.

SpreadTip: A further great use for the DIF function is the reduction of the memory a model consumes. If you have a model that is accumulating data as time goes on, soon the little memory indicator in the top right corner gets dangerously low. If there are areas of the model that are not going to change anymore, the formulas that created them are occupying valuable memory uselessly. Of course you can convert them to values one by one, using the # command symbol, or you can just DIF the area out to disk and bring it right back in again—the formulas will all have turned to values, and your memory counter should jump up a few notches!

APPLICATION SPREADSHEET

DIF Makes a DIFference!

So let us put this great capability to use, and we are going to do it in a simple consolidation exercise, that we have selected for its instant understandability. This model, the Monthly Expense Record and its companion template, yearly expense record, allow you to keep a record of your expenses by category. The monthly expenses are recorded for each item and transferred into the yearly expense record using DIF format, the year-to-date total is then computed, and the tax deductible expenses are moved into a separate account and totaled.

Now this is what one might call a "free-standing" model—it assumes that you will do a bit of preparatory work before sitting down to use it, possibly external to the computer. For instance, to enter a total figure for VISA CARD expenditures is one thing (the total of the check sent to VISA), but if you want to break down the actual expenses from that bill and allocate it to the types of charge: entertainment, clothing, travel, and so on, then that must be done externally, before you sit down to enter the data.

There is an alternative. You can associate the work here with a checkbook or spending management template (there is one in this book). As a check is written it is allocated to accounts, and using the DIF function, which this chapter explains, you can then take these totals and do the useful work we are about to show you.

We are, however, going to treat this as a free-standing model and make no assumptions as to how the data gets prepared before entry, we just assume that the breakdowns are available.

The Monthly Expense Record

In Figure 14.1 you will see a very comprehensive list of possible expenses that a family (or a small business for that matter) could have in a month. The first thing that we do is to divide the expenses into categories.

SpreadTip: You can use the MOVE capability in the early stages of model development to get things in the right order. We did this one by just sitting down at the machine and typing in entry after entry without thought of order or categorization. When we had all that we could think of, we started to /MOVE them

Where Did All the Money Go?

```
            A       B       C       D           E
 1 MONTHLY  HOUSEHOLD EXPENSE RECORD
 2 ================================================
 3
 4
 5
 6                       MONTH:      MARCH
 7                                   --------
 8 EXPENSES RELATING TO HOUSE             COMMENTS
 9 --------------------------             --------
10 MORTGAGE PRINCIPAL          540.00
11           INTEREST          375.00
12 TAXES                       100.00
13 GAS                          35.31
14 ELECTRICITY                  18.46
15 TELEPHONE                    42.73
16 WATER                        17.85
17 WOOD                         75.00
18 HOUSE INSURANCE             200.00   QRTLY PMT
19 MORTGAGE INSURANCE           50.00
20
21 SUB-TOTAL                  1454.35
22
23 OTHER HOUSEHOLD EXPENSES
24 ------------------------
25   IMPROVEMENTS                0.00
26   APPLIANCE REPAIR           35.00   WASHER
27   FURNITURE                  57.00   LAMP
28   MISCELLANEOUS              15.00   KITCN TLS
29
30 SUB-TOTAL                   107.00
31
32 TOTAL HOUSE EXPENSE        1561.35
33 ====================================
34
35 LIVING EXPENSES
36 ---------------
37   FOOD                      250.00
38   RESTAURANTS                65.00
39   DRY CLEANING               30.00
40   AMERICAN EXPRESS CARD     150.00
41     INTEREST                  0.00
42   VISA CARD                  75.00
43     INTEREST                  3.80
44   MASTER CARD                50.00
45     INTEREST                  2.25
46   SEARS                      55.00
47     INTEREST                  0.00
48   LIFE INSURANCE-HUSBAND     20.00
49   LIFE INSURANCE-WIFE        20.00
50   MEDICAL INSURANCE         228.00   QRTLY PMT
51   DOCTOR-HUSBAND              0.00
52   DOCTOR-WIFE                90.00
53   DRUGS                      35.00
54   DENTIST-HUSBAND            45.00
55   DENTIST-WIFE                0.00
56   CLOTHING-HUSBAND          175.00   SUIT
57   CLOTHING-WIFE              35.00   BLOUSE
58   CHURCH TITHE               50.00
59   OTHER CONTRIBUTIONS        10.00   LIONS CLB
60   CASH                      200.00
61   MISCELLANEOUS              17.00   MAG. SUB
62
63 TOTAL LIVING EXPENSES      1600.00
64 ====================================
65
```

Figure 14.1: Monthly Expense Record (part 1 of 2)

```
                       A          B         C            D          E
             5              MONTHLY HOUSEHOLD EXPENSE RECORD
             6                     MONTH:    MARCH
             7                               --------
             8  EXPENSES RELATING TO HOUSE              COMMENTS
             9  -------------------------               --------
            10  MORTGAGE PRINCIPAL           540.00
            11           INTEREST            375.00
            12  TAXES                        100.00
            13  GAS                           35.31
            14  ELECTRICITY                   18.46
            15  TELEPHONE                     42.73
            16  WATER                         17.85
            17  WOOD                          75.00
            18  HOUSE INSURANCE              200.00 QRTLY PMT
            19  MORTGAGE INSURANCE            50.00
            20
            21  SUB TOTAL                   1454.35
            22
            23  OTHER HOUSEHOLD EXPENSES
            24  ------------------------
            25   IMPROVEMENTS                  0.00
            26   APPLIANCE REPAIR             35.00    WASHER
            27   FURNITURE                    57.00    LAMP
            28   MISCELLANEOUS                15.00 KITCN TLS
            29
            30  SUB TOTAL                    107.00
            31
            32  TOTAL HOUSE EXPENSE         1561.35
            33  ======================================
            34
            35  LIVING EXPENSES
            36  ---------------
            37   FOOD                        250.00
            38   RESTAURANTS                  65.00
            39   DRY CLEANING                 30.00
            40   AMERICAN EXPRESS CARD       150.00
            41       INTEREST                  0.00
            42   VISA CARD                    75.00
            43       INTEREST                  3.80
            44   MASTER CARD                  50.00
            45       INTEREST                  2.25
            46   SEARS                        55.00
            47       INTEREST                  0.00
            48   LIFE INSURANCE-HUSBAND       20.00
            49   LIFE INSURANCE-WIFE          20.00
            50   MEDICAL INSURANCE           228.00 QRTLY PMT
            51   DOCTOR-HUSBAND                0.00
            52   DOCTOR-WIFE                  90.00
            53   DRUGS                        35.00
            54   DENTIST-HUSBAND              45.00
            55   DENTIST-WIFE                  0.00
            56   CLOTHING-HUSBAND            175.00    SUIT
            57   CLOTHING-WIFE                35.00    BLOUSE
            58   CHURCH TITHE                 50.00
            59   OTHER CONTRIBUTIONS          10.00 LIONS CLB
            60   CASH                        200.00
            61   MISCELLANEOUS                17.00 MAG. SUB
            62
            63  TOTAL LIVING EXPENSES       1600.00
```

Figure 14.1: Monthly Expense Record (part 2 of 2)

around until they were in the order we wanted, then we inserted the category headings, underlines, and so on.

The next thing that we had to decide was if we wanted the model to show one month only, or whether we wanted to have the whole year appear. Naturally this would be only a matter of adding columns, but we had decided that we needed to deal with one month at a time due to the number of entries we had to make each month, and the limited amount of memory we had in our machine (anyway if we did a whole year we would not have so much DIFfing to show

Where Did All the Money Go?

you!). Before entering any data we save the model containing the expense category labels to disk with a suitable name, like BLANKMONTH. This is so that we can call it in each time we start a new month, ready for data.

The rest of the Monthly Expense Record is fairly easy (if time-consuming). We enter the actual expenses in each category in column D, leaving blanks where there were no entries for the month. If there were any comments necessary to explain the expenditure, we enter those in column E next to the item. At the end of the list for each category we entered a formula that summed the expenses in each major type. For example, to determine the Total Living Expenses at D63 we have the formula:

@SUM(D37...D40,D42,D44,D46,D48...D61)

SpreadTip: One gets so used to using the SUM formula as a straight range that it is possible to forget that it will work on any "list," which can be a mixture of single cell locations or ranges, like this last formula is. Use it this way when the values you want are not contiguous. For instance in a column that has several subtotals in it, you can exclude them by using the various separate ranges:

SUM(A1...A3,A19...A25,A29...A42)

or get your SUM by adding up ONLY the subtotals

SUM(A4,A26,A43)

We have used this method in this model just to demonstrate. In some cases, a major category has two or more subcategories such as the House Expense group, which has two subgroupings, Total Automobile and Total Commuting. In these cases, we have summed the subgroup, and then added these subtotals together to get the Total for the expense type. The formula at D81 for Subtotal Automobile is

@SUM(D71,D73...D78)

(we were careful not to add the car loan interest twice); the formula at D88 for Subtotal Commute

@SUM(D84...D86)

and the formula at D90 for Total Transportation is

@SUM(D81,D88)

The completed data are saved to disk with a suitable filename, such as MARCHEXP or even just MARCH, especially if the diskette is dedicated to this particular procedure. We assume that we now have a diskette with the months of JANUARY, FEBRUARY, and MARCH duly completed.

The Yearly Expense Record

Now we need the consolidation model into which all this stuff is going to come together. You can see this model in Figures 14.2 and 14.3. We start by reloading the file saved previously as BLANKMONTH, the one that has all that category typing neatly laid out in the right order and pattern. Now we are going to add a feature before the data come in.

We not only want a record of all the expenses for the year, but we also want to know which of those expenses are tax deductible items. Get out Schedule A for Form 1040 and look at what kinds of expenses qualify as tax deductions.

```
          A        B        C         D        E        F        G        H        I    ...   AB
 1 YEARLY    HOUSEHOLD EXPENSE RECORD
 2 ================================================================================
 3
 4                    (TOTALS IN COLUMN AB)
 5
 6                 MONTH:    JANUARY           FEBRUARY            MARCH
 7                           --------          --------            -----
 8 EXPENSES RELATING TO HOUSE         COMMENTS          COMMENTS          COMMENTS  TOTALS
 9 --------------------------         --------          --------          --------
10 MORTGAGE  PRINCIPAL        495.00             520.00              540.00          1555.00
11           INTEREST         420.00             395.00              375.00          1190.00
12 TAXES                      100.00             100.00              100.00           300.00
13 GAS                         47.98              32.80               35.31           116.09
14 ELECTRICITY                 23.72              25.17               18.46            67.35
15 TELEPHONE                   35.64              55.83               42.73           134.20
16 WATER                       18.33              16.43               17.85            52.61
17 WOOD                         0.00               0.00               75.00            75.00
18 HOUSE INSURANCE              0.00               0.00              200.00QRTLY PMT  200.00
19 MORTGAGE INSURANCE          50.00              50.00               50.00           150.00
20
21 SUB-TOTAL                 1190.67            1195.23             1454.35          3840.25
22
23 OTHER HOUSEHOLD EXPENSES
24 ------------------------                                                          --------
25 IMPROVEMENTS               50.00BTHRMFIXT      0.00                0.00             50.00
26 APPLIANCE REPAIR            0.00               0.00               35.00  WASHER    35.00
27 FURNITURE                 350.00 CFEE TBL      0.00        LAMP   57.00  LAMP     407.00
28 MISCELLANEOUS              85.35FRPLCSCRN     37.00        PAINT  15.00KITCN TLS  137.35
29
30 SUB-TOTAL                 485.35              37.00              107.00           629.35
31
32 TOTAL HOUSE EXPENSE      1676.02            1232.23             1561.35          4469.60
33 ================================================================================
34
```

Figure 14.2: Yearly Expense Record (part 1 of 3)

Where Did All the Money Go?

```
         A         B         C        D        E         F        G        H         I     ...   AB
35 LIVING EXPENSES
36 ----------------------                                                                       ---------
37 FOOD                                235.31            197.30           250.00                 682.61
38 RESTAURANTS                         103.45            153.78            65.00                 322.23
39 DRY CLEANING                         27.00             32.00            30.00                  89.00
40 AMERICAN EXPRESS CARD               101.20             77.83           150.00                 329.03
41   INTEREST                            0.00              0.00             0.00                   0.00
42 VISA CARD                            60.00             75.00            75.00                 210.00
43   INTEREST                            2.75              3.80             3.80                  10.35
44 MASTER CARD                          50.00             50.00            50.00                 150.00
45   INTEREST                            2.25              2.14             2.25                   6.64
46 SEARS                                 0.00              0.00            55.00                  55.00
47   INTEREST                            0.00              0.00             0.00                   0.00
48 LIFE INSURANCE-HUSBAND               20.00             20.00            20.00                  60.00
49 LIFE INSURANCE-WIFE                  20.00             20.00            20.00                  60.00
50 MEDICAL INSURANCE                     0.00              0.00           228.00QRTLY PMT        228.00
51 DOCTOR-HUSBAND                        0.00              0.00             0.00                   0.00
52 DOCTOR-WIFE                           0.00              0.00            90.00                  90.00
53 DRUGS                                23.00             15.00            35.00                  73.00
54 DENTIST-HUSBAND                       0.00              0.00            45.00                  45.00
55 DENTIST-WIFE                         45.00              0.00             0.00                  45.00
56 CLOTHING-HUSBAND                     23.00 UNDRWEAR     0.00           175.00       SUIT      198.00
57 CLOTHING-WIFE                       189.99 SUIT         5.00 STKNGS     35.00       BLOUSE    229.99
58 CHURCH TITHE                         50.00             50.00            50.00                 150.00
59 OTHER CONTRIBUTIONS                   0.00             15.00 HRT FUND   10.00 LIONS CLB        25.00
60 CASH                                250.00            300.00           200.00                 750.00
61 MISCELLANEOUS                        29.00 MAG. SUB     0.00            17.00 MAG. SUB         46.00
62
63 TOTAL LIVING EXPENSES              1226.95           1010.91          1600.00                3837.86
64 ====================================  ========         ========         ========              ========
65
```

Figure 14.2: Yearly Expense Record (part 2 of 3)

Down at the end of the expense listing (A112) we input the labels for the Income Tax Record portion of the Yearly model as shown in Figure 14.3. The general tax categories came from Schedule A, then we went back through the expense record list and assigned the specific tax record labels.

The formulas for the Income Tax Record section simply consist of calls to the location in which the particular expense is found in the monthly listing (which is currently blank). For example, the tax deductible item "Dentist–wife" in row 122, has the formula for the month of January

(D52)

which is the location of the wife's dental expenses for the month of January.

After we have all of the tax formulas in place for January, they are copied into the columns for the other twelve months. We used every other column in the model for the actual entries, because we want to bring in the comments each month as from the Monthly format. At this time we put in all the other headings,

```
         A         B         C         D        E       F        G        H         I      ... AB
     66 TRANSPORTATION EXPENSE
     67 --------------------------                                                               ---------
     68 AUTOMOBILE
     69
     70    AUTOMOBILE ONE
     71    LOAN PAYMENT                       250.00          250.00          250.00               750.00
     72    INTEREST                           155.00          150.00          145.00               450.00
     73    GAS                                 47.80           65.25           55.61               168.66
     74    REPAIR                               0.00           30.50 OIL CHNG  25.00 FLAT TIRE      55.50
     75    MISCELLANEOUS                        0.00
     76
     77    AUTOMOBILE TWO
     78    GAS                                 73.50           52.00           67.89               193.39
     79    REPAIR                               0.00            0.00           91.87 TUNEUP         91.87
     80    MISCELLANEOUS                       83.00    TAXES                                       83.00
     81
     82 SUB-TOTAL AUTOMOBILE                  609.30          397.75          490.37              1497.42
     83
     84 COMMUTING
     85    STATION PARKING                     35.00           35.00           35.00               105.00
     86    TRAIN TICKET-HUSBAND                95.00           95.00           95.00               285.00
     87    TRAIN TICKET-WIFE                   95.00           95.00           95.00               285.00
     88
     89 SUB-TOTAL COMMUTE                     225.00          225.00          225.00               675.00
     90
     91 TOTAL TRANSPORTATION                  596.30          622.75          715.37              1934.42
     92 ==========================         ========        ========        ========             ========
     93
     94 VACATION EXPENSES
     95 --------------------------         --------        --------        --------             --------
     96    AIRPLANE TICKETS                     0.00          140.00 WASH DC    0.00               140.00
     97    HOTEL                                0.00           65.00            0.00                65.00
     98    RENTAL CAR                           0.00           27.00 TAXI       0.00                27.00
     99    RESTAURANTS                          0.00          230.00            0.00               230.00
    100    ENTERTAINMENT                        0.00           70.00            0.00                70.00
    101    MISCELLANEOUS                        0.00           35.00                                35.00
    102
    103 TOTAL VACATION                          0.00          567.00            0.00               567.00
    104 ==========================         ========        ========        ========             ========
    105
    106 TOTAL EXPENSES FOR MONTH            3499.27         3432.89         3876.72             10808.88
    107
    108 ==========================         ========        ========        ========             ========
    109
    110 =========================================================================================
    111
```

Figure 14.2: Yearly Expense Record (part 3 of 3)

total locations, etc. for the eventual arrival of the various months of data from the separate files residing on our diskette.

When all is done the model is saved to disk as YEAR (just so we do not lose it!).

Transferring the Data

Now we come to the DIFfing part of the process, and we have to "go back in time" a bit. We said that each month, when the data was entered, the model was

Where Did All the Money Go?

```
            A         B         C         D       E         F        G         H       I   ...    AB
    112 INCOME TAX RECORDS
    113                                       JANUARY           FEBRUARY            MARCH
    114 ===========================================================================================
    115
    116 MEDICAL EXPENSES
    117 ------------------------------------------------------------------------------------------
    118   MEDICAL INSURANCE                      0.00              0.00             228.00        228.00
    119   DOCTOR-HUSBAND                         0.00              0.00               0.00          0.00
    120   DOCTOR-WIFE                            0.00              0.00              90.00         90.00
    121   DENTIST-HUSBAND                        0.00              0.00              45.00         45.00
    122   DENTIST-WIFE                          45.00              0.00               0.00         45.00
    123   DRUGS                                 23.00             15.00              35.00         73.00
    124
    125 TOTAL MEDICAL                           68.00             15.00             398.00        481.00
    126 ---------------------------------     -------           -------            -------       -------
    127
    128 TAXES
    129 ---------------------------------     -------           -------            -------       -------
    130
    131   REAL ESTATE                          100.00            100.00             100.00        300.00
    132   MOTOR VEHICLE                         83.00                                              83.00
    133   PERSONAL PROPERTY                                                                         0.00
    134
    135 TOTAL TAXES                            183.00            100.00             100.00        383.00
    136 ---------------------------------     -------           -------            -------       -------
    137
    138 INTEREST EXPENSE
    139
    140   MORTGAGE                             420.00            395.00             375.00       1190.00
    141   AMERICAN EXPRESS                       0.00              0.00               0.00          0.00
    142   VISA                                   2.75              3.80               3.80         10.35
    143   MASTERCARD                             2.25              2.14               2.25          6.64
    144   SEARS                                  0.00              0.00               0.00          0.00
    145   AUTO LOAN                            155.00            150.00             145.00        450.00
    146
    147 TOTAL INTEREST                         580.00            550.94             526.05       1656.99
    148 ---------------------------------     -------           -------            -------       -------
    149
    150 MISCELLANEOUS                                                                               0.00
    151
    152 ===========================================================================================
    153
```

Figure 14.3: Income Tax Records

saved to disk with the name of the month as the filename. This was saved with the regular procedure. There is something else that was done at that time, that we did not mention. The column of figures, the actual dollar amounts, along with the comments about each expense is also saved as a DIF file, using the DATA SAVE procedure outlined earlier in this chapter.

The cursor is positioned on the month name in D6. Then we type /S#S (for Storage DIF Save), and answer the questions that VisiCalc asks. To the question "FILE FOR SAVING?" we write MAR.DIF.

SpreadTip: We add the suffix .DIF to all our DIF files in order to distinguish them from regular VisiCalc files. This prevents us from trying to load a

DIF file as a regular VisiCalc file. There is no harm done if you do inadvertently load a DIF file as a normal file. What will happen is that VisiCalc will try to read the file, and then will write EOD in the upper right-hand corner of your spreadsheet, indicating a file type mismatch. To correct this, simply load the file again using the DIF procedure this time.

The second question is "LOWER RIGHT?" and we enter E106, the last location at which there is information that we want to save (remember, we are saving the comments along with the expenses). The next VisiCalc question is whether we want to save the information as a row (R) or a column (C). Because the information is in two columns, we respond with the C for column format. A few whirs and clicks, and the data are saved in the DIF Format.

So now we want to do the consolidation, and as we said, we assume that we already have the DIF data for two months on the diskette in addition to the March data we just saved. We load the model that we created for the yearly totals, called YEAR. We want the January information to go in the first month's column, so we place the cursor at D6. To load the DIF file, we type /S#L (/STORAGE, DIF, LOAD), and again answer the various questions. "FILE FOR LOADING?":JAN.DIF. R or C for row or column: C. VisiCalc enters the stored data beginning at the cursor location and in a few seconds the January column is completely filled in.

Each time a DIF file is loaded into VisiCalc, a recalculation takes place, so that the formulas in the Income Tax Record section, and Totals column are automatically updated. The same procedure is followed for the FEB.DIF and MAR.DIF files with a few quick keystrokes and the first three months are added to the YEAR file.

OtherCalcs

Multiplan

In Multiplan there is an easier way to do a consolidation like this using the eXternal File Linking command. You have to name the cells on the Monthly files and then use the eXternal Linking command to bring them into the Yearly file. You may find that the Yearly consolidation file will not fit into the memory of your computer as it is so large. What you will have to do if this is the case, is enter three months' worth of monthly data on one file and then consolidate this quarterly information into your yearly template using eXternal File Linking. The OtherCalcs Multiplan section of the last chapter explained the file linking procedure in greater detail. You may wish to go back to that chapter and review the procedure.

SuperCalc³

SuperCalc³ supports the use of DIF so that you could use the same procedure shown here to accumulate your expense files. There is, however, another way to consolidate files and that is with the /Load Part File command. With this command you can combine all of the monthly information into the yearly report without have to go through the bother of using DIF. You have to remember the range that the Monthly information occupies in the Monthly spreadsheet; but then you simply place the cursor on the cell in the Yearly spreadsheet where the data you wish to bring in should begin, and you type /L filename P fromrange RET RET and the data comes in, in value form.

Out of Commission

15

SPREADSHEET FUNCTIONS: LOOKUP, IF, NA
FEATURED PROGRAM: VisiCalc
TEMPLATE FUNCTION: Preparing Commission Statements

BACKGROUNDER

There are many different applications in this book, aimed at different business solutions. We do not envisage any particular businessperson being the prime target for most of the models we use as illustrations, examples, and utilities. This one, however, tends towards sales.

The sales manager has several different areas of interest that are exclusively functions of that job, and one of them (in many companies) is working out the commission report for the reps or salespeople who are out there in the field, pushing the products, so that checks may be sent. In some companies this may be done by payroll or by the accounts payable group, but the information most frequently comes from the sales department.

We are going to look at a simple model that helps with this job, and in the process demonstrate a method for doing virtually any kind of report preparation that requires a value based on a scale of values. In order to do this we are going to set up a hypothetical situation, to be able to better follow the process.

APPLICATION SPREADSHEET

The Commission Calculator

Our imaginary company has several different products, each of which either pays a standard (but possibly different in each case) commission, or pays a "house" scale of commissions that decreases as volume grows.

The Sales Managers, together with the marketing group, design the various sales promotions that will take place each month. They decide together, perhaps because of a promotion that the company is running, if a product or products will be paid on the "deceleration" house scale or the standard product commission.

Take a look at Figure 15.1. There is a finished commission statement, ready to be sent to payroll to pay the sales rep, Charles Brown, his commission for May. His total sales for the month were $88,400.00, and his total commission earnings were $9,265.00. Let's take a look at how he got it, and how the commission calculator figured it out.

In column C is a code. This refers to the four standard commission rates the company pays on its products, coded 0 through 3, and a code 4 that tells VisiCalc to use a different figure for commission.

```
              A           B           C         D          E            F
 1                            COMMISSION REPORT   NOVEMBER  1984
 2
 3   SALESPERSON NAME:    CHARLES BROWN
 4   TERRITORY :          MIDWEST
 5
 6
 7   PRODUCT       SALES            COMMISSION      COMMISSION $'S
 8                                CODE    RATE     STRAIGHT    HOUSE
 9
10   GIZMO       14567.00          1      .075     1092.53     0.00
11   WIDGIT      10567.00          2      .1       1056.70     0.00
12   THNGAMAJIG   9567.00          3      .125     1195.88     0.00
13   DOHICKEY    13910.00          4      NA          0.00  1766.00
14   GADGET      14000.00          1      .075     1050.00     0.00
15   WTCHMCALIT   4789.00          2      .1        478.90     0.00
16   DOODAD      21000.00          3      .125     2625.00     0.00
17
18
19   TOTALS      88400.00                          7499.00  1766.00
20   COMMISSION EARNED THIS MONTH......................    9265
21            PERCENT OF SALES....   10.48              --------
22   DRAW AMOUNT.........    8000    CHECK AMOUNT...   1265
```

Figure 15.1:   Commission Report

In the next column (for the reference of Charles when he is checking his statement) the model brings down the commission rate that applies to the code. In the next column, providing the code is not 4, the straight percent of sales is inserted (column B times column D), and in the last column, if the code is indeed 4, the result of the sliding scale calculation is inserted. The rest of the totalling is obvious.

The Work Area

Take a look now at the work area illustrated in Figure 15.2. At the top we have a simple LOOKUP table, in which VisiCalc can find the current commission rate represented by the codes, for use in column D. Since 4 is the code for a different payment method, we insert @NA, which lets VisiCalc print NA in the RATE column in the Commission Report when applicable (VisiCalc is writing "Not Available"—we are reading it as "Not Applicable"). The formula in column D, on the first calculation line (row 13) is:

@LOOKUP (C13, H3...H7)

VisiCalc looks up the code in the table, and brings back the commission rate listed.

	H	I	J	K	L	M	N	O
1	CODE	TABLE						
2	0	.05						
3	1	.075						
4	2	.1						
5	3	.125						
6	4	NA						
7								
8								
9								
10	WORK AREA							
11			1-5K	5001-10K	10001-15K	15001-20K	20K & UP	TOTAL
12			.15	.125	.1	.075	.05	
13		14567	750.00	625.00	456.70	0.00	0.00	1831.70
14		10567	750.00	625.00	56.70	0.00	0.00	1431.70
15		9567	750.00	570.88	0.00	0.00	0.00	1320.88
16		13910	750.00	625.00	391.00	0.00	0.00	1766.00
17		14000	750.00	625.00	400.00	0.00	0.00	1775.00
18		4789	718.35	0.00	0.00	0.00	0.00	718.35
19		21000	750.00	625.00	500.00	375.00	50.00	2300.00

Figure 15.2: Work Area

Figuring Out the Sliding Scale

But what about the "House Commission"? The sliding scale works like this: on the first $5,000 in sales of the selected product 15 percent is paid. On the next $5,000, the commission goes down to 12.5 percent, on the next to 10 percent and so on, in $5,000 increments, until $20,000 is reached, when a straight 5 percent is paid on the amount over that.

Obviously the sales figure must then be broken down, since for instance on a sale of $7,500, we are going to pay 15 percent on the first $5,000 and 12.5 percent on the $2,500 remaining.

The bottom area of the Work Area does this, and there are some interesting formulas in there to do the work. We will stay in row 13 as we look at the formulas in the different columns, and by the way, we brought over the sales figure to this area in column I just for convenience during development—we could have used the column B entry directly in the following formulas. In column J, the formula is

@IF(I13>5000),750,(I13*J12)

SpreadTalk: Take a look at I13. If it is greater than 5,000, just insert 750 here, otherwise calculate I13 times J12 (which is the commission rate on sales 5,000 and under). The 750 figure is the default commission paid on the first complete 5,000, and is 15 percent.

In column K the formula is:

@IF((I13>10000),625,
     (@IF(((I13 − 5000)*K12)<1,0,(I13 − 5000)*K12)

It may look intimidating but VisiCalc understands this kind of talk! It takes a look at I13 again and if it is greater than 10,000 it inserts 625, which is of course the commission on the second 5,000 at 12.5 percent. If, on the other hand, it is less than 10,000, then it checks to see if the result of the commission calculation will be a negative quantity (if so it uses zero), and deducts 5,000 (on which we have paid commission in column J), and pays the commission rate on the portion of the second 5,000.

The formulas in columns L through N are similar, with only the greater than amounts changed to reflect the 5,000 increment on which the column is working. The formula in column N is simply

@IF((I13>20000),(I13 − 20000)*N12,0

which after the foregoing is probably quite obvious. The last column, O, is a simple @SUM addition across to get the total commission.

Back to the Commission Report...

So in the main Commission Report, if column D finds a 4 in the code column, it returns NA from the list (@LOOKUP table entry). If column F finds a 4 it picks up the total from column O and brings it over with the simple formula

@IF(C18=4,(O18),0)

The Draw

The only other small feature of this model concerns the draw. It is an obvious calculation to figure out the commission less the draw equals the check amount. But what if he doesn't make his draw—the report, against which payroll is going to pay, will show a negative amount, which will make it look as if poor old Charles has to write the company a check!

Since this is not the Ebenezer Scrooge Co., Inc., we have a simple formula to check the result of the Check Amount calculation and insert zero if it is less than 1 (that is negative)—and Charles gets to make it up next month, since the payroll records will also be tracking his year-to-date performance. Can you figure it out? Put this sentence into VisiCalcese: if the result of adding the two commissions, and then subtracting the draw is less than 1 (or zero if you like), insert zero, otherwise insert the result of the addition and subtraction.

SUMMARY

Even given the limited memory of the APPLE, it would be easy to design expansion of this matrix so that in fact it became a running record of the salesman's activities for the year, as well as printing out a payroll slip each month.

OtherCalcs

Multiplan

This program is simple to translate into Multiplan. All of the formulas work in the same manner. You will need to change the Lookup formula structure slightly, though. The formula would read

LOOKUP(RC[−1],R3C8:R7C9)

SuperCalc³

To use this model in SuperCalc all you would need to do is change the syntax of the Lookup formula. In SuperCalc this formula should be

    LOOKUP(C13,H3:H7)

16

Projecting Is Quite a Project...

SPREADSHEET FUNCTIONS: AVERAGE, COUNT, SQRT, SUM
FEATURED PROGRAM: VisiCalc
TEMPLATE FUNCTION: Linear Regression Analysis

BACKGROUNDER

This model performs linear regression analysis on entered data points. After the regression is completed, data points along the line can be predicted by the model. Now all that may seem like gobbledegook to the uninitiated—after all, we did not all graduate top of the class in math! Simply stated it is the capability to take a known, smaller series of numbers and plot them so that there can be an accurate prediction of other, unknown numbers.

This kind of work is done frequently in engineering firms by the data analysts. These people "crunch" the numbers the engineers bring in after they have done their studies on the ground and collected the data. But marketing people and salespeople can use the function too—they must also predict or forecast end results based on initial data.

This model then, while based on a manufacturing example, is applicable to many different kinds of uses and as we explain it you will see how it can, perhaps, be used in your business, too.

Pre-spreadsheeting, the job had to be done with a calculator (before that with a slide rule—anyone remember the "slipstick"?). The calculator method has a lot of drawbacks though, because you have to enter the numbers two or three times to check if the answer is correct. There is a high probability for error, with the repetitive entry of numbers, and sometimes it is difficult to be sure that you have entered all of the them correctly because as in most calculators, the contributing numbers disappear when they have been processed.

If you have a computer, however, there is a way to do this work with aid of a spreadsheet, since the three mathematical processes you need are built in to most of them. The three functions are:

Count: which is the ability to count across a row or down a column, counting the total of the number of entries (rather than the total OF the entries)

Square Root: a single entry command that figures the square root of a value (expressed as SQRT)

Average: which uses part of count—adding the total of a range of entries and then dividing by the number of them

Nearly all spreadsheet programs worth the name have these functions, and all of those featured by us in this book do.

APPLICATIONS SPREADSHEET

Take a look at Figure 16.1, which illustrates the the displayed part of the model, in which data is entered and the results appear. In the bottom right of the screen, in the area starting at K11, you can enter a desired X or Y value in cells B17 or B19, and after the initial data are entered you can recalculate to have an immediate confirmation of what the predicted value will be appear in L13 or L16.

The two columns, labelled X and Y, represent the data to be examined and from which predictions will be made. In our model they are the the number of pieces of a product that will be manufactured, in the X column, and some historical prices for the product at the different levels in the Y column.

The rest of the model, including the formulas in Figure 16.2, is the work area, in which the spreadsheet program does the lion's share of the calculating.

SpreadTip: We have used a useful windowing technique here that qualifies as a tip. Since the sequence of calculations in the model is left to right, if we place the results area directly beside the data area, we will have to do extra recalcs because of the forward references (this will not be true in Multiplan as it calculates in Natural Order). We have placed a window in the model and displayed the data entry area in the left hand one and the results area in the right. VisiCalc continues to do its thing in the hidden portion of the model and we get an instant response to changing X or Y without having to track around the matrix.

```
              A              B                    K           L

 1  LINEAR REGRESSION                   1
 2                                      2  PARAMETER VALUES
 3  DATA POINT ENTRY                    3  ------------------
 4        X              Y              4  X MU        941.20
 5  ==========================          5  Y MJ        173.40
 6          103         260.00          6  X STD DEV   687.20
 7          145         235.00          7  Y STD DEV    55.67
 8          500         221.00          8  SLOPE M    -.078613
 9          576         200.00          9  Y INTERCE   247.39
10          684         177.00         10  CORR.COE   -.970441
11          923         163.00         11  ##################
12         1006         148.00         12  X GUESS        400
13         1487         132.00         13  Y PREDICT   215.95
14         1983         105.00         14  ------------------
15         2005          93.00         15  Y GUESS     235.00
16                                     16  X PREDICT      158
17  ENTER X->           400            17  ------------------
18                                     18
19  ENTER Y->           235            19
```

Figure 16.1: Data Entry and Results Area

```
              E          F          G           H          I

 4        X SQR      Y SQR       X*Y        COUNT        10
 5  =====================================   SUM X      9412
 6        10609      67600      26780       SUM Y      1734
 7        21025      55225      34075       SUM X SQ  13108714
 8       250000      48841     110500       SUM Y SQ    328566
 9       331776      40000     115200       SUM XY     1297924
10       467856      31329     121068
11       851929      26569     150449
12      1012036      21904     148838
13      2211169      17424     196284
14      3932289      11025     208215
15      4020025       8649     186465
16
17
```

Figure 16.2: Calculation Area

If it does not strain the imagination too much, imagine that our manufacturer makes a precise part that has hand-tooling involved, so the variation in price at different quantity levels is not large. Also imagine that because of the special nature of the work he gets orders that may be "irregular"—13 pieces, say, or maybe 2011 pieces. What he wants to be able to do is predict the price for ALL levels between those for which he has proven information.

The formula that models a linear relationship is

$$y = mx + b$$

Where

y	=	the cost for each to be determined
m	=	the slope or gradient of increase in cost
x	=	the quantity to be manufactured
b	=	the *y-intercept* or where the predicted line would intercept the y axis

To determine m, the slope, for a regression line is pretty straightforward, but takes a few interim calculations. The formula is

$$(SUMxy - (SUMx*SUMy)/n))/ \\ (((SUMx*x) - (SUMx*SUMx))/n)$$

In this formula, n represents the number of known values from which we will be predicting. The formula for b, the *y-intercept* value is

$$((-m*SUMx) + SUMy)/n$$

We will come back to these two formulas later, since there are several interim values required in order to do the total linear regression analysis. We have decided to let the spreadsheet program do them step by step—advanced spreadsheet users will be able to combine some of the interim calculations into other formulas, but our method allows us to explain it step by step.

The first step to solving these equations is to calculate the sum of the x and y values, and some squares and square root relationships. We put labels for the items COUNT, SUM X, SUM Y, SUM X SQ, SUM Y SQ, and SUM XY in column H, then put the formulas for each of these items into the corresponding area of column I. (See Figure 16.2.)

In the COUNT cell at I3, is the VisiCalc formula:

@COUNT(A5...A14)

SpreadTalk: This counts the number of x values, or data points, or ns, that are to be evaluated. This could later be changed if a larger number of data points were examined. All that has to be done is to change A14 in the formula to whatever the end of the column A range was.

SUM X is

@SUM(A5...A14)

and SUM Y is

@SUM(B5...B14)

To get the SUM of the X SQUARES, we first have to square all of the x values. We do this in column E by multiplying each cell value by itself, with a formula similar to

(A5*A5)

Similarly we square the y values in column F, and then in column I we add the columns in the cells opposite the labels as shown, using

@SUM(E5..E14)

and

@SUM(F5...F14)

The last value we need is the SUM X times Y. We have the spreadsheet multiply all the x values by the y values in column G, and then use

@SUM(G5...G14)

to find the total.

Now the calculation of the regression statistics can get started and we will find the answers we need in columns K and L. In L3, the value called "X MU" is the average of the x value inputs. The formula that calculates this value is

@AVERAGE(A5...A14)

Y MU at L4 is the average of the y values, and was obtained with a similar formula

@AVERAGE(B5...B14)

Now we will start to use the values we precalculated in column I to figure out the Standard Deviation, the formulas for which are a little more complex. There are two formulas for calculating a Standard Deviation. One uses the *number of x values*, and one uses the *number of x values minus one*. When you are taking the Standard Deviation of a whole population, that is, you have sampled every value, you use the formula with n. In most cases you have only a sample

Projecting Is Quite a Project . . .

of a population to work with and in those cases you use the formula that looks at $n-1$. The formula that we use here

$$\text{STDDEV} = \sqrt{\frac{\text{SUM of } X^2 - \left(\frac{(\text{sum of } X)^2}{n}\right)}{n-1}}$$

Substitute n into the divisor of this formula if you are interested in the whole population.

In Spreadsheet formula language for our model, the formula for the Standard Deviation of x is

@SQRT((I7 − ((I5∗I5)/I4))/(I4 − 1))

which was placed at L6 in our model.

SpreadTalk: Take the sum of the X^2 values (I7) and subtract the quantity: sum of the X's squared divided by n (I5 squared divided by I4). Divide this quantity by $n-1$ (I4 − 1) and then take the square root.

The formula used to determine the Standard Deviation of the y values at L7 is similar,

@SQRT((I8 − ((I6∗I6)/I4))/(I4 − 1))

Substituting the Sum of the Y^2's and Sum of Y's for the Sum of the X^2's and Sum of X's.

The next step is to calculate m and b. We mentioned the two key formulas earlier in this chapter, and now we have all the components we need in either column L or column I. We put the formula to calculate m at L8, and it reads:

(I9 − ((I5∗I6)/I4))/(I7 − ((I5∗I5)/I4))

The formula for the *y-intercept*, b, is placed in L9, and reads

(((−L8∗I5) + I6)/I4)

Once this value, the slope of the values, has been determined, we are now able to do predictions: by inserting theoretical values for x and y values in column B, opposite the labels, we get the projected values. To predict y values the formula is

$((L8*L12)+L9)$

at L13. The formula to predict x values, at L16, is

$((L15-L9)/L8)$

The layout of the total model is a combination of Figures 16.1 and 16.2.

SUMMARY

Now our manufacturer can outlook what the projected manufacturing cost will be for virtually any quantity of product ordered. The answers will be statistically sound and once again a spreadsheet program can create a model that can be saved to disk and used over and over. Of course one of the side benefits is that a table can be created to cover, say, ten unit or twenty unit increments, and that can be used in hard copy for reference by different departments.

OtherCalcs

Multiplan

In Multiplan, there is a built-in Standard Deviation formula. You can therefore avoid having the X SQR and Y SQR columns in the model. Moving the answer column over to J or column 10, the formula in R6C10 for the X STD DEV would become:

STDEV(R6C1:R15C1)

and the formula for Y STD DEV in R7C10 would become

STDEV(R6C2:R15C2)

This formula uses the $n-1$ convention, so that if you were evaluating a whole population you would have to enter a formula similar to the ones used in VisiCalc.

SuperCalc[3]

In SuperCalc[3], the model would be constructed in the same manner as the VisiCalc model as there is no built-in Standard Deviation formula.

17

Breaking a Date

SPREADSHEET FUNCTIONS: LOOKUP, INT, IF
FEATURED PROGRAM: VisiCalc
TEMPLATE FUNCTION: Project Scheduling Application

BACKGROUNDER

We have commented before that some spreadsheet programs do not have date arithmetic, a built-in function that allows dates to be calculated and manipulated. As early users of VisiCalc, who were somewhat hampered in this way, we saw several systems developed to calculate dates, and have others in this book. We like this one because, though it seems complex, it is really very simple.

This template helps you to plan work projects that have several stages or sequential parts. Just specify the project's starting date and the number of days required for each stage, and VisiCalc calculates the dates of all the intermediate deadlines automatically. In the model, all deadlines are "rounded off" so that they never fall on weekends. You can also override any VisiCalc determined deadline by directly entering the desired date, and VisiCalc will calculate further deadlines from the entered date.

Using the principles outlined here you will be able to incorporate this date management facility into other models for other purposes. The template described here is an example of this project scheduling model. We have labelled the steps in the project as Task 1, Task 2, etc. The actual tasks must be entered in the order in which they naturally occur, and must not overlap.

APPLICATIONS SPREADSHEET

The Project Scheduler

The template works on the basis that each day in a period spanning many years has a unique number, by implementing a numbers scheme that assigns a number to a given date in the twelve year period from January 1, 1981 to December 31,1992: January 1, 1981 = 1; January 2, 1981 = 2; and so on.

Any production schedule that falls within this 12-year period can be planned with our template. Simple changes to the @LOOKUP table shown in Figure 17.4, will allow you to adapt the template to other time periods.

Even though the actual calculations performed to determine the completion dates for each step are rather complex, we want this template to be easy to use and to appear simple. The part of the template that is shown in Figure 17.1 is all that appears on the screen when the model is loaded into the computer. The actual area shown will be dictated by the computer you are using. If your computer allows displays of 80 characters, you may have to adjust the template display.

To use the template, the Starting Date is entered in B26 and C26. The cell format at B26 is set to /F$ in order to allow the display of two decimal places. The date entry at B26 is the Month and Day written as Month.Day. For example, the starting date in Figure 17.1 is November 24th, written as 11.24. The year is entered at C26, just as it would normally appear, 1984 in Figure 17.1.

	A	B	C		O	P
21	PROJECT SCHEDULING			21		
22	--------------------			22		
23				23		
24		START DATE		24		
25		--------------		25		
26	PROJECT	11.24	1984	26	11.24	1984
27	"ZERO"			27		
28			WORKING	28		
29	TASK		DAYS REQD	29	DUE DATE	
30	--------------------			30	--------------	
31	ONE		3	31	11.27	1984
32	TWO		10	32	12.11	1984
33	THREE		3	33	12.14	1984
34	FOUR		5	34	12.21	1984
35	FIVE		12	35	1.03	1985
36	SIX		1	36	1.09	1985
37	SEVEN		25	37	2.13	1985
38	EIGHT		1	38	2.14	1985
39	NINE		14	39	3.06	1985

Figure 17.1: Input and Results Screen

Breaking a Date

The tasks to be completed during the project are entered, starting at A31. The days required to complete each task are added in column C. When this information is entered, a forced recalculation will cause the Project Due Dates to appear in columns O and P.

SpreadTip: When entering data into a spreadsheet model (or even when entering formulas during development), get into the habit of setting the automatic recalculation function OFF. This will speed the entries since you will not have to wait after each Return or Enter while the program recalculates the total model. It is unlikely that you will want to see the results of interim values during the process but if you do want to examine a specific result in one particular cell, there's an easy way . . .

SpreadTip: To examine a result when the /Global Recalc Automatic is off, go to the cell and go through the motions of /Editing the formula, but without actually changing it. In VisiCalc you would type /E and then immediately hit Return. Most all programs recalculate a cell after editing and you will see that result change, without having to wait for the whole model to be redone.

Note that we have suggested setting a vertical window in the display that allows one to see the Due Dates next to the Working Days input.

Calculating the Due Dates

What are the calculations that have to take place in order for VisiCalc to determine the Due Dates? This model uses a @LOOKUP Table that takes the Date entered as the Starting Date, and converts this date to a Day Number, adds the first project Days Required and then converts this back to the Month/Day format and places this number in column O.

There are many intermediate steps that take place during this calculation. These steps occur off the screen, in columns D though J, and columns Q through T. Take a look at Figure 17.1. The first thing that happens is that the Starting Date is written into O26 and P26. Then at Q26 (Figure 17.2), the formula

@LOOKUP(P26,B1...M1)

LOOKsUP the Year in the Table. This gives the Day Number for the first day of that particular year; 1096 for 1984.

The formula in R26 determines the Day Number; the beginning of the year for the first day of the Starting Date month:

@IF(P26/4 = @INT(P26/4),
    @LOOKUP(O26,B6...M6,
        @LOOKUP(O26,B11...M11)

```
            Q        R       S        T

    26     1096     305      23      1424
    27
    28     YEAR    MONTH    DAY     TOTAL
    29     OFFST   OFFST   OFFST    OFFST
    30     ---------------------    1424
    31     1096     305      26      1427
    32     1096     335      10      1441
    33     1096     335      13      1444
    34     1096     335      20      1451
    35     1462       0       7      1469
    36     1462       0       8      1470
    37     1462      31      12      1505
    38     1462      31      13      1506
    39     1462      59       5      1526
```

Figure 17.2: Offset Calculator

This number is not the same in all years due to Leap Year, so . . .

SpreadTalk: First the formula establishes if it is a Leap Year. If the result of dividing the year by four equals the integer of the same division (indicating there is no decimal remainder and therefore the division is exact), it is a Leap Year. If it is, the first day of the month number is @LOOKedUP in B6. . .M6, and if it is not, then in B11. . .M11.

Now that the Day Number from January 1, 1981 is known in Q26, and the number of days from that date to the first of the month for the starting date is known (R26), we need to know how many days into the month the starting date is so that we can get the exact Day Number for the Starting Date. This calculation is performed in S26 by the formula

$$(O26 - @INT(O26)) * 100 - 1$$

SpreadTalk: Multiply the day decimal number by 100 to get a whole number, and then subtract 1 because the Month calculation at R26 has already accounted for the first day of the month.

The Day Number for the Starting Date can now be calculated at T26 by adding up the numbers in Q26, R26, and S26

$$(Q26 + R26 + S2)$$

This number is then transferred—called over by T30

Breaking a Date   153

(+T26)

for use in the formula at E31.

Adjusting for Weekends

With the Starting Date Day Number known, VisiCalc can now determine the completion date for the first task. These calculations take place in columns D through J, which are shown in Figure 17.3. The process begins at D31, where the number of Calendar Days necessary to complete the task is computed using the formula

@INT(C31/5)*7 + C31 − (5*@INT(C31/5))

SpreadTalk: For tasks that take more than a week (established by dividing the duration of the task by five), this formula adds the additional days necessary to account for nonworking weekends. The formula at E31 determines if there is an additional Weekend Adjustment needed to the project ending on a Friday.

@IF(−7*@INT(4 + D31 + T30/7) + 4 + D31 + T30<
(−7*@INT(4 + T30/7) + 4 + T30),2,0)

At F31, the number of Calendar days and the Weekend Adjustments are added to the Starting Date Number by the formula

T30 + D31 + E31

	D	E	F	G	H	I	J
26							
27		ADDIT			DAYS		DAYS
28	CALEND	WKND	TOTAL		FROM		AFTER
29	DAYS	ADJUST	DAYS	YEAR	JAN 1	MONTH	FIRST
30	---	---	---	---	---	---	---
31	3	0	1427	1984	331	11.01	26
32	14	0	1441	1984	345	12.01	10
33	3	0	1444	1984	348	12.01	13
34	7	0	1451	1984	355	12.01	20
35	16	2	1469	1985	7	1.01	7
36	1	0	1470	1985	8	1.01	8
37	35	0	1505	1985	43	2.01	12
38	1	0	1506	1985	44	2.01	13
39	18	2	1526	1985	64	3.01	5

Figure 17.3:   Weekend and Year-end Adjustment Area

The formula in column G LOOKsUP the Total Days from column F in order to determine what year the next deadline occurs in:

@LOOKUP(F31,B2...M2)

SpreadTalk: Read the Day Numbers from the @LOOKUP table in row 2 of Figure 17.4, and return the Year below it.

In column H, VisiCalc subtracts out the Year's "contribution,"

F31 − @LOOKUP(G31,B1...M1)

leaving the number of days the new deadline occurs past January 1st.

The Month in which the new deadline occurs is determined in column I:

@IF(G31/4 = @INT(G31/4),
   @LOOKUP(H31,B7...M7),
   @LOOKUP(H31,B12...M12)

SpreadTalk: First the Leap Year condition is determined, and then the Month is looked up using the LOOKUP Table at B7...M7, or B12...M12

The calculations in column J find the number of days the new deadline is after the first of the month.

@IF(G31/4 = @INT(G31/4),
   @LOOKUP(H31,B6...M6),
   @LOOKUP(H31,B11...M11)

	A	B	C	D	E	F	G	H	I	J	K	L	M
1	YEAR	1981	1982	1983	1984	1985	1986	1987	1988	1989	1990	1991	1992
2	TO/FR	1	366	731	1096	1462	1827	2192	2557	2923	3288	3653	4018
3	DAYS	1981	1982	1983	1984	1985	1986	1987	1988	1989	1990	1991	1992
4													
5													
6	LEAP	1	2	3	4	5	6	7	8	9	10	11	12
7	YEAR	0	31	60	91	121	152	182	213	244	274	305	335
8	MONTHS	1.01	2.01	3.01	4.01	5.01	6.01	7.01	8.01	9.01	10.01	11.01	12.01
9													
10													
11	NON-	1	2	3	4	5	6	7	8	9	10	11	12
12	LEAP	0	31	59	90	120	151	181	212	243	273	304	334
13	YEAR	1.01	2.01	3.01	4.01	5.01	6.01	7.01	8.01	9.01	10.01	11.01	12.01

Figure 17.4:   Date LOOKUP Tables

SpreadTip: A note for those who may be entering this into VisiCalc or SuperCalc[3]: Set your order of recalculation to ROWS, so that no multiple recalcs are necessary.

The Rest of the Deadlines

Now that the first deadline has been calculated, VisiCalc moves back to columns Q through T to begin the process all over again for the succeeding deadlines. The formulas that appear in row 31, columns D...J and columns Q...T are replicated down the columns to row 39. As each deadline is calculated, formulas at columns O and P display the Due Dates. The formulas at column O are in the form:

+I31+(J31/100)

which display the Month and Day as a number with two decimals. The cell format for the column is set to /F$, so that the whole date is displayed. The formulas in column P simply transfer the year number from column J.

Manual Adjustments

For some projects, one or more of the stages must be completed by a certain date. If this is the case, the Due Date desired can be directly input into columns O and P. Before using the recalculate key, press the "shift window" key (;) and enter the dates in one or more rows of columns O and P (don't forget to enter both the Month.Day and the Year!).

When the Recalculation function is called, VisiCalc does not revise these new manually input dates. Instead, it uses each one as a new starting date for calculating all subsequent deadlines. In column G (Year), VisiCalc looks up Total Days in the years table to determine in which year the next deadline falls.

If you use this "manual override" feature often, sometimes the dates in columns O and P will appear out of order. This reflects an inconsistency in the scheduling. The days required take you past the manually input Due Date. VisiCalc can't help when this happens—you must go back an change something in the schedule.

Note with caution that when you place an "override " date in columns O and P, you destroy the formulas that would allow VisiCalc to calculate a date in those cells. To undo this override, you must restore the appropriate formulas, by either reloading the template from disk storage, or replicating the formulas from a row you haven't altered.

SUMMARY

This model is very complex in its construction and calculations. Representative formulas that went into the model are listed at the end of the chapter. Once the template is built, however, it is remarkably simple to use, and should be very useful to those who need to schedule projects with many stages.

OtherCalcs

Multiplan

This model has been demonstrated in VisiCalc, but it will be keyed in identically to a Multiplan model, using the correct syntax for Multiplan expressions.

SuperCalc³

SuperCalc³ has built-in date arithmetic, that enables it to manage dates written in the format MM,DD,YY as direct values. It is worth becoming familiar with this particular attribute of SuperCalc³ as it can be most useful.

We have created a template in SuperCalc³ that is shown in Figures 17.5 and 17.6. This model is somewhat less complex than the VisiCalc and Multiplan model as the date functions automatically calculate the dates for you. You still must be concerned with adjustments in schedules for weekends though, that our model does for you.

	A	B		E	F
1	ENTER		1		
2	START DATE	5/ 6/85	2		
3			3	TASK	TASK
4		DAYS TO	4	START	END
5		COMPLETE	5	DAY	DAY
6	TASK 1	3	6	5/ 6/85	5/ 8/85
7	TASK 2	4	7	5/ 9/85	5/14/85
8	TASK 3	5	8	5/15/85	5/21/85
9	TASK 4	10	9	5/22/85	6/ 4/85
10	TASK 5	8	10	6/ 5/85	6/14/85
11	TASK 6	2	11	6/17/85	6/18/85
12	TASK 7	4	12	6/19/85	6/24/85
13	TASK 8	5	13	6/25/85	7/ 1/85

Figure 17.5: SuperCalc³ Entry and Results Screen

Breaking a Date

	C	D
1		
2		
3	CUMULATVE	WEEKEND
4	PROJECT	ADJUSTMNT
5	DAYS	DAYS
6	3	0
7	7	2
8	12	0
9	22	4
10	30	2
11	32	0
12	36	2
13	41	0

Figure 17.6: SuperCalc[3] Work Area

Take a look at Figure 17.5. Here you see The Entry and Results areas that appear to be very similar to the VisiCalc model. The starting date is entered at B2 using the formula:

DATE(05,06,85)

SpreadTalk: Enter the Starting date using the DATE built-in function that takes the form DATE(MM,DD,YY).

The days scheduled to complete each task are entered in column B. In column C of the work area, the formula at B6:

+B6+C5

finds a running total of the number of days on the project. This formula is /Replicated relatively down the column. In column D we make an adjustment for weekend days using the formulas:

D6	=	INT(+C6/7)*2
D7	=	INT(+C7/7)*2 − SUM(D6:D6)
D8	=	INT(+C8/7)*2 − SUM(D6:D7)
D9	=	INT(+C9/7)*2 − SUM(D6:D8)
D10	=	INT(+C10/7)*2 − SUM(D6:D9)
D11	=	INT(+C11/7)*2 − SUM(D6:D10)
D12	=	INT(+C12/7)*2 − SUM(D6:D11)
D13	=	INT(+C13/7)*2 − SUM(D6:D12)

SpreadTalk: Divide the running total figure by 7 to find the number of weeks for this task. Multiply the integer portion of the weeks by 2 to add the proper number of weekend days. Because we may have already adjusted for some weekends, subtract those adjustments (SUM(D6:D8)) from the number just calculated.

To find the task starting and ending days in columns E and F, we begin by bringing over our entered starting date, and place this at E6. Then we find the ending date for this task in column F using the formulas similar to this one at F6:

IF(WDAY(E6 + D6 + B6 − 1) = 7,E6 + D6 + B6 + 1,
　　IF(WDAY(E6 + D6 + B6 − 1) = 1,E6 + D6 + B6 + 1,E6 + D6 + B6 − 1))

SpreadTalk: Here we are using the built-in formula WDAY(datevalue) to determine if the ending day (E6 + D6 + B6 − 1) falls on a Saturday (WDAY = 7) or Sunday (WDAY = 1). If either of these cases is true, two additional days are added to the ending day (the ending day formula is Project Days (B6) plus Additional Weekend Days (D6) plus Start Date (E6) minus one— since we have not subtracted the one in the formula E6 + D6 + B6 + 1, we are in essence adding two additional days). If no additional adjustment is needed, then the Ending Date is calculated using E6 + D6 + B6 − 1.

The Starting date for the second task uses the formula:

IF(WDAY(F6) = 6,F6 + 3,F6 + 1)

SpreadTalk: Check to see whether the preceding task ended on a Friday (WDAY = 6). If so, add three more days (the weekend plus the day after the end date) or just add one to get us to the next day.

The rest of the starting and ending formulas are identical to the ones just outlined, and are replicated down the columns. Because of the small amount of space this model takes up it is ideally suited for using as a utility structure within other models.

Making the Quota 18

SPREADSHEET FUNCTIONS: DIF Overlays/Consolidation
FEATURED PROGRAM: VisiCalc
TEMPLATE FUNCTION: Sales Territory Management

BACKGROUNDER

One of the functions that made Multiplan an early hit was the presence of a capability that had not been available up until that time: the ability to link spreadsheet files. By this we mean to be able to tell the spreadsheet program to bring in data from one or a series of reports and collate them into a new, summary report, which is automatically updated for changes as it is loaded. For instance, the financial reports of several divisions could be assembled into the company report using this facility.

The SuperCalc family of templates has this capability in another fashion. Here, the files or portions of files can be called in and added to or subtracted from existing data in the file. The only proviso is that the component reports be in an identical format to one another. The programs that have this function load one template on top of another, adding (or subtracting) each incoming cell to the total resident in the corresponding cell in the computer, until eventually they are all totaled. Needless to say, after the process is complete then the resident model, the "totals" report, can be modified or manipulated as one wishes.

VisiCalc did not have this function, and still does not, even in the Advanced version, so we had to devise ways around it. What VisiCalc had that made it all possible was the DIF function (see Chapter 14), permitting us to do overlays.

The purpose of these models is to allow the user to track sales performance for an entire region during a year and develop the next year's quotas for individual territories from the previous year's data. Customized reports for each sales territory can be printed with a minimum number of model changes.

If you have a spreadsheet program that contains a consolidation function you may be wondering why you should read this chapter at all. It is useful in that the discipline and methodology of organizing the work and the procedure for carrying out are the same for consolidating as for using DIF files and overlays. Anyway you enjoy reading about spreadsheet programs conceptually, don't you?

APPLICATION SPREADSHEET

We developed this template in response to one of our friend's needs for a model that would help him project the new year's sales quotas for his sales force. Jim was responsible for supervising the entire sales force for the five regions the company had. This job involved keeping track of how the sales force was performing during the year, and also setting up new sales quotas for the following year. The bookkeeping for the job took nearly all of his time. He was desperate to figure out how he could make this task simpler.

Entering the Data

Jim's needs were not terrifically complicated. He received every year at the end of the year a report that summarized the activity of the sales force in each of his regions. It was an easy matter to computerize this report procedure once we had visualized the entire system. Each product sold in the region was listed, and then as the sales force sent in their quarterly performance reports, the numbers were entered in the appropriate location in the model shown in Figure 18.1. The data were actually sent in quarterly, and what you don't see in the figure is the quarterly report areas that stretch out to AN18. The model contains formulas in columns A through H that summarize all of this quarterly information. So at the end of the year, our friend could call up each region and they would either send him a disk with the report, or could send him the appropriate file over a modem.

The region report has several crossfoot checks to make sure that the data entered are accurate, and that the totals are correct. In Figure 18.1, row 15 contains an entered total that is the total given to the region manager by the salesperson. Row 17 contains a checksum formula that sums the sales numbers for each column to make sure that the numbers were entered correctly. An example of the formula that would be placed at J17, the first column in the First Quarter Report is:

(@SUM(J7...J13)

Making the Quota   161

	A	B	C	D	E	F	G	H
1	REGION SALES FOR:		1983					
2								
3								
4	NEW	TERR	TERR	TERR	TERR	TERR	TERR	REGION
5	ENGLAND	300	301	304	314	340	350	TOTAL
6	-----------	-----	------	------	-----	------	------	-------
7	PRODUCT 1	1123	2759	22267	8994	23762	34428	93334
8	PRODUCT 2	3363	8277	9937	3627	9681	15500	50391
9	PRODUCT 3	2365	5810	13359	8821	23941	44116	98412
10	PRODUCT 4	26040	63984	30206	8246	22533	43734	194743
11	PRODUCT 5	498	1225	14584	6411	17006	11245	50969
12	PRODUCT 6	2492	6123	3090	18932	52944	120085	203666
13	PRODUCT 7	17360	42656	14725	403	1120	4172	80437
14		-----	------	------	-----	------	------	-------
15	ENTRED TOT	53246	130834	108169	55435	150988	273280	478131
16								
17	CHECK SUM	53246	130834	108169	55435	150988	273280	771952
18								

Figure 18.1:   Region Summary

If the numbers in row 15 match the numbers in row 17, all the entries are correct. In column AP, the totals for each product for each quarter are summed using the formula

@SUM(J7...O7,R7...W7,Z17...AE7,AH7...AM7)

These are compared in column AQ with the region total from the yearly summary report, which is in column H. The Formula at AQ is

(H7 − AP7)

If the result is zero, the totals match. If this is not the case, there is an error in the data to search for.

Saving the Region Information

Once the Region Managers had all of the data entered and had checked to make sure it was accurate, and the yearly totals were correct, they saved the summary portion of the file (columns A...H) as a DIF file. To do this they put the cursor at A1 and hit /S#S (/Storage DIF Save). They entered an abbreviation for their region name and yr (NE84 for example) and hit return. When asked R (row) or C (column) or Return, they hit return to save the information in a block. This procedure allowed them to save only the actual figures that our friend was interested in, that is, the yearly summary, and speed up the process of data transfer. The summary file was sent out through a modem, and Jim saved each of the reports as they came in in separate files called REGIONYR#.

An example of a completed report for a region is shown in Figure 18.1. This file was saved with the filename "NE84," and he was ready to begin the sales quota forecasts for New England for the following year.

The Forecasting Template

We set up for our friend a blank forecasting template called BLNKQUOTAS and saved it on a separate disk. From setting up the blank region reports we knew that none of them extended below row 18, so we began the forecasting model in row 21. This allowed us to take advantage of the overlay feature of VisiCalc to combine the regional reports with the forecast reports. You will see how this works in a minute.

Figure 18.2 illustrates the blank forecasting template. Quotas have to be sent out to each of the salespeople in a region, the target figure against which they were working and against which their sales efforts would be evaluated. Jim wanted a fast way to enter the territory reports from the last year, calculate the quotas for each salesperson, and get a printed copy of the report.

This template gave him the flexibility needed. Before he entered any sales data though, he had to decide what percent the quota would be of last year's sales, and we created a space for him to enter this information for each product in B38...B44. Then he had to decide what percent of the quota could be expected to be met for each quarter. This information he entered in the table we created starting at E58. Once these data were entered (he could change it for specific territories if the seasonal sales pattern varied later if he desired) he was ready to do the first report.

With the Sales Quota Projection model already loaded into the machine, our friend moved the cursor to A1 and typed

/S#L   NE84   Return   Return

SpreadTalk: This loaded the New England Sales Summary Report right on top of the Quota Report model! VisiCalc allows this overlaying of models for combining templates, but maybe it is worth reviewing the ground rules.

The templates (we'll call them the "resident" and the "incoming" templates) must match suitably. By this we mean that the incoming entries that are meant to replace resident entries must be in the same cell location—the incoming data will ALWAYS replace the resident, if both cells have data in them. On the other hand, a blank cell in the incoming will leave the resident's cell data undisturbed, and vice versa, an occupied incoming will slip neatly into an empty resident cell. When the models are combined, the data for both models are available for use.

Making the Quota   163

```
         A           B            C          D         E         F          G          H          I          J
20
21   SALES QUOTA PROJECTIONS
22   ----------------------
23
24   PUT TERRITORY NUMBER HERE---->
25   PRINT FROM HERE---------------------->         GRINCH PRODUCTION CORPORATION
26           TO J49                                 -----------------------------
27
28   ENTER TODAY'S DATE:         26
29   ENTER MONTH NUMBER:         11       REGION:
30   ENTER PROJ YR HERE:       1985                               TERRITORY QUOTA FOR:      1985
31   IS REGION CORRECT? CHECK F29        TERRITORY:      0
32
33              QUOTA       QUOTA FOR    ============================================================
34              EXPECTED    NEW YEAR                 1ST QTR    2ND QTR    3RD QTR    4TH QTR     1984
35              INC/DEC     (PREV YR=     BRAND       QUOTA      QUOTA      QUOTA      QUOTA     QUOTA
36   PRODUCT    PERCENT        1984)     ============================================================
37   ------------------------------
38   PRODUCT 1     10            0       PRODUCT 1      0          0          0          0         0
39   PRODUCT 2     15            0       PRODUCT 2      0          0          0          0         0
40   PRODUCT 3      8            0       PRODUCT 3      0          0          0          0         0
41   PRODUCT 4    100            0       PRODUCT 4      0          0          0          0         0
42   PRODUCT 5      0            0       PRODUCT 5      0          0          0          0         0
43   PRODUCT 6      0            0       PRODUCT 6      0          0          0          0         0
44   PRODUCT 7     -5            0       PRODUCT 7      0          0          0          0         0
45
46
47                                        QUOTA         0          0          0          0         0
48                                       ============================================================
49                                       PROJECTION DATE:         2 -26
50
51
52
53
54
55                                                   PERCENT OF QUOTA TO BE SOLD EACH QUARTER
56                                       PRODUCT      1ST QTR    2ND QTR    3RD QTR    4TH QTR
57                                       ---------------------------------------------------
58                                       PRODUCT 1      25         25         25         25
59                                       PRODUCT 2      25         30         20         25
60                                       PRODUCT 3      25         25         25         25
61                                       PRODUCT 4      22         18         30         30
62                                       PRODUCT 5      30         15         25         40
63                                       PRODUCT 6      18         26         35         21
64                                       PRODUCT 7      20         24         30         26
```

Figure 18.2: Blank Quota Report

One other item to note is that the formats in the resident model will be the formats used in the combined report. It is important then, that the column widths, etc. are compatible so that the information appears the same in both reports. In this example we are combining a DIF file with a regular VisiCalc model. This procedure will work for combining two regular VisiCalc files too, though you must remember that any information on the resident file will be overwritten by the incoming data.

To develop the sales quota forecasts, some additional work must be done. The forecast is done by territory within a region so the first step is to select which territory will be used for the forecast. We suggested that this work be done in order from left to right so that it would be easier to keep track of what territories were complete. To complete the report after loading the sales data, Jim had to make some manual entries and changes. Then it was necessary to write the number of the selected territory at D24. The date was entered in C28...C30. A31...C31 reminded him to make sure that the region name is correct on the body of the report.

The next step was to edit the formulas in C38...C44. These formulas multiply the sales figures from the summary report up top, by the new quota for the year for each product. To make these formulas correct he had to edit the first formula, C38, to use the correct column number for the territory. For Territory 301, which is in C7...C13, he changed the C38 formula,

(B7*(1+(B38/100)))

to read

(C7*(1+(B38/100)))

He then replicated this from C39...C44, making the references relative. All he had to do was recalculate, and the report was complete, and ready for printing.

The Quota Formulas

The formulas in the body of the report multiply the yearly quota determined in C38 by the Percent of Quota from the table. A typical formula for this is the one at F38 that reads:

(C38*(F58/100)

The formulas in J38...J44 sum up the quarterly quotas, so he can check these against column C to be sure that the percentage numbers from the table were correct. When he is satisfied with the numbers, our friend can print out the report by moving the cursor to E25 and beginning the /Print command, prints out the report, indicating the Lower Right coordinate of J49.

Starting a New Territory

To do the next territory, he enters the new number at D24, edits the formulas in C38...C44, recalculates, and the next report is complete! He can do the entire forecast for the New England Region in less than an hour! What a DIFference! The results of his work with the second NE Territory, 301, can be seen in Figure 18.3.

Making the Quota   165

```
          A           B           C           D           E           F           G           H           I           J
 1   REGION SALES FOR:            1983
 2
 3
 4   NEW           TERR        TERR        TERR        TERR        TERR        TERR        REGION
 5   ENGLAND        300         301         304         314         340         350        TOTAL
 6   ----------------------------------------------------------------------------------
 7   PRODUCT 1     1123        2759       22267        8994       23762       34428        93334
 8   PRODUCT 2     3368        8277        9937        3627        9681       15500        50391
 9   PRODUCT 3     2365        5810       13359        8821       23941       44116        98412
10   PRODUCT 4    26040       63984       30206        8246       22533       43734       194743
11   PRODUCT 5      498        1225       14584        6411       17006       11245        50969
12   PRODUCT 6     2492        6123        3090       18932       52944      120085       203666
13   PRODUCT 7    17360       42656       14725         403        1120        4172        80437
14                ------      ------      ------      ------      ------      ------      ------
15   ENTRED TOT   53246      130834      108169       55435      150988      273230       478131
16
17   CHECK SUM    53246      130834      108169       55435      150988      273280       771952
18   ----------------------------------------------------------------------------------
19
20
21   SALES QUOTA PROJECTIONS
22   -----------------------
23
24   PUT TERRITORY NUMBER HERE---->      301
25   PRINT FROM HERE---------------->                       GRINCH   PRODUCT  CORPORATION
26         TO  J49                                          ------------------------------------
27
28   ENTER DAY'S DATE:            26
29   ENTER MONTH NUMBER:          11        REGION:    NE
30   ENTER PROJ YR HERE:        1985                                      TERRITORY QUOTA FOR:    1985
31   IS REGION CORRECT?  CHECK  F29        TERRITORY:   301
32
33              QUOTA      QUOTA FOR       ================================================================
34              EXPECTED   NEW YEAR                      1ST QTR    2ND QTR    3RD QTR    4TH QTR     1985
35              INC/DEC   (PREV YR=        BRAND         QUOTA      QUOTA      QUOTA      QUOTA       QUOTA
36   PRODUCT    PERCENT       1984)        ================================================================
37   ----------------------------------
38   PRODUCT 1       10        3035        PRODUCT 1       759        759        759        759        3035
39   PRODUCT 2       15        9518        PRODUCT 2      2380       2855       1904       2380        9518
40   PRODUCT 3        8        6275        PRODUCT 3      1569       1569       1569       1569        6275
41   PRODUCT 4      100      127968        PRODUCT 4     28153      23034      38390      38390      127968
42   PRODUCT 5        0        1225        PRODUCT 5       367        184        306        490        1347
43   PRODUCT 6        0        6123        PRODUCT 6      1102       1592       2143       1286        6123
44   PRODUCT 7       -5       40523        PRODUCT 7      8105       9726      12157      10536       40523
45
46                                         ----------------------------------------------------------------
47                                         QUOTA         42434      39718      57228      55409      194789
48                                         ================================================================
49                                         PROJECTION DATE:          11 -26
```

Figure 18.3:   Completed Projection

Finishing the Other Regions

When Jim is finished with one region, he blanks out the sales summary report by replicating a Blank cell into the area A1...J18. He then /S#Loads the next region's report into the top of his sales quota model and can begin again.

SpreadTip: When you have a section of a report that you want to erase in VisiCalc, it is easiest to /Replicate a blank cell into the cells that you want to erase (make sure that the cell is blank though, it can waste a lot of memory space when you replicate unnecessary format commands). This saves time as opposed to /Blanking every cell, and saves headaches that can be caused by deleting rows that may ruin some of your formulas.

He then /S#Loads the next region's summary into that location, and he is ready to start again.

SpreadTip: When you wish to blank a cell that contains a /Format command, either before or after you use the /Blank command, set the format to /F Default. This will get rid of extraneous /Format commands residing in otherwise empty cells.

SUMMARY

This system of blank report templates, blank summary templates, and overlays can be used in virtually any situation where you have to consolidate information and print out customized reports. For VisiCalc users, use of the DIF function can save time and memory when dealing with large amounts of data. The only thing you have to remember about DIF is that it saves the current value of the formula and not the formula itself, so be sure your numbers are right before DIFfing.

OtherCalcs

SuperCalc[3]

In SuperCalc[3] this procedure will work similarly. You will want to use the file /Save Filename Part Values Range command and the file /Load Filename Consolidate command, though, to achieve the same effects.

To do this, /Save the Region summary range using

/Sfilename,PVA1:H18   Return

After loading the Quota Forecasting report model, make sure the range from A1:H18 is blank. Place the cursor at A1 and type

/Lfilename,C   Return

and the Region report should appear.

Multiplan

In Multiplan, you need to link the region report with the quota report. Just link one region report summary with the quota report. Then when you need to change regions, use the eXternal Use command to use the name of another file as the base for the linked cells. To do this, after loading the Quota model, type X, U, the new filename, and Return. The new numbers should appear like magic. This will work only if the region files are set up in exactly the same format.

Once the region numbers are present on the spreadsheet you can proceed in the same manner to update the reports for each territory.

19

Keeping the Salaries Secret

SPREADSHEET FUNCTIONS: INT
FEATURED PROGRAM: VisiCalc
TEMPLATE FUNCTION: Display Security System and Salary Finder

BACKGROUNDER

In the average office, one of the problems of the CRT screen is that it is difficult to prevent people from seeing what is displayed. We all know people with the talent for reading stuff upside down, and the necessity for covering up the papers on the desk when one of them is around. But the CRT makes it very difficult, and all you can really do is rearrange the furniture in the office so that they cannot even view it.

But there is another way, and that is to conceal your data behind symbols, and switch it on only when you want to see it. In giving you this great capability in this chapter, we are also going to add another feature—the ability to switch on only selected data, so that what you want to read or review is not buried in a welter of other data.

This is a useful and appealing application. While it uses math (the @INT function) it does not produce financial reports, it merely helps you find selected information that meets certain criteria! And there's only one formula in the whole thing!

APPLICATION SPREADSHEET

The Salary Finder

Here's the hypothesis (developed to illustrate the idea—you will have to use your own creativity to find a way in which to use the application!): you are the personnel manager of a small advertising agency. We have staff members in different departments, all of whom have been with the company varying lengths of time and are paid, of course, different salaries.

When we are considering the hiring of a new person we want to be able to review the salaries and histories of others in the same department, so that we can judge what to pay the new people. But there is a great need here for security. Since this model contains the salaries of all the people in the company, it is sensitive material, and we cannot afford to have it displayed even for a moment if there is the chance someone unauthorized will see it.

Look at Figure 19.1—baffling, isn't it? And that is what a stranger sees when you are temporarily away from the keyboard doing other things. Just a screen full of the lopsided chevrons that VisiCalc uses to indicate that the value is too large to be displayed. The secret lies in the top left-hand corner, under "Locate:." The value of "1" in A2 is what switches the screen off (or perhaps we should say "the security screen on"), and conceals the data. Naturally you would omit this explanatory entry from your spreadsheet.

```
         A         B        C        D        E        F        G        H        I        J        K
 1   LOCATE:     ART    WRITERS   PROD.    ACC.    BOOK-   CLERKS
 2       1       DEPT             DEPT    EXECS   KEEPING
 3  (ALL OFF,    .01      .02      .03     .04      .05     .06
 4    USE 1)
 5
 6  SALARY/WK   1974     1975     1976    1977     1978    1979    1980    1981    1982    1983
 7  ADD TO        1        2        3       4        5       6       7       8       9      10
 8
 9     220    >>>>>>>  >>>>>>>  >>>>>>>  >>>>>>>  >>>>>>>  >>>>>>>  >>>>>>>  >>>>>>>  >>>>>>>  >>>>>>>
10     270    >>>>>>>  >>>>>>>  >>>>>>>  >>>>>>>  >>>>>>>  >>>>>>>  >>>>>>>  >>>>>>>  >>>>>>>  >>>>>>>
11     320    >>>>>>>  >>>>>>>  >>>>>>>  >>>>>>>  >>>>>>>  >>>>>>>  >>>>>>>  >>>>>>>  >>>>>>>  >>>>>>>
12     370    >>>>>>>  >>>>>>>  >>>>>>>  >>>>>>>  >>>>>>>  >>>>>>>  >>>>>>>  >>>>>>>  >>>>>>>  >>>>>>>
13     420    >>>>>>>  >>>>>>>  >>>>>>>  >>>>>>>  >>>>>>>  >>>>>>>  >>>>>>>  >>>>>>>  >>>>>>>  >>>>>>>
14     470    >>>>>>>  >>>>>>>  >>>>>>>  >>>>>>>  >>>>>>>  >>>>>>>  >>>>>>>  >>>>>>>  >>>>>>>  >>>>>>>
15     520    >>>>>>>  >>>>>>>  >>>>>>>  >>>>>>>  >>>>>>>  >>>>>>>  >>>>>>>  >>>>>>>  >>>>>>>  >>>>>>>
16     570    >>>>>>>  >>>>>>>  >>>>>>>  >>>>>>>  >>>>>>>  >>>>>>>  >>>>>>>  >>>>>>>  >>>>>>>  >>>>>>>
17     620    >>>>>>>  >>>>>>>  >>>>>>>  >>>>>>>  >>>>>>>  >>>>>>>  >>>>>>>  >>>>>>>  >>>>>>>  >>>>>>>
18     670    >>>>>>>  >>>>>>>  >>>>>>>  >>>>>>>  >>>>>>>  >>>>>>>  >>>>>>>  >>>>>>>  >>>>>>>  >>>>>>>
19     720    >>>>>>>  >>>>>>>  >>>>>>>  >>>>>>>  >>>>>>>  >>>>>>>  >>>>>>>  >>>>>>>  >>>>>>>  >>>>>>>
20     770    >>>>>>>  >>>>>>>  >>>>>>>  >>>>>>>  >>>>>>>  >>>>>>>  >>>>>>>  >>>>>>>  >>>>>>>  >>>>>>>
```

Figure 19.1:   What the Stranger Sees

Look at the matrix in Figure 19.2. This is the "finder display." Across the top, for reference, is the "code" for each of our departments, expressed as a decimal fraction. In A2, under "Locate:," is entered the department whose personnel and salaries we are looking for.

When you enter, for instance, .03 as we have done, and do a recalc, some of the "greater than" symbols (we will refer to them from now on as LSC for "lop-sided chevrons") disappear and in their place appears a value. This value represents the Employee Number (in our agency everyone has one) on the left of the decimal, and the amount that must be added to the range figure in the left-hand column to establish his or her salary per week.

Get it? The first person, employee number 266, earns $445.00 per week, the 420 from the left plus the 25 after the decimal.

We asked to see the employees in the Production Department and there they are, listed by the year in which they joined the company. (We have filled in only the first three years of employees, we are sure you can imagine the rest!)

In Figure 19.3, just to prove it works, we changed the department to .04, the Account Executives, and you can see that the Producers disappeared behind their LSC's, and out from behind came the Execs!

The Data Storage Matrix

So how does all this work? The secret lies in another part of the model where we have stored the data. In Figure 19.4 you can see an area of the matrix starting

	A	B	C	D	E	F	G	H	I	J	K
1	LOCATE:	ART	WRITERS	PROD.	ACC.	BOOK-	CLERKS				
2	.03	DEPT		DEPT	EXECS	KEEPING					
3	(ALL OFF,	.01	.02	.03	.04	.05	.06				
4	USE 1)										
5											
6	SALARY/WK	1974	1975	1976	1977	1978	1979	1930	1931	1932	1933
7	ADD TO	1	2	3	4	5	6	7	8	9	10
8											
9	220	>>>>>>>>	>>>>>>>>	>>>>>>>>	>>>>>>>>	>>>>>>>>	>>>>>>>>	615.13	>>>>>>>>	>>>>>>>>	>>>>>>>>
10	270	>>>>>>>>	>>>>>>>>	134.18	>>>>>>>>	415.13	>>>>>>>>	>>>>>>>>	715.13	>>>>>>>>	>>>>>>>>
11	320	>>>>>>>>	>>>>>>>>	>>>>>>>>	>>>>>>>>	>>>>>>>>	>>>>>>>>	>>>>>>>>	>>>>>>>>	855.30	>>>>>>>>
12	370	>>>>>>>>	>>>>>>>>	>>>>>>>>	>>>>>>>>	>>>>>>>>	>>>>>>>>	>>>>>>>>	>>>>>>>>	>>>>>>>>	>>>>>>>>
13	420	266.25	115.13	>>>>>>>>	>>>>>>>>	>>>>>>>>	515.13	>>>>>>>>	>>>>>>>>	>>>>>>>>	>>>>>>>>
14	470	>>>>>>>>	>>>>>>>>	>>>>>>>>	>>>>>>>>	>>>>>>>>	>>>>>>>>	>>>>>>>>	>>>>>>>>	>>>>>>>>	>>>>>>>>
15	520	>>>>>>>>	>>>>>>>>	>>>>>>>>	>>>>>>>>	>>>>>>>>	>>>>>>>>	>>>>>>>>	>>>>>>>>	>>>>>>>>	915.13
16	570	>>>>>>>>	>>>>>>>>	>>>>>>>>	>>>>>>>>	>>>>>>>>	>>>>>>>>	>>>>>>>>	>>>>>>>>	>>>>>>>>	>>>>>>>>
17	620	>>>>>>>>	55.30	>>>>>>>>	>>>>>>>>	455.30	555.30	>>>>>>>>	755.30	831.18	>>>>>>>>
18	670	>>>>>>>>	>>>>>>>>	>>>>>>>>	>>>>>>>>	>>>>>>>>	>>>>>>>>	>>>>>>>>	>>>>>>>>	>>>>>>>>	>>>>>>>>
19	720	>>>>>>>>	>>>>>>>>	>>>>>>>>	>>>>>>>>	>>>>>>>>	>>>>>>>>	>>>>>>>>	>>>>>>>>	>>>>>>>>	>>>>>>>>
20	770	>>>>>>>>	>>>>>>>>	>>>>>>>>	>>>>>>>>	>>>>>>>>	>>>>>>>>	>>>>>>>>	>>>>>>>>	>>>>>>>>	>>>>>>>>

Figure 19.2: Finding the Production Department

Keeping the Salaries Secret   171

```
          A        B         C         D         E         F         G         H         I         J         K
  1   LOCATE:    ART      WRITERS    PROD.     ACC.      BOOK-     CLERKS
  2      .04    DEPT                 DEPT     EXECS     KEEPING
  3  (ALL OFF,   .01       .02       .03       .04       .05       .06
  4    USE 1)
  5
  6  SALARY/WK  1974      1975      1976      1977      1978      1979      1980      1981      1982      1983
  7  ADD TO       1         2         3         4         5         6         7         8         9        10
  8
  9    220    >>>>>>>>  >>>>>>>>  >>>>>>>>  >>>>>>>>  >>>>>>>>  >>>>>>>>  >>>>>>>>  >>>>>>>>  >>>>>>>>  >>>>>>>>
 10    270    >>>>>>>>  >>>>>>>>  >>>>>>>>  >>>>>>>>  >>>>>>>>  >>>>>>>>  >>>>>>>>  >>>>>>>>  >>>>>>>>  >>>>>>>>
 11    320    >>>>>>>>  >>>>>>>>  >>>>>>>>  >>>>>>>>  >>>>>>>>  >>>>>>>>  >>>>>>>>  >>>>>>>>  >>>>>>>>  >>>>>>>>
 12    370    >>>>>>>>  >>>>>>>>  >>>>>>>>  >>>>>>>>  >>>>>>>>  >>>>>>>>  >>>>>>>>  >>>>>>>>  >>>>>>>>  >>>>>>>>
 13    420    >>>>>>>>  >>>>>>>>  >>>>>>>>  >>>>>>>>  >>>>>>>>  >>>>>>>>  >>>>>>>>  >>>>>>>>  >>>>>>>>  >>>>>>>>
 14    470    >>>>>>>>  >>>>>>>>  >>>>>>>>  >>>>>>>>  >>>>>>>>  >>>>>>>>  >>>>>>>>  >>>>>>>>    822.26    998.40
 15    520    >>>>>>>>  >>>>>>>>  >>>>>>>>  >>>>>>>>  >>>>>>>>  >>>>>>>>  >>>>>>>>  >>>>>>>>  >>>>>>>>  >>>>>>>>
 16    570    >>>>>>>>  >>>>>>>>    134.00  >>>>>>>>  >>>>>>>>  >>>>>>>>  >>>>>>>>  >>>>>>>>    813.45  >>>>>>>>
 17    620    >>>>>>>>  >>>>>>>>  >>>>>>>>  >>>>>>>>  >>>>>>>>  >>>>>>>>  >>>>>>>>  >>>>>>>>  >>>>>>>>  >>>>>>>>
 18    670    >>>>>>>>  >>>>>>>>  >>>>>>>>  >>>>>>>>  >>>>>>>>  >>>>>>>>  >>>>>>>>  >>>>>>>>  >>>>>>>>  >>>>>>>>
 19    720     93.40    >>>>>>>>  >>>>>>>>  >>>>>>>>  >>>>>>>>  >>>>>>>>  >>>>>>>>  >>>>>>>>    897.20  >>>>>>>>
 20    770     66.30    122.26    192.16    398.40    422.26    522.26    698.40    722.26  >>>>>>>>  >>>>>>>>
```

Figure 19.3:   Looking for the Account Executives

```
          AA       AB        AC        AD        AE        AF        AG        AH        AI        AJ        AK
  1   LOCATE:    ART      WRITERS    PROD.     ACC.      BOOK-     CLERKS
  2      .06    DEPT                 DEPT     EXECS     KEEPING
  3             .01       .02       .03       .04       .05       .06
  4
  5
  6  SALARY/WK  1974      1975      1976      1977      1978      1979      1980      1981      1982      1983
  7  ADD TO       1         2         3         4         5         6         7         8         9        10
  8
  9    220   109.4302        0    113.4502  309.0003  484.1406        0    615.1303  737.1505  842.1001  966.3005
 10    270   110.2801  284.1406  134.1803        0    415.1303  584.1406        0    715.1303  834.1505        0
 11    320        0        0        0    341.1001        0        0    641.1001        0    855.3003  986.1905
 12    370        0        0    197.2001  366.3005        0        0    666.3006        0        0        0
 13    420   266.2503  115.1303  199.2002        0        0    515.1303        0        0    891.2205        0
 14    470   284.0502  146.1005        0        0    499.2302  546.1005        0    799.2002  822.2604  998.4004
 15    520        0    141.1001        0    342.1001  441.1001  541.1001  645.1001  741.1001        0    915.1303
 16    570        0    134.1505  134.0004        0    434.1505  534.1505        0    734.1505  813.4504        0
 17    620        0     55.3003  136.1906  386.1906  455.3003  555.3003  686.1906  755.3003  831.1803        0
 18    670        0        0        0        0        0        0        0        0        0        0
 19    720    98.4004  191.2205        0        0    491.2205  591.2205        0    791.2205  897.2004  999.2002
 20    770    66.3004  122.2604  192.1604  398.4004  422.2604  522.2604  698.4004  722.2604  899.2002        0
```

Figure 19.4:   Hidden Data

over in column AA. We put it so far away to make construction easier, since this area is called by the template to get the information it requires to display, and since it corresponds it was easier to to know where we had to look—all the column B references are in column AB, D's in column AD, and so on.

Take a look at the structure of the value in this data matrix. It is of special construction. The integer part is the employee number. The first two digits after the decimal are the amount that is required to calculate the salary and the last two digits represent the department. We break this value up when we bring it over to our "finder" display on the left...

This magical switched-on display is created by the use of a simple formula, which is first found in B9:

@IF((AB9*100 − @INT(AB9*100) = A2),
(AB9 − (A2/100)),999999999)

SpreadTalk: Just follow in the formula above as we examine what it does. If the number in AB9, our first employee's data, is multiplied by 100, it has the effect of moving the decimal two places to the right, therefore leaving the department code digits on the right of the decimal. So, for example, the first one, 109.2501, becomes 10925.01.

First our formula checks to see if decimal amount (the result of subtracting the now-larger integer portion from the rest of it) equals the value we have entered under "Locate:." If it does not, then it enters the 999 million-odd, which because it is too large to display, gives us our LSC.

On the other hand, if it does match, then VisiCalc subtracts the located value divided by 100 (which adds two zeros to the left of it, or in our first example, .0004) from the complete employee value, thus stripping off the department code, and passes this value to the matrix. Thus we get the information we want for the department we have selected. Simple, huh?

This formula is /Replicated everywhere as (R)elative, with only the A2 value (N)o Change.

SUMMARY

And there you have it! A very simple way to hide data that is not for public viewing. In addition, you have a template which makes it easy to find all of the people (or items) that fall into a specific category.

OtherCalcs

Multiplan

Multiplan will display "oversized" numbers as #### symbols repeating across the cell. This will work in the same manner as the VisiCalc template without any other special changes.

SuperCalc³

In SuperCalc³ as in VisiCalc the display for large numbers is the lopsided chevron (>>>>). The model will work as is in SuperCalc. You may, however, want to simply use the Hide format in SuperCalc to hide your display. This command is part of the /Format command, and to use it you type /F, identify the area to be formatted, then press H for hidden format and return.

20

Green Eyeshades and Cuff Protectors

SPREADSHEET FUNCTIONS: SUM, DIF
FEATURED PROGRAM: VisiCalc
TEMPLATE FUNCTION: A Ledger System in a Spreadsheet

BACKGROUNDER

No book that sets out to be "compleat" would indeed be so if it omitted the regular, mundane bookkeeping tasks. Can one do regular bookkeeping on a computer using a spreadsheet?

You certainly can, and this chapter is addressed to all of you who meet some basic requirements. And it is worth knowing what those are!

We, the writers of this book, are so caught up in spreadsheeting that we sometimes wonder if there are any limitations to the wonderful programs—but there are some. While they can do (almost) anything, there are some things for which perhaps they are better off not being used.

If you want to satisfy a CPA and do integrated accounts receivable, accounts payable, and general ledger, then save up your money and buy a good bookkeeping program. One of the best costs only around $495.00 and is just super! Spreadsheets can do all the "motions" of bookkeeping but you will be so involved with disk swapping, DIFfing out and in, and suffering from memory limitations, that it will not be worth it.

But . . . If you just want to keep track of your expenditures, allocate them to various accounts so that at tax time you will have a printout that will help prepare your return and (maybe) satisfy the Internal Revenue Service, then we'll look at a way in this chapter. The resulting model may be suitable, for instance, for single businesspeople (like perhaps independent salespeople), or even a small home business.

The ledger accounting method in this chapter has been used by several people we know of, all of them independent businesspeople that have several different sources of income, and must keep track of their expenditures, not for tax purposes necessarily, but to know just how they are doing on the costs side against the income they get.

The model will be quite suitable for a household account. Of course, there are the home accounting programs, sometimes called "checkbook managers" or "household budgeting" packages. But they cost extra money and you may find that the following method is all you need. However, if this model is just too simplistic for you, read the next chapter. We take this system and upgrade it to a higher level of automation, and add some features.

What we have developed for this book is an adaptation of the procedure we use for InterCalc, the International Spreadsheet Users Group, which we manage—it is a checkbook register that permits distribution of expenses (checks) and income (deposits) to a number of accounts, the periodic analysis of activity and, of course, a printed report whenever you want one (and at tax time).

The Monthly Entries

Depending on the amount of activity you anticipate, you may want to limit each template to a month, carrying forward the balances in each column by means of a DIF procedure at the end of the preceding month. Meanwhile look in our illustration, which shows a typical month, February (see Figure 20.1).

This is the February "page," and it shows a BROUGHT FWD—which came from January. To save space in the illustration we have made all the figures integers, just in case you thought we did very neat earning and spending! We also had to split the ledger into three pieces. Let's review the first two figures of the sheet briefly (Figures 20.1 and 20.2), ignoring for now the Summary and Analysis section at the bottom (Figure 20.3).

Anyone who has done "big green ledger" type bookkeeping will recognize the format. The first column is the date of the transaction, necessary for audit trail purposes. In the second column is the check number or an ID for any other type of entry— the two-digit ones are deposits. We number the customer copy of the deposit slips when we go to the bank and insert this number, which enables them to be found again if there's a question later.

We always annotate the deposit slips in case there's income in a split deposit from more than one of the "accounts." We also do this with checks that cover more than one expense account. For instance, the interest on the bank statements (NOW account) is indicated by the month credited.

```
                A       B       C        D       E       F       G       H
         1                      CHECK REGISTER & MINI-GENERAL LEDGER
         2
         3                                        -     ---INCOME-----
         4                TRANSACTION                 SOURCE SOURCE SOURCE
         5       DATE      DEP/CHK    PAID   REC'D    ONE    TWO    THREE
         6      ------------------------------------------------------------
         7             BROUGHT FWD...  6558   10739   5315    640   4517
         8
         9       FEB  5     42                150            150
        10       FEB  7    1529           46
        11       FEB  8    1530          295
        12       FEB  9     43                450            450
        13       FEB 10     44               1600                  1600
        14       FEB 10     45                660    660
        15       FEB 11    1535          335
        16       FEB 14    1536          227
        17       FEB 15   INT JAN              66
        18       FEB 16     47                497                   497
        19       FEB 20    1537          340
        20       FEB 21    1538          231
        21       FEB 24    1539          275
        22       FEB 27     48                840    540    300
        23       FEB 28    1540          117
        24       FEB 28    1541          311
        25
        26
        27
         :
         :
         :
       190  TOTALS         DATE       8734   15002   6515   1540   6614
       191  =======        ============================================
       192
       193  DOUBLE ENTRY PROOF...       0       0
       194                 ============================================
```

Figure 20.1: Check Register and Income Ledger

The next two columns, D and E, are simply the "in" and "out" of the accounts—paid and received. The four columns under "Income" represent (in our for instance) each of our clients, the sources of all our income, and the remaining columns (shown in Figure 20.2) are a series of expense account columns, reflecting the "general ledger" requirements—there are actually more in my template so we have shown only a few. You can have almost as many as you like, but the memory you have and the number of transactions will decide for you.

The Summaries

The key to the ease of use of this model is the way it summarizes itself. Way down at the bottom, in row 190, is the TOTALS TO DATE line (see Figure 20.1 and 20.2), followed by the remainder of the Summary and Analysis section (see Figure 20.3). One can go straight to entering new transactions at any time, with-

```
                I     J      K     L     M     N     O     P      Q

        1
        2
        3                  -----BUSINESS EXPENSES-----       OTHER   PROOF
        4     INT-          SECRE- PRINT- MESS-   TELE-      EXPENSE  COL
        5     EREST  AUTO  TARIAL   ING  ENGERS  PHONES      (PERS)
        6     ------------------------------------------------------
        7     267    494    938    680    490    351         3635
        8
        9
       10             46                                                  0
       11                    240     55                                   0
       12                                                                 0
       13                                                                 0
       14                                                                 0
       15            335                                                  0
       16                    145                              92          0
       17     66                                                          0
       18                                                                 0
       19                    300           40                             0
       20                                                     231         0
       21                     75           200                            0
       22                                                                 0
       23                     25     92                                   0
       24                                  311                            0
       25
       26
       27
        :
        :
        :
      190     333    875   1693    827    730    662         3948
      191     ========================================       =======
      192
      193
      194     =====================================================
```

Figure 20.2: Expense Ledger and Proof Column

out having to /Insert Rows. The cursor is set over the underline beneath the headings in column A and a /Titles Horizontal command is given—this keeps the column headings visible—now you can go down to the last empty line and always see the titles.

Note that in Figure 20.1 and 20.2 there are many blank rows left between the last data line and row 190.

When the details of a transaction are entered, with the amount under the "paid" or "rec'd" column, it is carried out to the applicable account with /Replicate—reducing the chance of keying errors. This is the "simple" method, that is most suitable if the number of accounts is relatively small. Since there are no formulas in the columns to do the "carrying out," this method also saves memory. We have another method (covered in the next chapter) for handling the carrying out to the accounts automatically, useful when there are many of them, but as you will see this uses a lot of memory.

```
         A      B       C        D       E       F      G      H      I      J      K
       195            SUMMARY AND ANALYSIS
       196            --------------------
       197                  PERIOD ENDING FEB 28 TH 1984           BUDGET ANALYSIS
       198                                                         --------------
       199                                ACTUAL          BUDGET        OVER   UNDER
       200   REVENUES                     -------         -------       --------------
       201
       202          SOURCE ONE            6515            6000          515      0
       203          SOURCE TWO            1540            1550            0     10
       204          SOURCE THREE          6614            6000          614      0
       205          INTEREST               333             300           33      0
       206                                -------         -------       --------------
       207          TOTAL REVENUE        15002           13850   TOTAL  1162     10
       208                                -------         -------   NET 1152      0
       209
       210   EXPENSES
       211
       212          AUTO MILEAGE           875            1000            0    125
       213          SECRETARIAL SERVICES  1693            2500            0    807
       214          PRINTING/COPYING       827            1000            0    173
       215          MESSENGER SERVICES     730            1000            0    270
       216          TELEPHONES/TELEGRAMS   662             500          162      0
       217                                                                0      0
       218          PERSONAL & NONBUSINES 3948            3300          648      0
       219                                -------         -------       --------------
       220          TOTAL EXPENSES        8734            9300   TOTAL  809   1375
       221                                -------         -------     NET   0    566
       222
       223          BALANCE ON HAND       6268
```

Figure 20.3: Summary Area

Error Checking

There are two proofing methods against errors. The first is the column to the right, headed PROOF COL. In this column there is a simple formula:

$$(D10 - @SUM(J10...P10)) = (E10 - @SUM(F10...I10))$$

SpreadTalk: Add the expense columns and subtract them from the PAID column, then subtract the income columns from the REC'D column. See if the amounts on either side of the equals sign are the same (zero). If these results are anything but zero, there's a problem. This is a logical statement that will be TRUE or FALSE. At a glance you can see that all your entries are correctly carried over.

Similarly with the "Double Entry Proof" line at row 193:

$$@SUM(D7...D189) - @SUM(J190...P190)$$

Green Eyeshades and Cuff Protectors   179

SpreadTalk: Add the checks column and then subtract the totals across row 190 for expenses—a zero should result. Similarly with deposits and income columns.

Printing Out the Report

When you are ready to /Print, it is done in two pieces—first down to the last transaction line, and then /Print again at row 190 without touching the printer. Not shown in the illustration is an eight-line gap that is inserted first at row 62, then whenever necessary, so that the printer passes over the paper perforation—in our office we don't bother to repeat the column headings, although that is easy enough to do (just /Replicate the top rows).

At the end of a month, or every time you update the data, you will need to file the model for the period to disk as protection. But there is one more task to get ready for the next month (or the next page if you have a lot of transactions, and the matrix is filled)—you need the column totals to carry forward.

Carrying Forward with DIF

The mechanics of this discussion are really for those of you who are VisiCalc users/readers, but at the end of the chapter you will find the procedure for carrying out the task in your spreadsheet. By reading the following you will know what it is that we are trying to achieve.

To begin the carry forward procedure, the user must first DIF out the column totals. This is a simple procedure (see Chapter 14 for a more complete discussion of the DIF process). Key in /S#S with the cursor in D190, indicate that the end of the range is the rightmost column, and save by Rows.

You will remember that using the DIF procedure, values go out to disk only, no formulas. Since these can be recalled and placed anywhere within the matrix (VisiCalc DIF files do not store the location with the values), this makes it a very different capability from overlaying (as covered in Chapter 18). Rows saved can even be restored in columns, thus giving yet another option.

In this case, of course, since all we want to carry out are the column totals, we perform the DIF procedure on the single totals row at the bottom of the model, using a filename like "FEBTOTAL." When the blank month matrix is brought in, for March, then the DIF procedure is used to reload FEBTOTAL (/S#L FEBTOTAL), but this time on the top line of the matrix, just under the headings. If the /S#Saving and /S#Loading processes are used with the cursor in column D (saving from D109 for instance), the data will drop neatly into place beside the BROUGHT FORWARD text.

In order to start a new page or month, we call in the standard page model from the account disk, which is saved with just the top header lines and those below 190. The top is edited to suit the month, and the column totals brought in from the DIF file that we saved, with the familiar sequence:

/S#L   XXXTOTALS

and the model is almost ready for continued data entry.

Bringing It All Together

At the bottom of the last page of the model is where we do the "mini-general ledger workup" (see Figure 20.3). This is part of the standard page model that waits empty on the data disk for when we run out of memory on the current page. We generally leave it on the page we have completed as a checklist if we are reviewing.

The remainder of the summary at the bottom is fairly obvious. The Account totals under ACTUAL are simply carry-downs of the column totals, and we have entered a BUDGET figure so that the small analysis can be done. So there it is—a very fast and efficient system that is not sophisticated bookkeeping but satisfies three requirements: we can track every transaction (see comments regarding paperwork in the next section), we have a complete printout at every meeting with our accountant if there are questions, and we can analyze our activities in our thriving (and growing) business to see what we are spending relative to budget.

Incidentally the formula that produces the BUDGET ANALYSIS figure is simply a comparison of the two figures in ACTUAL and BUDGET. For instance, the formula beneath OVER is:

@IF(G202>E202,0,E202 – G202)

SpreadTalk: If the ACTUAL is greater than the BUDGET, insert the result of subtracting BUDGET from ACTUAL, otherwise insert zero. The formula in the UNDER column is vice versa.

The Simple Paper Work

A word about the paper work. If you can write "small" you can make nearly all the required notes in the regular checkbook register, in addition to the payee for a check note the account to which it was posted (to which you assigned the expense). All income is similarly annotated on the deposit slip, which you should number sequentially. File these in the bank's envelope when you have balanced the checkbook.

SUMMARY

In the next chapter we show you how to upgrade this system to automate it to a higher level of bookkeeping, which may interest those of you who have larger requirements (it includes an automatic checkbook balancing feature too, together with an automatic diagnostic against an imbalance being caused by a carelessly written transposition!).

OtherCalcs

SuperCalc³

In SuperCalc³, you would structure the model as shown in the figures for this chapter. The file combining procedure for carrying forward totals is slightly different, however. Here you would want to use the file /Save Filename Part Values Range command and the file /Load Filename Consolidate command, though, to achieve the same effects.

To do this, /Save the Totals range using

/Sfilename,PVD109:P109   Return

After loading the blank template for the next month, place the cursor at D7 and type

/Lfilename,C   Return

and the totals will be carried forward.

SuperCalc³ returns a value of 1 if the formula is true, and 0 if the formula is false. You may therefore wish to change the PROOF formula. Here you could use SuperCalc³'s Textual values to return the text True or False depending on the status of the formula. A typical formula would read:

IF(E7 = SUM(J7:N7,O7/.07,P7),("TRUE"),("FALSE"))

Multiplan

In Multiplan, you need to link the totals line from the previous month to the carried forward line for the current month. Just link one month's total line with the Brought Forward line on the blank template. Then SAVE the blank template with the linked cells. Then when you need to change totals for a new template, use the eXternal Use command to use the name of another file as the base for the linked cells. To do this, after loading the blank model, type X U the new filename and Return. The new numbers should appear like magic. This will work only if the monthly files are set up in exactly the same format.

Once the brought-forward numbers are present on the spreadsheet you can proceed in the same manner as outlined earlier to update your accounts.

21
Automating the Quill Pen

SPREADSHEET FUNCTIONS: IF, AND, OR, SUM
FEATURED PROGRAM: VisiCalc
TEMPLATE FUNCTION: Automated Mini-Ledger

BACKGROUNDER

There was a fair amount of manual work necessary to manage the general ledger system we looked at in the last chapter. The model served a purpose, probably at the most elementary level of bookkeeping, but we recognize that some of you may need more (and of course that some of you may also think that if you bought a computer let it compute—let it do more of the work!).

There is not much in the way of complicated construction in this model, and all you need is the IF and AND conditional logic formulation.

We will treat the explanation of this template as if it were a new one, so that you do not need to keep turning back the pages to the last chapter. While the format is the same as that covered before, there have been many changes to produce this new AUTOMATED MICRO-LEDGER.

Why automate? Well in the last mini-ledger we had you carrying out cash receipts and disbursements (deposits and checks) to ledger accounts manually—that is, entering them in a suitably labelled column, then typing them in again under various headings so that an account could be kept for each month of where the money came from and where it went.

Automating the Quill Pen

There can be errors in this and while we had built in a "proofing" function that made sure that you did not type in one of the figures incorrectly, we felt that this was a bit "steam operated" and not up to the standards of modern computing!

Additionally, while an accounting record is all very well, you were really duplicating a lot of work that you had already done in your checkbook, so we felt automating that function and including it in our Ledger was a worthwhile endeavor.

Take a look at Figure 21.1 and the familiarities if you read the last chapter will be obvious. Let's run across the top and see what we have.

The first columns are easy: the date of the transaction, a column for the check number (or the deposit slip number, which we faithfully add, as recommended in the paperwork advice we gave in Chapter 20, when we get back from the bank), the amount, an account code and the running balance.

	A	B	C	D	E	F	G	H	I	J	K
1			CHECK REGISTER & MINI-LEDGER								
2											
3								----------INCOME----------			
4			TRANSACTION		ACCOUNT			SOURCE	SOURCE	SOURCE	INT-
5		DATE	DEP/CHK	AMOUNT	CODE	CASH	THRU	ONE	TWO	THREE	EREST
6						BALANCE	BANK	10	11	12	13
7											
8			BROUGHT FWD...			4181		5315	640	4517	267
9											
10		FEB 5	42	150	11	4331	1	0	150	0	0
11		FEB 7	1529	46	1	4285	1	0	0	0	0
12		FEB 8	1530	240	2	4045	1	0	0	0	0
13		FEB 8	1530	55	3	3990	1	0	0	0	0
14		FEB 9	43	450	11	4440	1	0	450	0	0
15		FEB 10	44	1600	12	6040	1	0	0	1600	0
16		FEB 10	45	660	10	6700	1	660	0	0	0
17		FEB 11	1535	335	1	6365	1	0	0	0	0
18		FEB 14	1536	227	2	6138	1	0	0	0	0
19		FEB 15	INT JAN	66	13	6204	1	0	0	0	66
20		FEB 16	47	497	12	6701	1	0	0	497	0
21		FEB 20	1537	300	2	6401	1	0	0	0	0
22		FEB 20	1537	40	4	6361	1	0	0	0	0
23		FEB 21	1538	230	6	6131		0	0	0	0
24		FEB 24	1539	200	4	5931		0	0	0	0
25		FEB 24	1539	75	2	5856		0	0	0	0
26		FEB 27	48	540	10	6396	1	540	0	0	0
27		FEB 27	48	300	11	6696	1	0	300	0	0
28		FEB 28	1540	117	2	6579		0	0	0	0
29		FEB 28	1541	310	5	6269	1	0	0	0	0
30						6269					
31						6269					
32											
33			TOTALS	MONTH		6269		1200	900	2097	66
34				YEAR				6515	1540	6614	333

Figure 21.1: The Check Register and Income Accounts

Maintaining the Running Balance

Notice anything odd? We haven't included a separate column for checks and deposits, or even added a minus sign to the checks, indicating a deduction from our account. Why should we? Let the spreadsheet take care of it!

The secret in this little trick lies in the difference between deposit slip numbers and check numbers. All we have to do is make sure that the spreadsheet can identify the transaction from looking at this number—in our case if the number in the identifier column is less than 99, the spreadsheet knows that it is a deposit to be added to the running balance, if more than 100 it is a check and should be subtracted. The formula, expressed in SpreadTalk, is: IF column C is less than 99, calculate column F plus last amount in column D, but if it is more than 99, then calculate column F minus last amount in column D. Clear?

So the spreadsheet now knows how to make the adjustment in carrying a running balance, which is the amount we have available to spend in our checking account.

You will have to decide the system for your own model. If your checks are in the three digit range you are still okay but if not, then just arbitrarily add a digit to either the checks or the deposit slip number—anything will do as long as it is a decided difference that the spreadsheet can recognize. Also look out a little way into the future and see if the two number series will overlap in the near term—that could confuse things too!

Carrying Out to the Accounts

Continuing across the top of the model (and into Figure 21.2) we now come to the income and expense account columns—these were the ones to which formerly figures from the deposits and checks columns were manually typed, by tracking over and entering the figures in the right columns. Split deposits were mentally (or on the back of an envelope) calculated and the splits entered into the right places—all opportunities for error.

We have now automated all of this—and the key is the number beneath the column headings, two digits for income and one for expenses (of course you will adjust this to your own circumstances—if you have lots more expense columns than in our example, you are going to want to reverse this or even go to three digits). The important thing is that they are Values and not Labels of Text, so that the spreadsheet can use them in math.

The SpreadTalk for the formula in each column says (quietly, to itself): "let's see if the number in the Account code column is the same as the amount of the transaction, if not, not". In VisiCalc terms, for instance, a typical formula might look like this:

@IF(E29=Q6,D29,0)

Automating the Quill Pen

	L	M	N	O	O	Q	R	S
	\-\-\-\-\-BUSINESS EXPENSES\-\-\-\-\-\-					OTHER	OUTSTANDING	
		SECRE-	PRINT-	MESS-		TELE-EXPENSE	CHKS	DEPS
	AUTO	TARIAL	ING	ENGERS	PHONES	(PERS)		
	1	2	3	4	5	6		
	494	908	680	490	351	3635		
	0	0	0	0	0	0	0	0
	46	0	0	0	0	0	0	0
	0	240	0	0	0	0	0	0
	0	0	55	0	0	0	0	0
	0	0	0	0	0	0	0	0
	0	0	0	0	0	0	0	0
	0	0	0	0	0	0	0	0
	335	0	0	0	0	0	0	0
	0	227	0	0	0	0	0	0
	0	0	0	0	0	0	0	0
	0	0	0	0	0	0	0	0
	0	300	0	0	0	0	0	0
	0	0	0	40	0	0	0	0
	0	0	0	0	0	230	230	0
	0	0	0	200	0	0	200	0
	0	75	0	0	0	0	75	0
	0	0	0	0	0	0	0	0
	0	0	0	0	0	0	0	0
	0	117	0	0	0	0	117	0
	0	0	0	0	310	0	0	0
							0	0
							0	0
	331	959	55	240	310	230	622	0
	875	1867	735	730	661	3865		

Figure 21.2:   Expense Register and Outstanding Balances

where E is the Account Code, Q the column in which the evaluation is taking place, and D is the amount.

And that is it for the automatic account assignment in the top of the model. It works and you don't need to have a proofing column. You will almost certainly have set your spreadsheet for manual recalculation, so that you don't have to wait between entries for the screen to update. At this point one recalc will carry out the totals to their correct accounts.

SpreadTip: In SuperCalc[3] and Multiplan you could set the format for each entry to "display blank if zero" if you prefer the white space that eliminating the zeros will give you.

There are a couple of things to note. To maintain the automatic error protection against incorrect carrying out, you must enter split deposits or checks that are for more than one expense account to separate lines. No problem with this, just use the check or deposit slip number twice, as we have done.

Also note that you can use text in the transaction column *but only for deposits* or net additions to the bank account (like credits, interest earned, and so on). This is because most spreadsheets evaluate a text or label entry as zero, therefore the "if it's less than 99" question will work properly. But if you do it for a net deduction from the bank account, it will also be added rather than subtracted, and that is not what you want!

The formula in the check column typically looks like this, again from VisiCalc:

@IF(@AND(C31>99,G31<>1),D31,0)

SpreadTalk: If the transaction code is less than 99 AND the thru Bank column does not equal 1 (has not cleared), bring over the amount in D, otherwise insert zero. The formula for the deposits will be exactly the same except for the greater than symbol becoming less than.

So on the total line this column has the total of all checks and all deposits that have not cleared the bank. By the way the other totals down there are pretty obvious—the month totals are *excluding* the Brought Forward figures from last month, while the next line, year to date, *includes* the brought forwards.

There's only one more thing we need (and the model needs) to balance the checkbook and that is, of course, the total that the bank tells you it has in your account. Look at Figure 21.3 and you will see the place where we just type that in—accurately of course!

```
              A       B        C           D        E
35
36 CHECKBOOK RECONCILIATION
37
38 ENTER     BANK'S CLOSE FIGURE->         5647
39                   CHECKS OUTSTANDING     622
40                   DEPS OUTSTANDING         0
41                   MICRO-LEDGER BALANCE   6269
42                   ACCOUNT IN BALANCE    TRUE
43
44                   AMOUNT OF DIFFERENCE:    0
45
46 ADVISE TRANSPOSITION CHECK
```

Figure 21.3: Reconciliation Statement

Automating the Quill Pen   187

Checks and Balances

One recalc and the matrix tells you the facts—it is TRUE the account is in balance, or this is a FALSE statement. The formula that does this little service is probably an easy one for you—remember the boxes on the back of the statement? It is (banks closing figure) plus (checks not cleared) minus (deposits not cleared) equals (the Mini-ledger ending running balance).

Since this is entered as logical statement you get TRUE or FALSE in VisiCalc and Multiplan (SuperCalc just gives you a one or a zero, so you would want to rephrase the legend to something like "Account in Balance if Zero").

Just one more useful little service and we are done. In the old days of high desks and quill pens, the scribe that wrote the books in beautiful copperplate penmanship was often guilty of copying errors—and the transposition was probably the commonest of these. Since it is also about the commonest typing error too, particularly for two-finger typists, we use the same diagnostic trick that bookkeepers used in those days and CPAs use today, to help us sort out a problem.

If two digits have been transposed, 146 written as 164 or even 416, then the difference between the unbalanced numbers will be exactly divisible by nine. Trust us, it's true!

If you look at our last illustration in this chapter, Figure 21.4 you will see that we purposely transposed the amount figure 117 on Feb 28 to read 171—and

```
              A         B         C         D         E         F

27           FEB        27        48        300       11        6696
28           FEB        28        1540      171       2         6525
29           FEB        28        1541      310       5         6215
30                                                              6215
31                                                              6215
32           ------------------------------------------------
33                                TOTALS    MONTH               6215
34                                          YEAR
35
36  CHECKBOOK RECONCILIATION
37
38  ENTER    BANK'S CLOSE FIGURE->           5647
39           CHECKS OUTSTANDING              676
40           DEPS OUTSTANDING                0
41           MICRO-LEDGER BALANCE            6215
42           ACCOUNT IN BALANCE              FALSE
43
44           AMOUNT OF DIFFERENCE:           -108
45  ****** ****** ****** ****** ******
46  ADVISE TRANSPOSITION CHECK               ******
47  ****** ****** ****** ****** ******
```

Figure 21.4:   Transposition Error

note how the bottom of our model has changed. Our legend "ADVISE TRANSPOSITION CHECK" has been highlighted with a border of asterisks. Now you know at least one thing you can look for in finding the cause of the imbalance.

We did this with two steps—first we found the difference in the balance, how much we were off, then we examined this figure with the following formula, again from a VisiCalc model:

$$@IF((E44/9) = @INT(E44/9),8,0),0)$$

with the format set at /F*. In this example E44 is the difference figure, and we are saying that if this figure divided by nine is equal to the integer value of the same division (thus proving that there are no decimals and the division is exact), then use 8 and if it is not exact use zero.

Therefore the spreadsheet writes eight asterisks if an exact division is completed, and there is a reasonable chance that the error is a transposition. If there is a remainder, then zero asterisks will appear.

We entered this formula into all the locations surrounding the legend. Just to make it "pretty" we substituted a 3 for the 8 in the formula in the location at the beginning of the legend and in the column to the right of it.

One small point—this formula as written will also indicate a transposition if there is a zero in E44, which occurs if the account is in balance. To protect against this we modified the formula a bit as follows:

$$@IF(E44<>0,@IF(@INT(E44/9) = (E44/9),8,0),0)$$

Now the IF statement drops out to the final zero if it finds an account in balance, and only proceeds with the "divide by nine" trick if there is any other value there.

OtherCalcs

Multiplan

This model will work in much the same way in Multiplan. There are some ways in which the instructions would be different in this program, though. The replicating process in Multiplan is done with the Copy command. To replicate the formulas in the model down the columns you would either use the Copy From command to copy all of the cells in the first row into the rest of the data section, or you would use the Copy Down command to copy the first cell in a column Down into the rest of the column. You have to take care when constructing your formulas because you have to specify whether a reference is Relative or Absolute when you construct the first formula.

For example, our formula in column J which reads

@IF(F7=J3,E7,0)

would be written

IF(RC[−4]=R3C10,RC[−5])

Copying this formula down the column would be done using the following command keystrokes

C D 15 (Or however many rows you want) RETURN

The references to the Account Code column and the Amount columns are Relative with the Account Code number for column J (10) Absolute.

Another way to do this without having to remember all of the [−#] column references would be to assign names to the Account Code column and to the Amount column. To do this for the Account Code column, go to the appropriate column and type

N ACCTCDE TAB R7C6:R38C6 RETURN

Do the same procedure for the Amount column using the Name AMNT. Now the formula would read:

IF(ACCTCDE=R3C10,AMNT,0)

You could even Name the Account Code on top of column 10 something appropriate like INC. In this case the formula would be

IF(ACCTCDE=INC,AMNT,0)

If you are not fond of looking at all of the zeros in the empty cells in the account columns, you could have Multiplan write a blank space instead of a zero. To do this the formula in R7C10 would now be

IF(ACCTCDE=INC,AMNT," ")

The Name command can also be used to save some of the headaches when constructing the Summary Section in the model. If you Name each of the Account Totals, then reference the Name in the call down for the formula, you do not have to worry about editing the replicated cell references, or worry about whether the correct cell was being called on.

One final refinement in Multiplan is use of the Lock command to protect all of the formulas in the model so that they are not ever inadvertently written over.

SuperCalc³

There are no special differences between the VisiCalc model outlined here and the model in SuperCalc³. You may want to protect all of the formulas by using the /P command and specifying the range containing the formulas to be protected.

U1
Looks Like It's Getting Late!

SPREADSHEET FUNCTIONS: IF, LOOKUP
FEATURED PROGRAM: VisiCalc
TEMPLATE FUNCTION: Startup Schedule Forecaster

PURPOSE

This utility model allows the user to develop a schedule of start dates for a series of events, and to produce from them a variety of reports that depend on the start dates of each individual event. Thus the results of slips and accelerations in start dates can be "what-iffed."

UTILITY APPLICATION SPREADSHEET

Slipping Dates in a Store Opening Schedule

This example might be useful in an environment like the planning department in the headquarters of a retail chain.

We developed the application for another purpose (which was proprietary) but you will see that with some modifications, it can be used to do something that all businesspeople get involved with at some time or other—the forward planning that goes into the launch of a series of products, or some other sequential series of events, that may not may not have financial implications (this one does).

The situation we have represented here is the planning of the opening of a chain of stores. Each store has a "going income," which is the monthly volume it is expected to do when it is up and running. It also has a projected ramp up (period of improving performance) in contribution, that is used to forecast income until the "break-in" period is over, (a percentage of the going rate, based on experience).

It is assumed our planner is in a corporate position. Since each store in the chain has income and profit and loss contributions to make to the group as a whole, it is naturally important for the forward planning to be able to review the implications of a store being opened later, or earlier for that matter, than the planned date.

Our application allows the planning to take place, the examination of variations in the original start date plan, and as the stores eventually open, tracking the progress in terms of the actual numbers.

The Timing Analysis

In Figure U1.1 you will see a typical report. For the sake of readability we have labelled the eight events shown as "ACTIONS" —in here would go the name of the store, or its number, or some other identifier. They could, as you will see, be any kind of event. The model has been "rigged" in the illustration to show that they are at present sequential, the first one opens first, in January, the second in February, and so on. Therefore you can see that the income figures appear as a nice even slope across the model.

```
            A       B       C       D       E       F       G       H       I       J       K       L       M       N       O       P       Q
19  TIMING VERSUS INCOME ANALYSIS
20
21          GOING
22  INTRO  MONTHLY                                                                                                                       TOTAL
23  MONTH   SALES           JAN     FEB     MAR     APR     MAY     JUN     JUL     AUG     SEP     OCT     NOV     DEC    INCOME
24  ------------------------------------------------------------------------------------------------------------------------
25      1  110000 ACTION   16500   27500   60500   93500  110000  110000  110000  110000  110000  110000  110000  110000  1078000
26      2   46000 ACTION       0   16500   27500   25300   39100   46000   46000   46000   46000   46000   46000   46000   430400
27      3   82000 ACTION       0       0   16500   20500   45100   69700   82000   82000   82000   82000   82000   82000   643800
28      4   58000 ACTION       0       0       0    8700   14500   31900   49300   58000   58000   58000   58000   58000   394400
29      5   76000 ACTION       0       0       0       0   11400   19000   41800   64600   76000   76000   76000   76000   440800
30      6   41000 ACTION       0       0       0       0       0    6150   10250   22550   34850   41000   41000   41000   196800
31      7   38000 ACTION       0       0       0       0       0       0    5700    9500   20900   32300   38000   38000   144400
32      8   53000 ACTION       0       0       0       0       0       0       0    7950   13250   29150   45050   53000   148400
33
34              MONTHLY TOT 16500   44000  104500  148000  220100  282750  345050  400600  441000  474450  496050  504000  3447700
```

Figure U1.1:   Report Area

Looks Like It's Getting Late!

On the left side you can see the projected Going Monthly Sales, the income of each of the actions, which are of course different as they might well be in a real situation, in my case one store may have a higher potential because of location, competition and so on.

Elsewhere in the model, with a few keystrokes we can change the start month, and immediately have a new monthly and yearly income figure for the series. Let's look at how it is done.

The Work Area

Above the Report area in the model you can see there is a work area (Figure U1.2) into which we can enter our variables, the "what-ifs" we want to look at, and from these the model establishes some codes for the status of each event under the current scenario. This is the first analysis that VisiCalc makes of the situation, and it works out a useful figure for us—at what stage each event in development is at present.

The two left-hand columns then are the start month, entered as "1" for January, "2" for February and so on, and although it is not used directly in the work area we make potential data changes easier by entering the going income rate for each event in column B—this data can be carried elsewhere when VisiCalc needs it.

We will demonstrate the formulas on the top row of the model, row 4, and you will remember that they are replicated down the model. The formula in column D is

```
        A      B       C          D     E     F     G     H     I     J     K     L     N     O     P
 1  LAUNCH TIMING ANALYSIS
 2
 3  START MONTH EVALUATOR   (WORK AREA).
 4
 5   INTRO  GOING                  1     2     3     4     5     6     7     8     9    10    11    12
 6   MONTH  SALES                 JAN   FEB   MAR   APR   MAY   JUN   JUL   AUG   SEP   OCT   NOV   DEC
 7  ------------------------------------------------------------------------------------------------
 8     1   110000  ACTION          1     2     3     4     5     6     7     8     9    10    11    12
 9     2    46000  ACTION          0     1     2     3     4     5     6     7     8     9    10    11
10     3    82000  ACTION          0     0     1     2     3     4     5     6     7     8     9    10
11     4    58000  ACTION          0     0     0     1     2     3     4     5     6     7     8     9
12     5    76000  ACTION          0     0     0     0     1     2     3     4     5     6     7     8
13     6    41000  ACTION          0     0     0     0     0     1     2     3     4     5     6     7
14     7    38000  ACTION          0     0     0     0     0     0     1     2     3     4     5     6
15     8    53000  ACTION          0     0     0     0     0     0     0     1     2     3     4     5
```

Figure U1.2: Work Area

@IF(D5 = A8,D5,0)

Now you will see why we have a number above each month in addition to the label.

SpreadTalk: Compare the start month we entered in column A with the number above the month name to see if they are the same—if they are then carry down the month number, otherwise enter zero.

In column E there is a change:

@IF(E5 = A8,1,@IF(D8<1,0,D8 + 1))

SpreadTalk: Look to see if the start month in column A matches the month number at the top of the column, and if it does then enter a "1" (for the start month for this action). On the other hand if it does not match, then look at the preceding month to see if anything has started yet for this action. If there is a figure "less than 1" of course it hasn't started, so insert a zero. If things are on the way with this action, then add one to the preceding month's entry.

This formula is replicated across the model, thus building the sequence. The formula is either starting (opening) a sequence, or it is continuing one that has already started. So in the work area VisiCalc is building a pattern that will enable us to look at the matrix and establish just where each Action (store opening or whatever) is in the scheme of things! Now let's put the information to work.

How Much Will the Stores Make?

As you can see, the layout of the Report area (Figure U1.1) is the same as the work area (Figure U1.2); therefore, every position in it can look at a corresponding position in the work area and know what to do.

Now we can introduce the financial side of things. We mentioned earlier the varying contribution a store makes according to how long it has been open. We call this period the "ramp up." In our case we have a four month ramp up and if you look for a moment at Figure U1.3 you will see the information waiting to be used.

The LOOKUP table has thirteen values that can be looked up, including the zero at the top, which is important as you will see. In month one of a startup we assume an action will deliver ten percent of its eventual going rate. In month two it is twenty percent, and so on until in the fifth month we forecast it will be delivering its full potential.

Rather than doing these calculations in formulas in the report, which we could have done, we chose to make these ramp-up percentages a separate part of the model. In the LOOKUP table we can change assumptions easily, and then examine their implication on the income of the activities. As we have said else-

Looks Like It's Getting Late!

```
            S      T

      3  LOOKUP TABLES
      4
      5     0      0
      6     1      0.15
      7     2      0.25
      8     3      0.55
      9     4      0.85
     10     5      1
     11     6      1
     12     7      1
     13     8      1
     14     9      1
     15    10      1
     16    11      1
     17    12      1
```

Figure U1.3: LOOKUP Tables

where in this book, we like making variables, things that you might like to change in a "what-if" situation, very accessible so that they can be changed with the minimum fuss.

Back to the Report

There is really only one formula in the report area, replicated everywhere with suitable adjustment of the (R)elative and (N)o change entries. The formula in column D is

@IF(D8<=5,B25*@LOOKUP(D8,R5...R17),B25)

SpreadTalk: Look up to the corresponding position in the work area to see if the number there is less than or equal to five (our ramp up period). If the number meets this check, then look up the value from the work area in the LOOKUP table, and multiply the going rate from column B by the value brought back. On the other hand, if the work area number is greater than five, use the going rate unchanged.

Now you can see the importance of the zero in the LOOKUP table— if the Action has not yet started, then the value to be looked up will be less than five, zero, and it too must be looked up, even though the value brought back is also zero (and going rate times zero is still zero, so no money gets entered in the report). Without this first zero you would get back NA for not available— in this context incorrect.

Apart from some totalling with @SUM, that's it—a simple yet effective way of seeing the implications of changing start dates immediately, which can be adapted to many uses.

OtherCalcs

Multiplan

In Multiplan you will be able to use this model with only a couple of changes. The lookup formula in the Report area would become:

IF(R[−17]4<=5,R25C2*LOOKUP(R[−17]C,R5C18:R17C19,1),R25C2)

You may wish to name the column 2 variables something like GOINGRTE. Then your lookup formula would be:

IF(R[−17]4<=5,GOINGRTE
*LOOKUP(R[−17]C,R5C18:R17C19,1),GOINGRTE)

Then you can easily copy this formula into all other locations in your table.

The other change you will want to make is with the formulas in the work area that indicate whether work has started yet. The formula from column 5 would be written in Multiplan as follows (we have named the row five variables MNTH and the column 1 variables STRTMNTH:

IF(MNTH=STRTMNTH,1,IF(RC[−1]<1,0,RC[−1]+1))

This formula can them be copied into all other locations in this work area.

SuperCalc³

This model works very well in SuperCalc³ with no changes other than the normal formula syntax differences between SuperCalc³ and VisiCalc.

How Much on the Meter?

U2

SPREADSHEET FUNCTIONS: Math Operators
FEATURED PROGRAM: SuperCalc³
TEMPLATE FUNCTION: Metric/English Measure Conversions

PURPOSE

To develop a practical format for a conversion table. A template like this can also be set up to do conversions in other categories, such as currency rates or electrical units.

In business, technical, and educational settings it is often necessary to convert from one measurement standard to another. The applications spreadsheet model in this chapter is a handy reference guide for people who need to do frequent conversions from Metric to English units of measure and vice versa.

UTILITY APPLICATION SPREADSHEET

Metric/English and English/Metric Conversion Table

This particular template that performs Metric/English unit conversions was developed while we were working on a user guide for a product that was to be sold in both the U.S. and Europe. We had discovered that we would be required to convert hundreds of English measurements to Metric, so we set up this conversion template to make the task easier.

The complete template can be viewed in Figures U2.1 and U2.2. First we entered all the labels in the columns shown. The formulas for converting English units to Metric equivalents appear in column C. Each of these formulas takes the English unit entered in column B and multiplies or divides it by the appropriate converting factor. An example of one of these formulas is the formula at C19, which converts Miles to Kilometers, and reads

(B19*1.609)

```
          A         B         C         D

 1 ENGLISH/METRIC CONVERSION TABLES
 2
 3
 4 METRIC CONVERSION
 5 ------------------
 6 ENGLISH    ENGLISH   METRIC    METRIC
 7 UNIT       VALUE     RESULT    UNIT
 8 -----------------------------------
 9 LINEAR MEASURE
10 --------------
11 INCHES        1       .0254 MILLIMTR
12 INCHES        1      2.54   CENTIMTR
13 FEET          1     30.48   CENTIMTR
14 FEET          1      0.30   METERS
15 YARDS         1      0.91   METERS
16 MILES         1   1609.34   METERS
17 MILES         1      1.61   KILOMTRS
18
19 LAND MEASURE
20 ------------
21 SQ. INCH      1 6.452E-4 CENTIARE
22 SQ. YARD      1  .0383612 ARES
23 ACRE          1  .4046945 HECTARES
24 SQ. MILE      1 2.590674  SQKILOMT
25
26 WEIGHT MEASURE
27 --------------
28 GRAIN         1      .0648 GRAM
29 OUNCE         1    28.3495 GRAMS
30 POUNDS        1   453.59   GRAMS
31 100WEIGHT     1    45.36   KILOGRAM
32 TON           1   907.18   GRAM
33
34 LIQUID MEASURE
35 --------------
36 CUP           1     .2366 LITER
37 PINT          1     .4732 LITER
38 QUART         1     .9464 LITER
39 GALLON        1    3.7854 LITER
40
41 TEMPERATURES
42 ------------
43 DEG F         1   -17.22 DEG C
44
45 ====================================
```

Figure U2.1:   Converting from English to Metric

How Much on the Meter?   199

```
                    F         G         H         I
         1
         2
         3
         4  ENGLISH CONVERSION
         5  ------------------
         6  METRIC    METRIC    ENGLISH   ENGLISH
         7  UNIT      VALUE     RESULT    UNIT
         8  ------------------------------------
         9  LINEAR MEASURE
        10  --------------
        11  MILLIMTR      1       .03937 INCH
        12  CENTIMTR      1       .3937  INCH
        13  DECIMTR       1       3.937  INCH
        14  METERS        1       3.2808 FEET
        15  DECAMTR       1       32.808 FEET
        16  HECTOMTR      1       328.08 FEET
        17   KILOMTRS     1       .621   MILE
        18  MYRIAMETR     1       6.21   MILE
        19
        20  LAND MEASURE
        21  ------------
        22  CENTIARE      1       1549.9 SQ. INCH
        23  ARES          1       119.6  SQ.YARD
        24  HECTARES      1       2.471  ACRE
        25  SQKILOMTR     1       0.39   SQ. MILE
        26
        27  WEIGHT MEASURE
        28  --------------
        29  CENTIGRAM     1       .1543  GRAIN
        30  DECIGRAM      1       1.5432 GRAIN
        31  GRAM          1       15.432 GRAIN
        32  DECAGRAM      1       .3527  OUNCE
        33  HECTOGRAM     1       3.5274 OUNCE
        34  KILOGRAM      1       2.2046 POUNDS
        35  MYRIAGRAM     1       22.046 POUNDS
        36  QUINTAL       1       220.46 POUNDS
        37  METRICTON     1       2204.6 POUNDS
        38
        39  LIQUID MEASURE
        40  --------------
        41  CENTILITR     1       .338   FLUID OZ
        42  DECILITR      1       3.38   FLUID OZ
        43  LITER         1       1.0567 QUART
        44  DECALITER     1       2.64   GALLON
        45  HECTOLITR     1       26.418 GALLON
        46  KILOLITER     1       264.18 GALLON
        47
        48  TEMPERATURES
        49  ------------
        50  DEG C         1       33.80  DEG F
        51
        52  ========================================
```

Figure U2.2:   Converting from Metric to English

In case you want to use this model exactly as it appears and do not have a conversion table handy, the formulas which contain all the conversion factors are all listed in the Appendix.

The Metric to English conversions take place in the section from columns F through I shown in Figure U2.2. All we had to do to make use of the feature was to enter the unit we wanted to convert in the appropriate cell in column G, and the formula at column H does the conversion. The formulas in column H are similar to the ones in column C, in that they multiply or divide the entry in column G by the English conversion factor. A sample formula is the one at H39,

(G39*2204.6)

which converts Metric Tons to Pounds.

SUMMARY

That's all there is to it! After the template is set up, you enter the unit to convert in column B or column G, depending on whether you want to convert to Metric or English.

The recalculation key (!) is pushed, and the properly converted answer appears in column D or column H. One final note: displayed answers, in some cases, approximate the exact answer due to the rounding procedures in SuperCalc. They were accurate enough for our purposes, but if a more accurate answer is needed, you can set the format in the answer columns to General FC,D,G) and make the column width (/FC,D,15) as wide as is necessary to display desired number of digits.

OtherCalcs

Multiplan

The principles as illustrated in this model will work in the same manner in Multiplan.

VisiCalc

This model will work as shown in VisiCalc.

U3
Things Are Looking Up

SPREADSHEET FUNCTIONS: CHOOSE, LOOKUP
FEATURED PROGRAM: VisiCalc
TEMPLATE FUNCTION: Using LOOKUP Tables in Two
                               Dimensions

PURPOSE

Most spreadsheet programs provide a built-in function called LOOKUP which we have featured several times in this book. Most of the times we are using it in templates, however, the LOOKUPs are one-dimensional with only one list searched. In this chapter we illustrate how you can search more than one list for the correct value, adding a two-dimensional nature to the LOOKUP process.

UTILITY APPLICATION SPREADSHEET

For a change of pace we will take a look at how you can use the concept of two-dimensional LOOKUPs to LOOKUP tax amounts from the tables that come with Form 1040. One problem in using VisiCalc to do this is that the tax tables are based on income levels AND filing status. With two variables that can change it is hard to get a standard LOOKUP table to work. You not only want to have VisiCalc LOOKUP the tax, but you also want it to LOOK in the the correct table based on the filing status of the taxpayer. This ability could save you a tremendous amount of time.

Of course we would never tell you about something that we would like VisiCalc to do without showing you a way to accomplish the wish. We are persistent spreadsheeters and we will work on something until we come up with a solution that we can talk about, or we will never mention it in the first place. One day while puzzling over the tax table problem we thought to ourselves "There must be some way to choose the right table." Eureka! we had it, the CHOOSE function! We might be able to use the CHOOSE function in conjunction with the LOOKUP function to give the flexibility wanted.

After working on the formula for a while we were finally successful. This formula does use the CHOOSE function to select the proper table to look in, and then LOOKsUP the correct tax.

An entire tax model has been abbreviated here for reasons of space, but Figures U3.1 and U3.2 demonstrate the use we make of this formula. The big model (not shown here) calculates the taxable income for input at line 37 of Form 1040. This Two-Dimensional LOOKUP Table example uses this amount entered at C4, as the value to be compared to the search lists. The challenge to the problem is how to select which list to look in. The problem was solved by using a code which corresponds to the taxpayer filing status code which has been entered in this example at C12.

The real beauty of this model is that only one formula selects the table to look in and looks up the tax! The formula that is at C14 in Figure U3.1 reads:

```
@CHOOSE(C12,@LOOKUP(C4,D14...D33),
        @LOOKUP(C4,F14...F33),
           @LOOKUP(C4,H14...H33),
              @LOOKUP(C4,J14...J43))
```

```
                      A         B         C
 1
 2
 3  ENTER INCOME FROM
 4  LINE 37 FORM 1040>  41350.67
 5
 6  ENTER STATUS CODE AT C12
 7  1= SINGLE
 8  2= MARRIED FILING JOINT
 9  3= MARRIED FILING SEPARATE
10  4= HEAD OF HOUSEHOLD
11
12             CODE VALUE:          4
13
14  TAX PAYABLE:            10028
15                       ********
```

Figure U3.1: Entries and Results

Things Are Looking Up

	D	E	F	G	H	I	J	K
11	CODE	TAX	CODE	TAX	CODE	TAX	CODE	TAX
12	1	VALUE	2	VALUE	3	VALUE	4	VALUE
13	-----	-----	-----	----	-----	-----	-----	-----
14	41000	10723	41000	8663	41000	12858	41000	9898
15	41050	10743	41050	8680	41050	12880	41050	9917
16	41100	10763	41100	8698	41100	12902	41100	9935
17	41150	10783	41150	8715	41150	12924	41150	9954
18	41200	10803	41200	8733	41200	12946	41200	9972
19	41250	10823	41250	8750	41250	12968	41250	9991
20	41300	10843	41300	8768	41300	12990	41300	10009
21	41350	10863	41350	8785	41350	13012	41350	10028
22	41400	10883	41400	8803	41400	13034	41400	10046
23	41450	10903	41450	8820	41450	13056	41450	10065
24	41500	10924	41500	8838	41500	13078	41500	10083
25	41550	10947	41550	8855	41550	13100	41550	10102
26	41600	10969	41600	8873	41600	13122	41600	10120
27	41650	10992	41650	8890	41650	13144	41650	10139
28	41700	11014	41700	8908	41700	13166	41700	10157
29	41750	11037	41750	8925	41750	13188	41750	10176
30	41800	11059	41800	8943	41800	13210	41800	10194
31	41850	11082	41850	8960	41850	13232	41850	10213
32	41900	11104	41900	8978	41900	13254	41900	10231
33	41950	11127	41950	8995	41950	13276	41950	10250

Figure U3.2.: LOOKUP Table

SpreadTalk: The formula looks at C12 where the code is entered, and chooses the proper LOOKUP formula from the list according to the code value. For example, the code value in the figure is 4, so the LOOKUP formula used would be

@LOOKUP(C4,J14...J43)

because it is fourth in the CHOOSE list. The LOOKUP formula then compares the value of the taxable income from C4, to the selected search list, and returns the correct tax amount to C14.

The most tedious part of building the model that uses this formula, was the input of the entire detailed tax table from the 1040 package. Fortunately, once this task was completed it was very easy to input the formula that did all of the work. We hope your application of the Utility will use tables that are less tedious to build!

OtherCalcs

Multiplan

In Multiplan the LOOKUP formula is structured in such a way that the use of a simple IF statement and code numbers across that top of the columns of the

LOOKUP table to indicate which column is in use would solve the problem of LOOKUPs in two dimensions. Take a look at Figure U3.3. This is how the LOOKUP table would appear in Multiplan. You can leave out the extra search lists due to the fact that Multiplan allows you to search in non-adjacent columns. The formula that would be placed in R14C3 in Multiplan would be

IF(R12C3 = 1,LOOKUP(R4C3,R14C4:R33C5),
   IF(R12C3 = 2,LOOKUP(R4C3,R14C4:R33C6),
      IF(R12C3 = 3,LOOKUP(R4C3,R14C4:R33C7),
         IF(R12C3 = 4,LOOKUP(R4C3,R14C4:R33C8),

If this formula is too long to fit into your Multiplan program, you could shorten it by assigning Names to the code and income cells, and to the LOOKUP ranges. These names should be very short, but very meaningful.

SuperCalc³

In SuperCalc³ there is no CHOOSE function, so that you must use the same type of IF statement shown in the Multiplan explanation. You have to remember, however, that there must be a search list adjacent to each of the LOOKUP value columns. The tables for the model should be set up the same as the VisiCalc model shown in Figure U3.2.

	4	5	6	7	8
11	CODE	TAX	TAX	TAX	TAX
12		VALUE	VALUE	VALUE	VALUE
13	----	-----	-----	-----	-----
14	41000	10723	8663	12858	9898
15	41050	10743	8680	12880	9917
16	41100	10763	8698	12902	9935
17	41150	10783	8715	12924	9954
18	41200	10803	8733	12946	9972
19	41250	10823	8750	12968	9991
20	41300	10843	8768	12990	10009
21	41350	10863	8785	13012	10028
22	41400	10883	8803	13034	10046
23	41450	10903	8820	13056	10065
24	41500	10924	8838	13078	10083
25	41550	10947	8855	13100	10102
26	41600	10969	8873	13122	10120
27	41650	10992	8890	13144	10139
28	41700	11014	8908	13166	10157
29	41750	11037	8925	13188	10176
30	41800	11059	8943	13210	10194
31	41850	11082	8960	13232	10213
32	41900	11104	8978	13254	10231
33	41950	11127	8995	13276	10250

Figure U3.3: LOOKUP Table in Multiplan

U4
Doing the Impossible with LOOKUP

SPREADSHEET FUNCTIONS: LOOKUP, CHOOSE, IF
FEATURED PROGRAM: VisiCalc
TEMPLATE FUNCTION: An Automated Invoice System

PURPOSE

In our earlier chapters (Chapters 4, 9, and Utility 3) on using the LOOKUP function we mentioned two rules that had to be followed in order for LOOKUPs to work properly. First we said that the search list had to be in ascending order, and the return values list had to be adjacent to the search list. In this utility, we will show you a way to get around those two limitations (the first condition is still a limitation in Multiplan).

UTILITY APPLICATION SPREADSHEET

In this model we bring you an invoicing system that looks up parts listed in any order, determines the price, and adds up the invoice.

The way in which we do this is by using a combination of the LOOKUP Function and the CHOOSE function to accomplish this task. (in the OtherCalcs section at the end of this chapter we will show how to do this with SuperCalc[3] which does not have the CHOOSE option).

Why would anyone want to set up their LOOKUP lists in nonascending order, you may ask? Well consider a part numbering system that assigns numbers to different parts within various component systems. For example, our parts list is for a computer retail store. The dealer has parts listed in ascending order for disk drives, then another list for printer supplies in ascending order and another list in ascending order for software, but the entire list of numbers does not go from highest to lowest if you put all of the part numbers into one list. The Parts List is shown in Figure U4.1, column D of our model.

The invoice that is made up for each customer is shown in Figure U4.2, columns D through H. To make up an invoice the employee must enter the customer name, address, and phone in the appropriate columns and rows. Then the Part Numbers for the order are listed in column E with the number ordered entered alongside in column F. These numbers can be listed in any order in the column. All the sales clerk has to do then is recalculate a specified number of times (according to the instructions alongside the invoice), and the invoice is almost done. The amount paid is entered, another recalc is performed, and the invoice is complete and can be printed out!

This seems like a relatively easy system to operate, and it is. The formulas that perform the calculations are a bit more complex, however. To understand them let's go back to Figure U4.1 and take a more in-depth look. The LOOKUP equations in this model are not only LOOKingUP Part Numbers in Figure U4.1 that are not in ascending order, but the price list (column I) is not even adjacent to the part number list, another big No-No in VisiCalc!

After the customer data and order information are entered, the model

```
          A          B         C         D         E          F              G             H          I
 1 CALC.COUNT------>          10
 2 CURRENT
 3 LOOKUP---------->                    2340
 4
 5
 6                             PART               PART      !-------------------------------!       PRICE
 7                             TYPE              NUMBERS    !   WORK AREA DO NOT DISTURB    !       LIST
 8                            ---------          --------   !-------------------------------!     --------
 9                            DSKDRIVES            997                   1                     1    250.00
10                                                1007         0         2                     2    329.98
11                                                1056         0         3                     3    500.00
12                            PRNTR SUP           1008         0         4                     4     12.76
13                                                1250         0         5                     5      8.79
14                                                1357         0         6                     6     37.42
15                            SOFTWARE            1018         0         7                     7     39.99
16                                                1157         0         8                     8    257.00
17                                                2170         0         9                     9     99.00
18                                                2340         0        10                    10    650.00
```

Figure U4.1: Parts and Price List

Doing the Impossible with LOOKUP

```
          A         B       C       D        E       F         G          H         I
24  SET ZERO>       1              1004              COMPUTER WAREHOUSE
25                                                   94 DISK DRIVE
26                                                   TERMINAL, OR 97074
27
28                                                                          9  :   MONTH
29                                                                         20  :   DATE
30                                                                       1984  :   YEAR
31                                  CUSTOMER   NUMBER:    45
32                                  CUSTOMER     NAME:  FIRST    LAST
33                                                      TYRONE   PROGRAMMER
34                                  COMPANY      NAME:  DISKUS THROWERS
35                                  CUSTOMER ADDRESS:  18 BASIC WAY
36                                                      CITY     ST                ZIP
37                                                      TERMINAL,OR               97074
38                                  CUSTOMER    PHONE:  (503) 555-5555
39
40                                                         NO.       UNIT                 TOTAL
41                                  ITEM NO. PART NO.   ORDERED     PRICE                 PRICE
42                                  ----------------------------------------------------------
43                                        1     997        1        250.00                250.00
44                                        2    1007        1        329.98                329.98
45                                        3    1056        1        500.00                500.00
46                                        4    1008        1         12.76                 12.76
47                                        5    1250        1          8.79                  8.79
48                                        6    1357        1         37.42                 37.42
49                                        7    1018        1         39.99                 39.99
50                                        8    1157        1        257.00                257.00
51                                        9    2170        1         99.00                 99.00
52                                       10    2340        1        650.00                650.00
53
54                                                             TOTAL ORDER  $           1138.95
55                                                               SALES TAX                61.50
56                                                                                     --------
57                                                                   TOTAL  $           1200.45
58                                                             AMOUNT PAID               600.00
59                                                                                     --------
60                                                             BALANCE DUE  $            600.45
```

Figure U4.2: Invoice

works using successive recalculations to determine which Item No./Part No. is LOOKedUP. There is a Counter formula located in cell C1:

@IF(B24 = 0,0,C1 + 1)

SpreadTalk: This formula looks at the value in B24 to see if it's zero. If so, then no calculations will be done (or the invoice will be set back to zero). If there is any other input in B24, a one is added to the value in C1 each time the model is recalculated. With the first recalculation this number becomes one.

In cell C2 there is a LOOKUP equation which LOOKsUP the Count Number (the number just calculated in C1) in the Item Number list in column D of the Invoice. The equation for this is

@IF(B24 = 0,0,@LOOKUP(C1,D43...D52))

The result of this LOOKUP is a Part Number from the invoice written at C3. This part number is used in the equations in E10...E19 of Figure U4.1. An example of one of these equations is

@IF(D9 = C3,D9 + 1,0)

which is located at E10. This formula is replicated down the column from E10...E18 with the references to the D cell Relative.

SpreadTalk: If the Part Number in D9 equals the part number shown in C3, then a one is added to the Part Number and this number is placed in the appropriate cell in E10, otherwise a zero is written. Because there are similar formulas residing in the cells from E11...E19, during a recalc, some part number is written into one of the cells from E10...E19, unless the calculated part number from C3 does not exist in the list.

In Figure U4.1 the number that shows in column E, row 19 is 2341. This corresponds to the Part Number 2340 in D16. All the other E cells show a zero.

All that we have done so far is compare the count that is in C1 to the Item Number in the invoice. This item number is used to look up the Part number for the item from the invoice. In column E we add 1 to this number.

Now the equations in H9...H19 go to work. Let's look at the formula for H9:

@IF(B24 = 0,0,@IF(D43 = C1,@LOOKUP(E43,E9...E19),H9))

SpreadTalk: This says, assuming there is a number other than 0 in B24, and that H9 does not equal zero, if the Count No. (C1) is equal to the Item No. in D43, then LOOKUP the Part Number from E43 in the column E9...E18; otherwise just write H9. This equation is replicated down column H in Figure U4.1 (The Replicating instructions are N R N R N N N). Each of the equations in H9...H18 are evaluated in the recalculation, so that the Number from column F corresponding to the Part Number generated in E10...E18 in each recalc is written in the correct spot in H9...H18.

This number is then used by the equation in column G43...G52 to CHOOSE the appropriate price. The equations in G43...G52 take the number written in H9...H19 and find the Price based on its location in the Price list, column I9...I18. The CHOOSE function is used here.

In the CHOOSE equation @CHOOSE(VALUE,RANGE), the value returned is the sequence number in the CHOOSE equation range. That is, in an equation @CHOOSE(2,I9...I18) the second number from the range I9...I18 is chosen, for example, I10. So in the equation in G43:

@IF(F43 = 0,0,@IF(H9 = 0,0,@CHOOSE(H9,I9...I18)

Doing the Impossible with LOOKUP

SpreadTalk: First F36 is checked to determine if there was an order placed. Then if H9 is 0, there is a zero written at G36, otherwise the H9th price is chosen from the price list. In our example H9 is 1, therefore the first price in the list is chosen, $250.00.

To sum up (if it's possible), customer data and order information are entered into the invoice form. A starting digit is then placed in B24. Then a recalc is done. The counter in C1 is changed to 1. This 1 is used by the equation in C2 to LOOKUP a Part Number from the invoice adjacent to D43...D52, the Item No. column. This Part number is compared to the Part Number list in D9...D18, and whichever number it matches has a 1 added to it and is written one column over and one row down. This new list becomes a LOOKUP list for the equations in column H9...H18. In column H the part number is LOOKedUP from E9...E19, and a value from column F is written. This number is then used by the equations in G43...G53 of the invoice to CHOOSE the correct price from the list. More recalcs (equal to the last Item No. + 1) are done until the invoice is filled in. The invoice can then be printed out. After printing, a zero is inserted in B24 and the model is recalced once again to clear the invoice. Customer information must be erased and the Invoice number manually updated.

The rest of the formulas in the Invoice are easy to figure out. The formulas in I43...I52 multiply the Price per Part times the Number of Parts ordered. These amounts are summed up in I54. At I55 the sales tax is calculated based on this total, and I57 adds the tax to the Parts Total. The amount tendered is entered in I58, and the Balance due is calculated in I60.

After the Invoice is complete, the sales clerk follows the instructions listed for printing the invoice, and they are done. All that remains to be done is to clean up the invoice for the next user, and update the invoice number shown in D24.

SUMMARY

This utility model uses several techniques that are applicable to many other models. We showed you how you could get around the difficulties of having your LOOKUPs written in ascending order and in adjacent columns or rows. This model sounds very complicated, but it is not that difficult to execute. If you enter the example as shown here, you should gain a good understanding of the way this innovative LOOKUP system works.

OtherCalcs

Multiplan

The way in which Multiplan calculates a spreadsheet makes this model a bit trickier to design for this program. Because Multiplan proceeds with a "Natural" calculation mode, the simple Count formula used in the other programs to log the number of recalcs done and to determine which Part Number to LOOKUP, cannot be used. Instead, we have used at R1C3 the formula

IF(zero = 0,0,ITERCNT())

ITERCNT() is a special Multiplan built-in function that calculates the number of iterations that have been performed under the Iteration mode.

The Iteration mode is turned on when you enter the Options command and tab over three times to hit Yes. When this is done, Multiplan will continue to calculate all of the formulas in the model until they are complete every time you hit a recalc. If you don't use this option, any spreadsheet that contains circular references will not be able to recalc. Because this model contains numerous circular references we have chosen to use this recalculation mode. We have also chosen to use the Completion test option from the options mode.

In R51C11 we have placed the formula

ITERCNT()

In R52C11 we put the formula

OR(ZERO = 0,R[– 1]C = 12)

SpreadTalk: When the number of Iterations equals twelve, or when ZERO (the name for the SET ZERO cell) is turned to 0, then the recalculation mode is turned off. When in the Options mode, we tabbed over to the fourth option and entered R52C11 as the location of the completion test. When this condition is met, that is, one or the other of the conditions is true, recalculation stops.

The function that replaces the CHOOSE function in VisiCalc is the INDEX function. It is slightly different in construction than the CHOOSE function. The formulas in the Unit Price section of the invoice read similarly to this one found in R44C7:

IF(RC[– 1] = 0,0,IF(R10C8 = 0,0,INDEX(R9C9:R19C9,R10C8)))

It is much easier in Multiplan to construct formulas, especially long formulas, when you have assigned names to often-used variables. You can see here that we named a great number of variables in this model

NAME	LOCATION
ZERO	R25C2
COUNT	R1C3
TOTAL	R55C9

```
DUE     R61C9
LKUP    R3C3
```

There was also one rather odd aberration in Multiplan that we could not figure out. The LOOKUP formulas would not work in the Invoice unless there was a "DUMMY" line inserted at the top of the Parts and Price lists. Once we input a Dummy row at row 9 in the Parts List the formulas worked fine. If you are having difficulties implementing this system in Multiplan, write to us in care of *InterCalc, PO Box 4289, Stamford, CT 06907*, and we will send you a complete copy of the formulas and the printouts illustrating the working model in Multiplan.

SuperCalc³

Here is the solution for the SuperCalc users. To solve the CHOOSE problem we simply used another LOOKUP list in our Parts and Price List. The SuperCalc Parts and Price list is shown in Figure U4.3. We have moved the formulas that were in column H in the VisiCalc model, into column G. These formulas remain exactly the same as the VisiCalc formulas except the references to column H were changed to column G. In column H we input a new LOOKUP list from 1 to 10. Down in the Invoice section where the Unit Price is being determined in column G we have changed the formulas to make use of this new LOOKUP list. Now when the part number is converted to a list number in column G of the

```
    |   A    ||   B    ||   C   ||   D   ||   E   ||   F   ||   G   ||   H   ||   I   |
 1 |CALC.COUNT------>              9
 2 |CURRENT
 3 |LOOKUP---------->            1157
 4 |
 5 |
 6 |                    PART        PART    !-------------------------------!     PRICE
 7 |                    TYPE        NUMBERS ! WORK AREA DO NOT DISTURB       !     LIST
 8 |                    ---------   -------  !-------------------------------!     --------
 9 |                    ENGINE       997                1        2        1      .11
10 |                                1007        0       2        1        2     2.13
11 |                                1056        0       3        5        3      .51
12 |                    TRANSMISS   1008        0       4        7        4      .67
13 |                                1250        0       5        9        5     8.79
14 |                                1357        0       6        8        6     2.34
15 |                    TRIM        1018        0       7        8        7      .23
16 |                                1157        0       8        8        8      .45
17 |                                2170       1158     9        8        9     1.10
18 |                                2340        0      10        0       10      .75
```

Figure U4.3:   SuperCalc³ Parts and Price List

Parts and Price List, column G of the Invoice LOOKsUP this list number from the LOOKUP table in columns H and I of the Parts and Price list. A typical formula reads

IF(F36=0,0,IF(G9=0,0,LOOKUP(G9,H9:H18)))

This says to look at the Number Ordered. If this is zero write a zero; otherwise look at G9. If G9=0, write a zero; otherwise LOOKUP G9 in the LOOKUP list in H9:H18. A relatively easy solution to the CHOOSE problem.

U5
Find the Missing Piece

SPREADSHEET FUNCTIONS: EXP, LN
FEATURED PROGRAM: VisiCalc
TEMPLATE FUNCTION: Interest Calculator

PURPOSE

In many different businesses it is necessary to solve for a missing factor—you have three out of four components of a calculation and want to be able to figure out the one that's missing. You, of course, want to be able to do it regardless of which one is missing, on which side of the "equals" sign.

UTILITY APPLICATION SPREADSHEET

Our example of such a task is of interest to all who invest (or borrow): knowing three of four variables involved in an interest calculation—principal, interest rate, period, and yield—this template figures out the fourth variable for you, for continuous, daily, and monthly time frames.

Let us say that you have to calculate the yields offered for a Certificate of Deposit. This model was developed by a clever shortcut artist, to find the "missing value"—when she knew the other three values.

Let's further compound (intentional pun!) the problem by requiring our model to handle the possibility that the bank that issues these certificates offers three types of interest-compounding methods—continuous, daily, and monthly. Our model will calculate the "missing value" for each possible method as well.

214   Find the Missing Piece

```
              A          B        C        D        E        F

    1  INVESTMENT CALCULATOR
    2
    3  ---------------------------------------------------------------
    4  SUPPLY THESE        TO       TO       TO       TO
    5  VALUES              FIND     FIND     FIND     FIND
    6                      YIELD    PRINCIPAL INTEREST PERIOD
    7  ---------------------------------------------------------------
    8      PRINCIPAL                         ---
    9      INTEREST RATE                              ---
   10      PERIOD                                              ---
   11      YIELD                    ---
   12
   13 ---------------------------------------------------------------
   14 MISSING VALUE        YIELD PRINCIPAL INTEREST    PERIOD
   15 ---------------------------------------------------------------
   16 COMPOUNDING METHOD
   17
   18      CONTINUOUS      0.00     0.00     0.00     0.00
   19      DAILY           0.00     0.00     0.00     0.00
   20      MONTHLY         0.00     0.00     0.00     0.00
```

Figure U5.1:   Empty Matrix


```
              A          B        C        D        E        F

    1  INVESTMENT CALCULATOR
    2
    3  ---------------------------------------------------------------
    4  SUPPLY THESE        TO       TO       TO       TO
    5  VALUES              FIND     FIND     FIND     FIND
    6                      YIELD    PRINCIPAL INTEREST PERIOD
    7  ---------------------------------------------------------------
    8      PRINCIPAL       7000.00           ---
    9      INTEREST RATE   11.75                     ---
   10      PERIOD          3.00                              ---
   11      YIELD                    ---
   12
   13 ---------------------------------------------------------------
   14 MISSING VALUE        YIELD PRINCIPAL INTEREST    PERIOD
   15 ---------------------------------------------------------------
   16 COMPOUNDING METHOD
   17
   18      CONTINUOUS      9958.34  0.00    0.00     0.00
   19      DAILY           9957.77  0.00    0.00     0.00
   20      MONTHLY         9941.28  0.00    0.00     0.00
```

$7,000.00

Figure U5.2:   Searching for Yield

Find the Missing Piece   215

Look at Figure U5.1. As you can see there is a vertical column in the model that is designed to find each of the specific factors, which are listed in row 6. When we know what the missing variable is that we are looking for, we go to the column that will calculate that variable, and enter the known quantities on the requisite row.

To calculate the Yield for example, place the cursor at C8. Enter the first known value, Principal, then move down Column C and enter the Interest Rate, and Period. The calculated result will appear in C18...C20 after calling the re-calculation function twice (we need to call it twice because there is a forward reference in this model). The missing Yield is calculated for each different compounding method and appears in C18, C19, and C20.

The other options work similarly (and we have shown four illustrations, Figures U5.2-U5.5, using the same numbers to show that it works!).

This template derives the missing information using the following formulas in the results area, under COMPOUNDING METHOD. The first row of formulas (row 18) solves for the values under Continuous Interest Compounding rules:

Yield: @EXP(C10*(C9/100))*C8
Principal: @IF(@AND(D9=0,D10=0,D11=0),0,
           @EXP(@LN(D11)−(D10*(D19/100))))
Interest: @IF(@AND(E8=0,E10=0,E11=0),0,
           (@LN(E11/E18)/E10)*100)

```
              A       B           C         D         E          F

 1  INVESTMENT CALCULATOR
 2
 3  ----------------------------------------------------------------
 4  SUPPLY THESE        TO        TO        TO         TO
 5  VALUES              FIND      FIND      FIND       FIND
 6                      YIELD     PRINCIPAL INTEREST   PERIOD
 7  ----------------------------------------------------------------
 8        PRINCIPAL                          ---
 9        INTEREST RATE                     11.75
10        PERIOD                             3.00                ---
11        YIELD                   --- 10000.00
12
13  ----------------------------------------------------------------
14  MISSING VALUE       YIELD PRINCIPAL INTEREST       PERIOD
15  ----------------------------------------------------------------
16  COMPOUNDING METHOD
17
18        CONTINUOUS    0.00    7029.29    0.00        0.00
19        DAILY         0.00    7030.50    0.00        0.00
20        MONTHLY       0.00    7065.07    0.00        0.00
```

Figure U5.3:   Searching for Principal

```
              A         B         C         D         E         F

 1  INVESTMENT CALCULATOR
 2
 3  ------------------------------------------------------------------
 4  SUPPLY THESE        TO        TO        TO        TO
 5  VALUES              FIND      FIND      FIND      FIND
 6                      YIELD     PRINCIPAL INTEREST  PERIOD
 7  ------------------------------------------------------------------
 8          PRINCIPAL                       ---       7000.00
 9          INTEREST RATE                                       ---
10          PERIOD                                    3.00
11          YIELD                 ---                 10000.00
12
13  ------------------------------------------------------------------
14  MISSING VALUE       YIELD  PRINCIPAL  INTEREST    PERIOD
15  ------------------------------------------------------------------
16  COMPOUNDING METHOD
17
18          CONTINUOUS    0.00      0.00      11.89     0.00
19          DAILY         0.00      0.00      11.90     0.00
20          MONTHLY       0.00      0.00      12.07     0.00
```

Figure U5.4: Searching for Interest

```
              A         B         C         D         E         F

 1  INVESTMENT CALCULATOR
 2
 3  ------------------------------------------------------------------
 4  SUPPLY THESE        TO        TO        TO        TO
 5  VALUES              FIND      FIND      FIND      FIND
 6                      YIELD     PRINCIPAL INTEREST  PERIOD
 7  ------------------------------------------------------------------
 8          PRINCIPAL                       ---                 7000.00
 9          INTEREST RATE                             ---       11.80
10          PERIOD                                              ---
11          YIELD                 ---                           10000.00
12
13  ------------------------------------------------------------------
14  MISSING VALUE       YIELD  PRINCIPAL  INTEREST    PERIOD
15  ------------------------------------------------------------------
16  COMPOUNDING METHOD
17
18          CONTINUOUS    0.00      0.00      0.00      3.02
19          DAILY         0.00      0.00      0.00      3.02
20          MONTHLY       0.00      0.00      0.00      3.07
```

Figure U5.5: Searching for Period

Find the Missing Piece

Period: @IF(@AND(F8=0,F9=0,F11=0),0,
            (@LN(F11/F18)/(F19/100)

The second row (row 19) calculates the missing values using Daily Interest Compounding rules:

Yield: (C9/100)/360+1^(360*C10)*C8
Principal: @IF(@AND(D9=0,D10=0,D11=0),0,
              (@EXP(−360*@LN((D9/100)*D10/360+1)+
              @LN(D11))
Interest: @IF(@AND(E8=0,E10=0,E11=0),0,
              (@EXP(@LN(E11)−@LN(E8)/360)−1*360/E10)*100)
Period: @IF(@AND(F8=0,F9=0,F11=0),0,
              (@EXP(@LN(F11)−@LN(F8)/360)−1*360/(F9/100))

Finally, the last row of formulas in row 20 solves for the variables using Monthly Interest Compounding rules:

Yield: (C9/100)/12+1^(12*C10)*C8
Principal: @IF(@AND(D9=0,D10=0,D11=0),0,
              (@EXP(−12*@LN((D9/100)*D10/12+1)+@LN(D11))
Interest: @IF(@AND(E8=0,E10=0,E11=0),0,
              (@EXP(@LN(E11)−@LN(E8)/12)−1*12/E10)*100)
Period: @IF(@AND(F8=0,F9=0,F11=0),0,
              (@EXP(@LN(F11)−@LN(F8)/12)−1*12/(F9/100))

Those formulas look a bit intimidating, mostly because of the long AND statements that precede each active piece. Without the ANDs, however, the display in the principal, interest, and period columns will show ERROR if you are using that particular column. Since it not really an error (and the legend can scare someone not familiar with spreadsheets!), the AND expressions will insert zeros for the noncalculation of variables, looking much better on a printed report or display. Of course, we do not need one in the yield column because the formulas there automatically calculate to zero if there is no input variable.

SUMMARY

This is a very useful utility that will be of value to all investors or borrowers. The layout of the template, with the known variables and a column for searching for each missing one, is a tidy and organized way of managing the process—you can adapt it for any other project you have that requires similar "find the missing piece" calculations.

OtherCalcs

Multiplan

This program works as shown in Multiplan. Remember that in Multiplan the construction of the AND statement is similar to:

IF(AND(R8C5=0,R10C5=0,R11C5=0),0,
    (LN(R11C5/R18C5)/R10C5)*100)

SuperCalc³

AND statements in SuperCalc follow a similar syntax to Multiplan. An example formula would be:

IF(AND(E8=0,E10=0,E11=0),0,
    (LN(E11/E18)/E10)*100)

With SuperCalc³ for the Apple, you can choose Natural Order calculation which will calculate the model variables correctly each time you input new values. This way you will not have to do two manual recalculations to solve the forward references problem.

THE COMPLEAT APPLE SPREADSHEETER

Appendices

THE COMPLEAT APPLE SPREADSHEETER

Appendix I

The Spreadsheet FUNCTION Matrix

Use this chart to establish the equivalent function if the chapter you are reading is not demonstrated in your program.

Appendix I

```
SPREADSHEET COMMAND
   COMPARISON                       VisiCalc                    Advanced VisiCalc
-----------------------------------------------------------------------------------
EDITING
-----------------------
EDIT CELL CONTENTS                  /E(dit)                     /E(dit)
ENTER LABELS                        Letter or "                 Letter or "
ENTER VALUES                        Number + - . ( @            Number + - . ( @
ERASE CELL(S)                       /B(lank)                    /B(lank)
ERASE SCREEN                        /C(lear) Y(es)              /C(lear) Y(es)
GOTO LOCATION                       >Cell Address               >Cell Address

FORMATTING
-----------------------
CELLS
------
BAR GRAPH                           /F(ormat) *                 /F(ormat) *
COLUMN WIDTH                                                    /G(lobal)C(ol.width)#
COMMAS IN NUMBERS                                               /A(ttribute) V(alue) comma
DEFAULT                             /F(ormat) D(efault)         /F(ormat) D(efault)
DOLLARS AND CENTS                   /F(ormat) $                 /F(ormat) $
GENERAL                             /F(ormat) G(eneral)         /F(ormat) G(eneral)
HIDE VALUES                                                     /A(ttribute)H(ide)
INTEGER                             /F(ormat) I(nteger)         /F(ormat) I(nteger)
NEGATIVES IN PARENTHESES                                        /A(ttribute) V(alue) parenthesis
PERCENT                                                         /A(ttribute) V(alue) percent
PROTECT CELL ENTRIES                                            /A(ttribute) M(ode) P(rotect)
REPEATING LABELS                    /- character                /F(ormat) - character
TEXT LEFT                           /F(ormat) L(eft)            /F(ormat) L(eft)
TEXT RIGHT                          /F(ormat) R(ight)           /F(ormat) R(ight)
UNPROTECT CELL ENTRIES                                          /A(ttribute) M(ode) U(nprotect)
USER DEFINED - define                                           /F(ormat) = character
USER DEFINED - use                                              /F(ormat) character
VALUE LEFT                          /F(ormat) L(eft)            /F(ormat) L(eft)
VALUE RIGHT                         /F(ormat) R(ight)           /F(ormat) R(ight)

GLOBAL
-------
BAR GRAPH                           /G(lobal) F(ormat) *        /G(lobal) F(ormat) *
BORDER DISPLAY
COLUMN WIDTH                        /G(lobal) C(ol.Width) #     /G(lobal) C(ol.Width) C(ol.Width)#
COMMAS IN NUMBERS                                               /G A(ttribute) V(alue) comma
DEFAULT                             /G(lobal) F(ormat) D(efault) /G(lobal) F(ormat) D(efault)
DELETE COLUMN(S)                    /D(elete) C(olumn)          /D(elete) C(olumn)
DELETE ROW(S)                       /D(elete) R(ow)             /D(elete) R(ow)
DOLLARS AND CENTS                   /G(lobal) F(ormat) $        /G(lobal) F(ormat) $
FIXED TITLES - BOTH                 /T(itles) B(oth)            /T(itles) B(oth)
FIXED TITLES - CLEAR                /T(itles) N(one)            /T(itles) N(one)
FIXED TITLES - HORIZ.               /T(itles) H(orizontal)      /T(itles) H(orizontal)
FIXED TITLES - VERT.                /T(itles) V(ertical)        /T(itles) V(ertical)
GENERAL                             /G(lobal) F(ormat) G(eneral) /G(lobal) F(ormat) G(eneral)
HIDE VALUES                                                     /G(lobal) A(ttribute)H(ide)
INSERT COLUMN(S)                    /I(nsert) C(olumn)          /I(nsert) C(olumn)
INSERT ROW(S)                       /I(nsert) R(ow)             /I(nsert) R(ow)
INTEGER                             /G(lobal) F(ormat) I(nteger) /G(lobal) F(ormat) I(nteger)
MOVE COLUMN(S)                      /M(ove) Column...Column     /M(ove) Column...Column
MOVE ROW(S)                         /M(ove) Row...Row           /M(ove) Row...Row
NEGATIVES IN PARENTHESES                                        /G A(ttribute) V(alue) parenthesis
PERCENT                                                         /G A(ttribute) V(alue) percent
PROTECT CELL ENTRIES                                            /G A(ttribute) M(ode) P(rotect)
TEXT LEFT                           /G(lobal) F(ormat) L(eft)   /G(lobal) F(ormat) L(eft)
TEXT RIGHT                          /G(lobal) F(ormat) R(ight)  /G(lobal) F(ormat) R(ight)
UNPROTECT CELL ENTRIES                                          /G A(ttribute) M(ode) U(nprotect)
USER DEFINED - use                                              /G(lobal) F(ormat) character
VALUE LEFT                          /G(lobal) F(ormat) L(eft)   /G(lobal) F(ormat) L(eft)
VALUE RIGHT                         /G(lobal) F(ormat) R(ight)  /G(lobal) F(ormat) R(ight)
WINDOW - HORIZONTAL                 /W(indow) H(orizontal)      /W(indow) H(orizontal)
WINDOWS - CLEAR                     /W(indow) 1                 /W(indow) 1
WINDOWS - SYNCHRNIZED               /W(indow) S(ynchronized)    /W(indow) S(ynchronized)
WINDOWS - UNSYNCH                   /W(indow) U(nsynchronzed)   /W(indow) U(nsynchronzed)
WINDOWS - VERTICAL                  /W(indow) V(ertical)        /W(indow) V(ertical)
```

Appendix I

```
SPREADSHEET COMMAND
     COMPARISON                       SuperCalc3                      Multiplan
------------------------------------------------------------------------------------------
EDITING
-----------------------
EDIT CELL CONTENTS                      /E(dit)                         E(dit)
ENTER LABELS                               "                            A(lpna)
ENTER VALUES                      Number or + - ( .            Number, + - . ( or V(alue)
ERASE CELL(S)                           /B(lank)                        B(lank)
ERASE SCREEN                            /Z(ap)              T(ransfer) C(lear) Y(es)
GOTO LOCATION                       = Cell Address             G(oto) Name or Cell

FORMATTING
-----------------------
CELLS                          Level=Column, Row or Entry
------
BAR GRAPH                           /F(ormat) level,*              F(ormat) C(ells) *
COLUMN WIDTH                        /F(ormat) level,#              F(ormat) W(idtn)
COMMAS IN NUMBERS                   User-defined format          only global command
DEFAULT                             /F(ormat) level,D          F(ormat) C(ells) D(efault)
DOLLARS AND CENTS                   /F(ormat) level,$      F(ormat) C(ells) $ or F(ixed) 2
GENERAL                             /F(ormat) level,G          F(ormat) C(ells) G(eneral)
HIDE VALUES                         /F(ormat) level,H
INTEGER                             /F(ormat) level,I    F(ormat) C(ells) I(nt) or F(ixed) 0
NEGATIVES IN PARENTHESES            User-defined format          only global command
PERCENT                             User-defined format        F(ormat) C(ells) %
PROTECT CELL ENTRIES                    /P(rotect)             L(ock) C(ells) Locked
REPEATING LABELS                        character
TEXT LEFT                           /F(ormat) level,TL            F(ormat) C(ells) L(eft)
TEXT RIGHT                          /F(ormat) level,TR            F(ormat) C(ells) R(ignt)
UNPROTECT CELL ENTRIES                  /U(nprotect)             L(ock) C(ells) Unlocked
USER DEFINED - define                   /F(ormat) D
USER DEFINED - use                  /F(ormat) level,U,#
VALUE LEFT                          /F(ormat) level,L             F(ormat) C(ells) L(eft)
VALUE RIGHT                         /F(ormat) level,R             F(ormat) C(ells) R(ignt)

GLOBAL
-------
BAR GRAPH                         /F(ormat) G(lobal) *             F(ormat) D(efault) *
BORDER DISPLAY                    /G(lobal) B(orders)
COLUMN WIDTH                      /F(ormat) G(lobal) #         F(ormat) D(efault) W(idtn)
COMMAS IN NUMBERS             /F(ormat) G(lobal) User-defined   F(ormat) O(ptions) commas: Y
DEFAULT                         /F(ormat) G(lobal) D(efault)
DELETE COLUMN(S)                    /D(elete) C,range              D(elete) C(olumn)
DELETE ROW(S)                       /D(elete) R,range              D(elete) R(ow)
DOLLARS AND CENTS             /F(ormat) G(lobal) User-defined  F(ormat) D(efault) $ or F(ixed) 2
FIXED TITLES - BOTH                 /T(itles) B(otn)             W(indow) S(plit) T(itles)
FIXED TITLES - CLEAR                /T(itles) C(lear)              W(indow) C(lose)
FIXED TITLES - HORIZ.               /T(itles) H(orizontal)       W(indow) S(plit) H(orizontal)
FIXED TITLES - VERT.                /T(itles) V(ertical)         W(indow) S(plit) V(ertical)
GENERAL                         /F(ormat) G(lobal) G(eneral)     F(ormat) D(efault) G(eneral)
HIDE VALUES                     /F(ormat) G(lobal) H(ide)
INSERT COLUMN(S)                    /I(nsert), C                   I(nsert) C(olumns)
INSERT ROW(S)                       /I(nsert), R                   I(nsert) R(ows)
INTEGER                       /F(ormat) G(lobal) I(nteger)       F(ormat) D(efault) I(nt)
MOVE COLUMN(S)                        /M(ove) C                      M(ove) C(olumn)
MOVE ROW(S)                           /M(ove) R                      M(ove) R(ow)
NEGATIVES IN PARENTHESES      /F(ormat) G(lobal) User-defined   F(ormat) O(ptions) User-defined
PERCENT                       /F(ormat) G(lobal) User-defined     F(ormat) C(ells) %
PROTECT CELL ENTRIES                /P(rotect)                   L(ock) F(ormulas)
TEXT LEFT                     /F(ormat) G(lobal) TL(Text Left)   F(ormat) D(efault) L(eft)
TEXT RIGHT                   /F(ormat) G(lobal) TR(Text Right)   F(ormat) D(efault) R(ignt)
UNPROTECT CELL ENTRIES              /U(nprotect)                 L(ock) C(ells) Unlocked
USER DEFINED - use              /F(ormat) G(lobal) U#
VALUE LEFT                      /F(ormat) G(lobal) L(eft)       F(ormat) D(efault) L(eft)
VALUE RIGHT                     /F(ormat) G(lobal) R(ight)      F(ormat) D(efault) R(ignt)
WINDOW - HORIZONTAL                /W(indow) H(orizontal)      W(indow) S(plit) H(orizontal)
WINDOWS - CLEAR                    /W(indow) C(lear)              W(indow) C(lose)
WINDOWS - SYNCHRNIZED              /W(indow) S(yncnronized)       W(indow) L(ink)
WINDOWS - UNSYNCH                  /W(indow) U(nsynchronzed)      W(indow) C(lose)
WINDOWS - VERTICAL                 /W(indow) V(ertical)        W(indow) S(plit) V(ertical)
```

THE COMPLEAT APPLE SPREADSHEETER

Appendix II

The Spreadsheet COMMAND Matrix

Use this chart to establish the equivalent command if the chapter you are reading is not demonstrated in your program.

```
SPREADSHEET COMMAND
     COMPARISON              VisiCalc                        Advanced VisiCalc
-----------------------------------------------------------------------------------------
PRINTING
------------------------
PRINT TO DISK              /P(rint) F(ile) specify filename,  /P(rint) F(ile) specify filename,
                                            setup, range                       setup, range
PRINT TO PRINTER           /P(rint) P(rinter) specify setup,  /P(rint) P(rinter) specify setup,
                                                    range                             range

STORAGE
------------------------
DELETE A FILE              /S(torage) D(elete) filename Y(es) /S(torage) D(elete) filename Y(es)
LOAD A FILE                      /S(torage) L(oad) filename         /S(torage) L(oad) filename
QUIT THE PROGRAM                  /S(torage) Q(uit) Y(es)            /S(torage) Q(uit) Y(es)
RENAME A FILE               /S(torage) S(ave) new filename     /S(torage) S(ave) new filename
RETRIEVE SPECIAL FORMAT /S(torage) # L(oad) filename, range /S(torage) # L(oad) filename, range
SAVE A FILE                      /S(torage) S(ave) filename         /S(torage) S(ave) filename
SAVE IN SPECIAL FORMAT  /S(torage) # S(ave) filename, range /S(torage) # S(ave) filename, range

RECALCULATION CONTROL
------------------------
RECALC AUTOMATIC           /G(lobal) R(ecalc) A(utomatic)     /G(lobal) R(ecalc) A(utomatic)
RECALC MANUAL               /G(lobal) R(ecalc) M(anual)        /G(lobal) R(ecalc) M(anual)
RECALC ORDER COLUMN         /G(lobal) O(rder) C(olumn)         /G(lobal) O(rder) C(olumn)
RECALC ORDER ITERATION
RECALC ORDER NATURAL                                           /G(lobal) O(rder) N(atural)
RECALC ORDER ROW             /G(lobal) O(rder) R(ow)            /G(lobal) O(rder) R(ow)

COPYING
------------------------
CELL TO CELL                 /R(eplicate) Cell...Cell            /R(eplicate) Cell...Cell
RANGE TO RANGE           /R(eplicate) Row or Col. Range to  /R(eplicate) Row or Col. Range to
                                  Row or Col. range                  Row or Col. range

GRAPHICS
------------------------
CREATE GRAPH
  DATA RANGES
  FORMAT OPTIONS
  NAME
  RESET
  SAVE
  TYPE
  VIEW

DATABASE MANAGEMENT
------------------------
DATA TABLE 1
DATA TABLE 2
EXTRACT
FIND
INCREMENT NUMBERS
OCCURENCE COUNT
SORT
UNIQUE


KEYSTROKE MACROS AND
    SPECIAL COMMANDS
------------------------
DEFINE MACRO                  Enter keystrokes as labels      /K(eystroke Mem) = name, keystrokes
EDIT EXISTING MACRO      Load file saved as VC file and edit         /K(eystroke Mem) E(dit)
ERASE MACRO                          Delete print file        /K(eystroke Mem) C(lear) clears all
FORGET LAST KEYSTROKES
MOVE MACRO TO ANOTHER KEY                                     /K(eystroke Mem) = name, keystrokes
NAME CELL, RANGE OR MACRO
PRINT LIST OF MACROS
RECALL LAST KEYSTROKES                                            CTRL-K = name, keystrokes
SAVE TO FILE                       Save as Print file              Saved with spreadsheet
LINK SPREADSHEETS
execute MACRO               /S(torage) L(oad) print file                  CTRL-K name
```

Appendix II

SPREADSHEET COMMAND COMPARISON	SuperCalc3	Multiplan
PRINTING		
PRINT TO DISK	/O(utput) Display or Contents, D(isk)	P(rint) F(ile)
PRINT TO PRINTER	/O(utput) Display or Contents, P(rinter)	P(rint) P(rinter)
STORAGE		
DELETE A FILE	/D(elete) F(ile)	T(ransfer) D(elete)
LOAD A FILE	/L(oad)	T(ransfer) L(oad)
QUIT THE PROGRAM	/Q(uit) Y	Q(uit)
RENAME A FILE	/S(ave) oldfilename C(nange)	T(ransfer) R(ename)
RETRIEVE SPECIAL FORMAT		T(ransfer) O(ptions)S(ylk) T L(oad)
SAVE A FILE	/S(ave)	T(ransfer) S(ave)
SAVE IN SPECIAL FORMAT		T(ransfer) O(ptions)S(ylk) T S(ave)
RECALCULATION CONTROL		
RECALC AUTOMATIC	/G(lobal) A(utomatic)	O(ptions) recalc: Y
RECALC MANUAL	/G(lobal) M(anual)	O(ptions) recalc: N
RECALC ORDER COLUMN	/G(lobal) C(olumn)	
RECALC ORDER ITERATION	/G(lobal) I(terS) SC3 Release 2 onl	O(ptions) Iteration: Y
RECALC ORDER NATURAL	/G(lobal) N(at) SC3 Release 2 only	Always in Effect
RECALC ORDER ROW	/G(lobal) R(ow)	
COPYING		
CELL TO CELL	/C(opy) Cell:Cell	C(opy) Right or Down
RANGE TO RANGE	/(Replicate) Range:Range	C(opy) F(rom)
GRAPHICS		
CREATE GRAPH	/V(iew)	
DATA RANGES	/V(iew) D(ata)	
FORMAT OPTIONS	/G(lobal) G(raphics) or /V(iew) O(ptions)	
NAME	/V(iew) 1-9	
RESET		
SAVE	Saved with Spreadsheet	
TYPE	/V(iew) Pie, Bar, Stacked Bar, Line, Hi-Lo, X-Y, Area	
VIEW	/V(iew) Return or {F10}	
DATABASE MANAGEMENT		
DATA TABLE 1		
DATA TABLE 2		
EXTRACT	//D(ata) E(xtract)	
FIND	//D(ata) F(ind)	
INCREMENT NUMBERS		
OCCURENCE COUNT		
SORT	/A(rrange)	S(ort)
UNIQUE		
KEYSTROKE MACROS AND SPECIAL COMMANDS		
DEFINE MACRO	Enter keystrokes as labels	
EDIT EXISTING MACRO		
ERASE MACRO	Delete .XQT file	
FORGET LAST KEYSTROKES		
MOVE MACRO TO ANOTHER KEY		
NAME CELL, RANGE OR MACRO		N(ame)
PRINT LIST OF MACROS		
RECALL LAST KEYSTROKES		
SAVE TO FILE	Save as Print file with .XQT	
LINK SPREADSHEETS		eX(ternal) C(opy)
eXecute MACRO	/X(ecute) filename	

SPREADSHEET BUILT-IN FUNCTIONS COMPARISON

ARITHMETIC

	VisiCalc	Advanced VisiCalc	Multiplan	SuperCalc3
ABSOLUTE VALUE	@ABS(V)	@ABS(V)	ABS(V)	ABS(V)
ARCCOSINE	@ACOS(V)	@ACOS(V)		ACOS(X)
ARCSINE	@ASIN(V)	@ASIN(V)		ASIN(X)
ARCTANGENT-2 QUAD	@ATAN(V)	@ATAN(V)	ATAN(V)	ATAN(V)
ARCTANGENT-4 QUAD				
AVERAGE	@AVERAGE(LIST)	@AVERAGE(LIST)	AVERAGE(LIST)	AVERAGE(LIST)
COSINE	@COS(V)	@COS(V)	COS(V)	COS(V)
COUNT	@COUNT(LIST)	@COUNT(LIST)	COUNT(LIST)	COUNT(LIST)
DOT PRODUCT		@DOTPROD(RG1,RG2)		
EXPONENT	@EXP(V)	@EXP(V)	EXP(V)	EXP(V)
INTEGER VALUE	INT(V)	INT(V)	INT(V)	INT(V)
LOG BASE 10	@LOG10(V)	@LOG10(V)	LOG10(V)	LOG10(V)
MAXIMUM	@MAX(LIST)	@MAX(LIST)	MAX(LIST)	MAX(LIST)
MINIMUM	@MIN(LIST)	@MIN(LIST)	MIN(LIST)	MIN(LIST)
MODULO		@MOD(V1,V2)	MOD(V1,V2)	MOD(V1,V2)
NATURAL LOG	@LN(V)	@LN(V)	LN(V)	LN(V)
RANDOM NUMBERS				
ROUNDING		@ROUND(V,PRECISION)	ROUND(V,PRECISION)	ROUND(V,PLACES-VALUE)
SINE	@SIN(V)	@SIN(V)	SIN(V)	SIN(V)
SQUARE ROOT	@SQRT(V)	@SQRT(V)	SQRT(V)	SQRT(V)
STANDARD DEVIATION			STDEV(LIST)	
SUM	@SUM(LIST)	@SUM(LIST)	SUM(LIST)	SUM(LIST)
TANGENT	@TAN(V)	@TAN(V)	TAN(V)	TAN(V)
VARIANCE				

FINANCIAL

	VisiCalc	Advanced VisiCalc	Multiplan	SuperCalc3
FUTURE VALUE		@FV(I,N,PMT,PV)		FV(PYMNT,INT,PERIODS)
INTERNAL RATE OF RET		@IRR(INVSTMNT,RNG)		IRR(GUESS,RANGE)
NET PRESENT VALUE	@NPV(DR,RANGE)	@NPV(DR,RANGE)	NPV(RATE,LIST)	NPV(DISCOUNT,RANGE)
PAYMENT		@PMT(I,N,PV,FV)		PMT(PRINC,INT.RATE,PER)
PERIODS		@PERIODS(I,PMT,PV,FV)		
PRESENT VALUE		@PV(I,N,PMT,FV)		PV(PYMNT,INT,PERIOD)
RATE		@RATE(N,PMT,PV,FV)		

LOGICAL

	VisiCalc	Advanced VisiCalc	Multiplan	SuperCalc3
AND	@AND(LIST)	@AND(LIST)	AND(LIST)	AND(EXPR1,EXPR2)
IF	@IF(L,V1,V2)	@IF(L,V1,V2)	IF(L,V1,V2)	IF(V1,V2,V3)
OR	@OR(LIST)	@OR(LIST)	OR(LIST)	OR(EXPR1,EXPR2)
NOT	@NOT(L)	@NOT(L)	NOT(L)	NOT(EXPRESSION)
IS NOT AVAILABLE	@ISNA(V)	@ISNA(V)	ISNA(V)	ISNA(VALUE)
IS ERROR	@ISERROR(V)	@ISERROR(V)	ISERROR(V)	ISERR(VALUE)
IS NUMERIC				ISNUM(VALUE)
IS DATE				ISDATE(VALUE)
IS TEXTUAL VALUE				ISTEXT(VALUE)

Appendix II

SPREADSHEET BUILT-IN FUNCTIONS COMPARISON	VisiCalc	Advanced VisiCalc	Multiplan	SuperCalc3
CALENDAR				
ABSOLUTE DATE		@MDY OR @YMDY(MTH,DY,YR)		DATE(MM,DD,YY) or DVAL(DATE VALUE)
CALENDAR DAY		@DAY(ABSOLUTE DATE)		DAY(DATE VALUE)
CALENDAR MONTH		@MONTH(ABSOLUTE DATE)		MON(DATE VALUE)
CALENDAR YEAR		@YEAR(ABSOLUTE DATE)		YEAR(DATE VALUE)
DAY NUMBER				DAY(DATE VALUE)
MONTH NUMBER				MON(DATE VALUE)
YEAR NUMBER				YEAR(DATE VALUE)
JULIAN DATE				JDATE(DATE VALUE)
WEEKDAY NUMBER				NDAY(DATE VALUE)
HOURS,MINUTES,SECONDS		@HMS(HRS,MIN,SEC)		
HOURS		@HOUR(ABSOLUTE DATE)		
MINUTES		@MINUTE(ABSOLUTE DATE)		
SECONDS		@SECOND(ABSOLUTE DATE)		
TODAY'S DATE				TODAY
SPECIAL				
CHOOSE	@CHOOSE(V,LIST)	@CHOOSE(V,LIST)	INDEX(AREA,SUBSCRIPTS)	
LOOKUP	@LOOKUP(V,RANGE)	@LOOKUP(V,RANGE)	LOOKUP(VALUE,TABLE)	LOOKUP(VALUE,RANGE)
VERTICAL LOOKUP				
HORIZONTAL LOOKUP				
WITHOUT ARGUMENTS				
PI	@PI	@PI	PI	PI
NOT AVAILABLE	@NA	@NA	NA	NA
ERROR	@ERROR	@ERROR		ERROR
TRUE	@TRUE	@TRUE	TRUE	TRUE
FALSE	@FALSE	@FALSE	FALSE	FALSE
TEXT/VALUE CONVERSION				
COLUMN NUMBER			COLUMN	
COUNT OF TEXT CHARS			MID(T,S,C)	
LABEL TO VALUE			VALUE	
LENGTH OF TEXT IN NO.S			LEN(T)	
REPEAT TEXT			REPT(T,n)	
ROW NUMBER			ROW	
SIGN OF NUMBER			SIGN(V)	
VALUE TO LABEL		@LABEL	LABEL	
TEXTUAL VALUE				("9 CHARACTERS OF TEXT")

THE COMPLEAT APPLE SPREADSHEETER

Appendix III

KEY FORMULAS

The following pages show listings of the key formulas for each of the models demonstrated in this book, each illustrated in the VisiCalc syntax.

[Note: As the simplest from a syntax point of view we felt that translation would be easiest from VisiCalc syntax.]

Key Formulas for Template in Chapter 1

```
>A13:/F*@IF(F27=1,1,0)
>A14:/F*@IF(F27=2,1,0)
>A15:/F*@IF(@AND(F27=1,H27>=40),1,0)
>A16:/F*@IF(@AND(F27=2,H27>40),1,0)
>A17:/F*@IF(@AND(D27=1,H27>=40,I27>=12),1,0)
>A18:/F*@IF(@AND(D27=2,H27<40,I27>=12),1,0)
>A19:/F*@IF(J27>=30000,1,0)
>A20:/F*@IF(@OR(J27>=35000,L27<1974),1,0)
>A21:/F*@IF(@AND(H27>=30,H27<=40,@OR(I27=10,I27=11),J27>=35000),1,0)
>A27:/F*@IF(@AND(H27>=30,H27<=40,@OR(I27=10,I27=11),J27>=35000),1,0)

>B27:"Adamns
>C27:"Charles
>D27:"A.
>E27:(A27*J27
>F27:/FL1
>G27:/FR"2/29/44
>H27:/FR40
>I27:4
>J27:13500
>K27:4
>L27:1980
>M27:/F$@IF(@AND(J27>=20000,I27>=10),J27/12,0)
>N27:/F$@IF(@AND(J27<19999,I27<10,I27<>4),J27/52,0)
>O27:/F$@IF(I27=4,(J27/52)/35,0)
>P27:28
>Q27:/F$(O27*P27)

>D54:/FR"TOTAL
>E54:@SUM(E27...E52)
>L54:"MONTHLY TOT
>M54:/F$@SUM(M27...M52)
>N54:/F$@SUM(N27...N52)*4
>O54:/F$
>P54:/F$
>Q54:/F$@SUM(Q27...Q52)*4
>K56:"CASH REQUIR
>L56:"ED MONTHLY
>M56:/F$(M54+N54+Q54)
>L57:"   WEEKLY
>M57:/F$(N54+Q54)
```

Appendix III

Formulas for Template in Chapter 2

```
>F8:.00001
>G8:(F8+.00001
>H8:(G8+.00001
>I8:(H8+.00001
>J8:(I8+.00001
>K8:(J8+.00001
>L8:(K8+.00001
>M8:(L8+.00001
>N8:(M8+.00001
>O8:(N8+.00001

>A11:"MICRO
>B11:1000.13
>E11:(B11)
>F11:@IF(E11=@MAX(E11...E20),F8,E11)
>G11:@IF(F11=@MAX(F11...F20),G8,F11)
>H11:@IF(G11=@MAX(G11...G20),H8,G11)
>I11:@IF(H11=@MAX(H11...H20),I8,H11)
>J11:@IF(I11=@MAX(I11...I20),J8,I11)
>K11:@IF(J11=@MAX(J11...J20),K8,J11)
>L11:@IF(K11=@MAX(K11...K20),L8,K11)
>M11:@IF(L11=@MAX(L11...L20),M8,L11)
>N11:@IF(M11=@MAX(M11...M20),N8,M11)
>O11:@IF(N11=@MAX(N11...N20),O8,N11)
>P11:@MIN(F11...O11)*100000
>Q11:@MAX(E11...E20)

>A12:"MINI
>B12:900.34
>E12:(B12)
>F12:@IF(E12=@MAX(E11...E20),F8,E12)
>G12:@IF(F12=@MAX(F11...F20),G8,F12)
>H12:@IF(G12=@MAX(G11...G20),H8,G12)
>I12:@IF(H12=@MAX(H11...H20),I8,H12)
>J12:@IF(I12=@MAX(I11...I20),J8,I12)
>K12:@IF(J12=@MAX(J11...J20),K8,J12)
>L12:@IF(K12=@MAX(K11...K20),L8,K12)
>M12:@IF(L12=@MAX(L11...L20),M8,L12)
>N12:@IF(M12=@MAX(M11...M20),N8,M12)
>O12:@IF(N12=@MAX(N11...N20),O8,N12)
>P12:@MIN(F12...O12)*100000
>Q12:@MAX(F11...F20)

>R24:"PRODUCT
>S24:"QUANTITY
>T24:/FR"RANK
>U24:/FR"TOTAL
>R26:"MICRO
>S26:(B11)
>T26:(P11)
>U26:/F$(S26/(@SUM(S26...S35))*100
>R27:"MINI
>S27:(B12)
>T27:(P12)
>U27:/F$(S27/(@SUM(S26...S35))*100
>R28:"REGULAR
>S28:(B13)
>T28:(P13)
>U28:/F$(S28/(@SUM(S26...S35))*100
>R29:"SMALL
>S29:(B14)
>T29:(P14)
>U29:/F$(S29/(@SUM(S26...S35))*100
>R30:"MEDIUM
>S30:(B15)
>T30:(P15)
>U30:/F$(S30/(@SUM(S26...S35))*100
>R31:"LARGE
>S31:(B16)
>T31:(P16)
>U31:/F$(S31/(@SUM(S26...S35))*100
>R32:"SUPER
>S32:(B17)
>T32:(P17)
>U32:/F$(S32/(@SUM(S26...S35))*100
>R33:"JUMBO
>S33:(B18)
>T33:(P18)
>U33:/F$(S33/(@SUM(S26...S35))*100
>R34:"ULTRABIG
>S34:(B19)
>T34:(P19)
>U34:/F$(S34/(@SUM(S26...S35))*100
>R35:"MAGNUM
>S35:(B20)
>T35:(P20)
>U35:/F$(S35/(@SUM(S26...S35))*100
```

Formulas for Template in Chapter 2

```
>C6:/FI"OPENING BA
>D6:"ALANCE...
>E6:4032.56
>G6:/FI1
>H6:@IF(C6<1,+H5+E6,+H5-E6)
>I6:@IF(G6=1,@IF(C6<1,+I5+E6,+I5-E6),I5)
>A7:/FR+B1
>B7:/FL4
>C7:/FL101
>D7:/FL"RENTCO
>E7:/F$675
>F7:/FR6
>G7:/FR1
>H7:@IF(C7<1,+H6+E7,+H6-E7)
>I7:@IF(G7=1,@IF(C7<1,+I6+E7,+I6-E7),I6)
>J7:@IF(F7=J3,E7,0)
>K7:@IF(F7=K3,E7,0)
>L7:@IF(F7=L3,E7,0)
>M7:@IF(F7=M3,E7,0)
>N7:@IF(F7=N3,E7,0)
>O7:@IF(F7=O3,E7*.07,0)
>P7:@IF(F7=P3,E7,0)
>Q7:(E7=@SUM(J7...N7,(O7/.07),P7))
>S7:@IF(H7+H6=H6,H6,0)

>A40:"TOTALS
>F40:"CURRRENT
>G40:"BALANCE:
>H40:@MAX(S5...S39)
>J40:@SUM(J5...J39)
>K40:@SUM(K5...K39)
>L40:@SUM(L5...L39)
>M40:@SUM(M5...M39)
>N40:@SUM(N5...N39)
>O40:@SUM(O5...O39)
>P40:@SUM(P5...P39)
```

Appendix III

Key Formulas for Template in Chapter 4

```
>C4:75            >J5:/F$12         >O9:/FG.01
>D4:125           >K5:/F$13         >C10:/F$1
>E4:250           >L5:/F$14         >D10:/F$2
>F4:350           >M5:/F$16         >E10:/F$3
>G4:+F4+100       >C6:/F$12.5       >F10:/F$4
>H4:+G4+100       >N6:1             >G10:/F$5
>I4:+H4+100       >O6:/FG.005       >N10:+N9+1
>J4:+I4+100       >N7:+N6+1         >O10:/FG.015
>K4:+J4+100       >O7:/FG.006       >N11:+N10+1
>L4:+K4+100       >N8:+N7+1         >O11:/FG.018
>M4:1000          >O8:/FG.007       >D18:300
>C5:/F$3          >A9:"PER 100      >D19:2
>D5:/F$4.25       >C9:/F$.23        >D20:200
>E5:/F$6.25       >D9:/F$.43        >M45:/FI(D18)
>F5:/F$7.5        >E9:/F$.63        >M46:/FI(D20)
>G5:/F$9          >F9:/F$.83        >M47:(D19)
>H5:/F$10         >G9:/F$.93        >D49:+D18
>I5:/F$11         >N9:+N8+1
```

```
>M49:/F$@LOOKUP(M47,N6...N11)*(M45*M46)+@IF(((M45*M46)<1000),
     (@LOOKUP((M45*M46),C4...M4)),(((((M45*M46)-1000)/1000)*C6)+M5)

>M50:/F$@IF(D25=1,(@IF((((M45*M46)/100)*C9)
                                       <C10,C10,(((M45*M46)/100)*C9))),0)

>M51:/F$@IF(D26=1,(@IF((((M45*M46)/100)*D9)
                                       <D10,D10,(((M45*M46)/100)*D9))),0)

>M52:/F$@IF(D27=1,(@IF((((M45*M46)/100)*E9)
                                       <E10,E10,(((M45*M46)/100)*E9))),0)

>M53:/F$@IF(D28=1,(@IF((((M45*M46)/100)*F9)
                                       <F10,F10,(((M45*M46)/100)*F9))),0)

>D54:/F$@LOOKUP(D50,N6...N11)*(D49*D51)+(@IF(((D18*D20)<1000),
     (@LOOKUP((D18*D20),C4...M4)),(((((D18*D20)-1000)/1000)*C6)+M5)

>M54:/F$@IF(D29=1,(@IF((((M45*M46)/100)*G9)
                                       <G10,G10,(((M45*M46)/100)*G9))),0)

>D55:/F$@IF(D25=1,(@IF((((D18*D20)/100)*C9)
                                       <C10,C10,(((D18*D20)/100)*C9))),0)

>D56:/F$@IF(D26=1,(@IF((((D18*D20)/100)*D9)
                                       <D10,D10,(((D18*D20)/100)*D9))),0)

>D57:/F$@IF(D27=1,(@IF((((D18*D20)/100)*E9)
                                       <E10,E10,(((D18*D20)/100)*E9))),0)

>D58:/F$@IF(D28=1,(@IF((((D18*D20)/100)*F9)
                                       <F10,F10,(((D18*D20)/100)*F9))),0)

>D59:/F$@IF(D29=1,(@IF((((D18*D20)/100)*G9)
                                       <G10,G10,(((D18*D20)/100)*G9))),0)
```

Key Formulas for Template in Chapter 5

```
>B14:56
>E14:+B14
>F14:+B14
>G14:+B14
>H14:+B14
>J14:@CHOOSE(@COUNT(B14...B16),E14,@IF(@COUNT(B18...B19)=1,F14,G14),H14)
>K14:+J14
>B15:79.2
>E15:@SIN(E19)*B14/@SIN(E18)
>F15:+B15
>G15:+B15
>H15:+B15
>J15:@CHOOSE(@COUNT(B14...B16),E15,@IF(@COUNT(B18...B19)=1,F15,G15),H15)
>K15:+J15
>E16:@SIN(E20)*B14/@SIN(E18)
>F16:/F$@SQRT(F14*F14+(F15*F15)-(2*F14*F15*@COS(F20)))
>G16:/F$@SQRT(G14*G14+(G15*G15)-(2*G14*G15*@COS(G20)))
>H16:/F$+B16
>J16:@CHOOSE(@COUNT(B14...B16),E16,@IF(@COUNT(B18...B19)=1,F16,G16),H16)
>K16:+J16
>D18:@PI*B18/180
>E18:@IF(B18=0,@PI-@SUM(D18...D20),D18)
>F18:/F$@IF(D18=0,@ASIN(@SIN(F19)*F14/F15),D18)
>G18:/F$@ASIN(@SIN(G20)*G14/G16)
>H18:/F$@ACOS(H14*H14-(H15*H15)-(H16*H16)/(-2*H15*H16))
>J18:/FI@CHOOSE(@COUNT(B14...B16),E18,@IF(@COUNT(B18...B19)=1,F18,G18),H18)
>K18:+J18*180/@PI
>B19:/FI60
>D19:@PI*B19/180
>E19:@IF(B19=0,@PI-@SUM(D18...D20),D19)
>F19:/F$@IF(D19=0,@ASIN(@SIN(F18)*F15/F14),D19)
>G19:/F$@ASIN(@SIN(G20)*G15/G16)
>H19:/F$@ASIN(@SIN(H18)*H15/H14)
>J19:/FI@CHOOSE(@COUNT(B14...B16),E19,@IF(@COUNT(B18...B19)=1,F19,G19),H19)
>K19:+J19*180/@PI
>D20:@PI*B20/180
>E20:@IF(B20=0,@PI-@SUM(D18...D20),D20)
>F20:/F$@PI-F19-F18
>G20:@PI*B20/180
>H20:/F$@PI-H19-H18
>J20:/FI@CHOOSE(@COUNT(B14...B16),E20,@IF(@COUNT(B18...B19)=1,F20,G20),H20)
>K20:+J20*180/@PI
>F23:@SUM(F18...F20)
>G23:@SUM(G18...G20)
>J23:@SUM(J14...J16)
>K23:+J23
>K24:/F$+K14*K15*@SIN(J20)/2
>H25:/FG@PI/3
>K27:/FG@CHOOSE(@COUNT(B14...B16),1,@IF(@COUNT(B18...B19)=1,2.1,2.2),3)
```

Appendix III

Key Formulas for Template in Chapter 6

```
>J14:@SUM(F14...I14          >I21:(I17*C21)              >A25:/FL(A24+1)
>F15:(F14*C15                >J21:@SUM(F21...I21         >F25:@SUM(F20...F24
>G15:(G14*C15                >F22:(F17*C22)              >G25:@SUM(G20...G24
>H15:(H14*C15                >G22:(G17*C22)              >H25:@SUM(H20...H24
>I15:(I14*C15                >H22:(H17*C22)              >I25:@SUM(I20...I24
>J15:@SUM(F15...I15          >I22:(I17*C22)              >J25:@SUM(J20...J24
>F17:+F14-F15                >J22:@SUM(F22...I22         >A26:/FL(A25+1)
>G17:+G14-G15                >A23:/FL(A22+1)             >A27:/FL(A26+1)
>H17:+H14-H15                >F23:(F17*C23)              >F27:+F17-F25
>I17:+I14-I15                >G23:(G17*C23)              >G27:+G17-G25
>J17:+J14-J15                >H23:(H17*C23)              >H27:+H17-H25
>F21:(F17*C21)               >I23:(I17*C23)              >I27:+I17-I25
>G21:(G17*C21)               >J23:@SUM(F23...I23         >J27:+J17-J25
>H21:(H17*C21)               >A24:/FL(A23+1)             >A28:/FL(A27+1)
```

```
            >F28:@IF((G62<=0),(-1*G62),0)
            >G28:@IF((H62<=0),(-1*H62),0)
            >H28:@IF((I62<=0),(-1*I62),0)
            >I28:@IF((J62<=0),(-1*J62),0)
            >J28:@SUM(F28...I28
            >A29:/FL(A28+1)
            >F29:@IF(@ISERROR(F52),0,@IF((G62>0),+G62,0)
            >G29:@IF(@ISERROR(G52),0,@IF((H62>0),+H62,0)
            >H29:@IF(@ISERROR(H52),0,@IF((I62>0),+I62,0)
            >I29:@IF(@ISERROR(I52),0,@IF((J62>0),+J62,0)
```

```
>J29:@SUM(F29...I29          >A39:/FL(A38+1)             >J51:(I15+I32)*C51
>A30:/FL(A29+1)              >A40:/FL(A39+1)             >A52:/FL(A51+1)
>A31:/FL(A30+1)              >A41:/FL(A40+1)             >C52:/FL20
>F31:(F27+F28-F29)           >A42:/FL(A41+1)             >F52:+F46-F51-F55
>G31:(G27+G28-G29)           >G42:(F14*C42               >G52:+G46-G51-G55
>H31:(H27+H28-H29)           >H42:(G14*C42               >H52:+H46-H51-H55
>I31:(I27+I28-I29)           >I42:(H14*C42               >I52:+I46-I51-I55
>J31:@SUM(F31...I31          >J42:(I14*C42               >J52:+J46-J51-J55
>A32:/FL(A31+1)              >A43:/FL(A42+1)             >A53:/FL(A52+1)
>F32:(F31*C32)               >A44:/FL(A43+1)             >A54:/FL(A53+1)
>G32:(G31*C32)               >A45:/FL(A44+1)             >A55:/FL(A54+1)
>H32:(H31*C32)               >A46:/FL(A45+1)             >F55:(C55+C56)
>I32:(I31*C32)               >F46:@SUM(F41...F45         >G55:+C55+C56+F34
>J32:@SUM(F32...I32          >G46:@SUM(G41...G45         >H55:+C55+C56+G34
>A33:/FL(A32+1)              >H46:@SUM(H41...H45         >I55:+C55+C56+H34
>A34:/FL(A33+1)              >I46:@SUM(I41...I45         >J55:+C55+C56+I34
>F34:+F31-F32                >J46:@SUM(J41...J45         >A56:/FL(A55+1)
>G34:+G31-G32                >A47:/FL(A46+1)             >A57:/FL(A56+1)
>H34:+H31-H32                >A48:/FL(A47+1)             >A58:/FL(A57+1)
>I34:+I31-I32                >A49:/FL(A48+1)             >F58:+F46
>J34:+J31-J32                >A50:/FL(A49+1)             >G58:+G46
>A35:/FL(A34+1)              >A51:/FL(A50+1)             >H58:+H46
>A36:/FL(A35+1)              >G51:(F15+F32)*C51          >I58:+I46
>A37:/FL(A36+1)              >H51:(G15+G32)*C51          >J58:+J46
>A38:/FL(A37+1)              >I51:(H15+H32)*C51          >A59:/FL(A58+1)
```

```
            >G62:@IF(@ISERROR(G52),0,((F52+G52)*((C52/100)/4))
            >H62:@IF(@ISERROR(H52),0,(H52*((C52/100)/4))
            >I62:@IF(@ISERROR(I52),0,(I52*((C52/100)/4))
            >J62:@IF(@ISERROR(J52),0,(J52*((C52/100)/4))
```

Key Formulas for Template in Chapter 7

```
>G3:/FL(F3+1)
>H3:/FL(G3+1)
>I3:/FL(H3+1)
>J3:/FL(I3+1)
>K3:/FL(J3+1)
>L5:@IF(F7=1,F5,@IF(G7=1,G5,@IF(H7=1,H5,@IF(I7=1,I5,@IF(J7=1,J5,@IF(K7=1,K5,0)
>L6:@IF(F7=1,F6,@IF(G7=1,G6,@IF(H7=1,H6,@IF(I7=1,I6,@IF(J7=1,J6,@IF(K7=1,K6,0)
>L16:+C7+L9-L14
>F23:@IF(E23=0,0,+L5)
>G23:/FI@IF(F23>0,((F23+G22)*(1+(H13/100))),0)
>H23:/FI+F23*(1-(C6/100))
>I23:/FI@IF(H23=0,0,(I22+H23)*(1+((H13/100)*(1-(C6/100))))
>J23:/FI+G23-I23
>L23:/FI@IF(K23<59.5,+G23-(+G23*(C6/100)+(.1*G23))-I23,0)
>E24:/FL@IF(@OR(E23=L16,E23=0),0,E23+1)
>F24:@IF(E24=0,0,+L5)
>G24:/FI@IF(F24>0,((F24+G23)*(1+(H13/100))),0)
>H24:/FI+F24*(1-(C6/100))
>I24:/FI@IF(H24=0,0,(I23+H24)*(1+((H13/100)*(1-(C6/100))))
>J24:/FI+G24-I24
>K24:/FI@IF(F24>0,@IF(K23<=C7,K23+1,0),0)
>L24:/FI@IF(K24<59.5,+G24-(+G24*(C6/100)+(.1*G24))-I24,0)
>E25:/FL@IF(@OR(E24=L16,E24=0),0,E24+1)
>F25:@IF(E25=0,0,+L5)
>G25:/FI@IF(F25>0,((F25+G24)*(1+(H13/100))),0)
>H25:/FI+F25*(1-(C6/100))
>I25:/FI@IF(H25=0,0,(I24+H25)*(1+((H13/100)*(1-(C6/100))))
>J25:/FI+G25-I25
>K25:/FI@IF(F25>0,@IF(K24<=C7,K24+1,0),0)
>L25:/FI@IF(K25<59.5,+G25-(+G25*(C6/100)+(.1*G25))-I25,0)
>E26:/FL@IF(@OR(E25=L16,E25=0),0,E25+1)
>F26:@IF(E26=0,0,+L5)
>G26:/FI@IF(F26>0,((F26+G25)*(1+(H13/100))),0)
>H26:/FI+F26*(1-(C6/100))
>I26:/FI@IF(H26=0,0,(I25+H26)*(1+((H13/100)*(1-(C6/100))))
>J26:/FI+G26-I26
>K26:/FI@IF(F26>0,@IF(K25<=C7,K25+1,0),0)
>L26:/FI@IF(K26<59.5,+G26-(+G26*(C6/100)+(.1*G26))-I26,0)
```

Appendix III

Key Formulas for Template in Chapter 8

```
>G6:/F$@IF(G4=C4,C6,@IF(G4=D4,D6,@IF(G4=E4,E6,@IF(G4=F4,F6,0)
>G7:/FI@IF(G4=C4,C7,@IF(G4=D4,D7,@IF(G4=E4,E7,@IF(G4=F4,F7,0)
>B8:"TAX RATE:%
>G8:/FI@IF(G4=C4,C8,@IF(G4=D4,D8,@IF(G4=E4,E8,@IF(G4=F4,F8,0)
>G9:/FI@IF(G4=C4,C9,@IF(G4=D4,D9,@IF(G4=E4,E9,@IF(G4=F4,F9,0)
>G10:/FI@IF(G4=C4,C10,@IF(G4=D4,D10,@IF(G4=E4,E10,@IF(G4=F4,F10,0)
>G11:/FI@IF(G4=C4,C11,@IF(G4=D4,D11,@IF(G4=E4,E11,@IF(G4=F4,F11,0)
>G12:/FI@IF(G4=C4,C12,@IF(G4=D4,D12,@IF(G4=E4,E12,@IF(G4=F4,F12,0)
>H17:/FL(G4)
>D22:+G7

>E22:/FI+D22*(1+(E15/100))      >G23:/FI+F23*(1+(G15/100))
>F22:/FI+E22*(1+(F15/100))      >H23:/FI+G23*(1+(H15/100))
>G22:/FI+F22*(1+(G15/100))      >E24:/FI+D24*(1+(E15/100))
>H22:/FI+G22*(1+(H15/100))      >F24:/FI+E24*(1+(F15/100))
>E23:/FI+D23*(1+(E15/100))      >G24:/FI+F24*(1+(G15/100))
>F23:/FI+E23*(1+(F15/100))      >H24:/FI+G24*(1+(H15/100))

>D26:(+G9-(@MAX(D25...H25)))/@MAX(D20...H20)
>E26:(+G9-(@MAX(D25...H25)))/@MAX(D20...H20)
>F26:(+G9-(@MAX(D25...H25)))/@MAX(D20...H20)
>G26:(+G9-(@MAX(D25...H25)))/@MAX(D20...H20)
>H26:(+G9-(@MAX(D25...H25)))/@MAX(D20...H20)
>D28:(D22+D25)-@SUM(D23...D26)
>E28:(E22+E25)-@SUM(E23...E26)
>F28:(F22+F25)-@SUM(F23...F26)
>G28:(G22+G25)-@SUM(G23...G26)
>H28:(H22+H25)-@SUM(H23...H26)

>D29:-(G8/100)*D28              >F35:@SUM(D34...F34)
>E29:-(G8/100)*E28              >G35:@SUM(D34...G34)
>F29:-(G8/100)*F28              >H35:@SUM(D34...H34)
>G29:-(G8/100)*G28              >D36:-G9+D35
>H29:-(G8/100)*H28              >E36:+D36+E35
>D30:(D28-D29)                  >F36:+E36+F35
>E30:(E28-E29)                  >G36:+F36+G35
>F30:(F28-F29)                  >H36:+G36+H35
>G30:(G28-G29)                  >D37:/FI+H35
>H30:/FI(H28-H29)               >D38:+D37-G9
>D32:(D26+D30)                  >B40:@NPV(G6/100,D32...H32)-G9
>E32:(E26+E30)
>F32:(F26+F30)
>G32:(G26+G30)
>H32:/FI(H26+H30)
>D34:/FI(D32)*(1/(1+(G6/100))^D20)
>E34:/FI(E32)*(1/(1+(G6/100))^E20)
>F34:/FI(F32)*(1/(1+(G6/100))^F20)
>G34:/FI(G32)*(1/(1+(G6/100))^G20)
>H34:/FI(H32)*(1/(1+(G6/100))^H20)
>D35:@SUM(D34...D34)
>E35:@SUM(D34...E34)
```

```
Key Formulas for Template in Chapter 9

>P7:/F$+M7*@IF(@AND(D9>=1,D9<=5),1,@IF(@OR(D9>=6,D9<=10),.9,@IF(D9>11,.8,@ERROR))
>P8:/F$+M8*@IF(@AND(D10>=1,D10<=5),1,@IF(@OR(D10>=6,D10<=10),.9,@IF(D10>11,.8,@ERROR))
>A9:@LOOKUP(C9,N7...N18)
>B9:/F$@IF(@ISNA(A9),0,C9-A9)
>H9:@IF(B9=0,C9,(C9*(-@ABS(B9)))
>I9:/F$@LOOKUP(H9,O7...O18)
>J9:(D9)
>K9:/F$@IF(H9<0,@ERROR,@IF(@AND(H9=0,@ISNA(I9)),0,(I9*J9)))
>P9:/F$+M9*@IF(@AND(D11>=1,D11<=5),1,@IF(@OR(D11>=6,D11<=10),.9,@IF(D11>11,.8,@ERROR))
>A10:@LOOKUP(C10,N7...N18)
>B10:@IF(@ISNA(A10),0,C10-A10)
>H10:@IF(B10=0,C10,(C10*(-@ABS(B10)))
>I10:/F$@LOOKUP(H10,O7...O18)
>J10:(D10)
>K10:/F$@IF(H10<0,@ERROR,@IF(@AND(H10=0,@ISNA(I10)),0,(I10*J10)))
>P10:/F$+M10*@IF(@AND(D12>=1,D12<=5),1,@IF(@OR(D12>=6,D12<=10),.9,@IF(D12>11,.8,@ERROR))
>A11:@LOOKUP(C11,N7...N18)
>B11:@IF(@ISNA(A11),0,C11-A11)
>H11:@IF(B11=0,C11,(C11*(-@ABS(B11)))
>I11:/F$@LOOKUP(H11,O7...O18)
>K11:/F$@IF(H11<0,@ERROR,@IF(@AND(H11=0,@ISNA(I11)),0,(I11*J11)))
>P11:/F$+M11*@IF(@AND(D13>=1,D13<=5),1,@IF(@OR(D13>=6,D13<=10),.9,@IF(D13>11,.8,@ERROR))
>A12:@LOOKUP(C12,N7...N18)
>B12:@IF(@ISNA(A12),0,C12-A12)
>H12:@IF(B12=0,C12,(C12*(-@ABS(B12)))
>I12:/F$@LOOKUP(H12,O7...O18)
>K12:/F$@IF(H12<0,@ERROR,@IF(@AND(H12=0,@ISNA(I12)),0,(I12*J12)))
>P12:/F$+M12*@IF(@AND(D14>=1,D14<=5),1,@IF(@OR(D14>=6,D14<=10),.9,@IF(D14>11,.8,@ERROR))
>A13:@LOOKUP(C13,N7...N18)
>B13:@IF(@ISNA(A13),0,C13-A13)
>H13:@IF(B13=0,C13,(C13*(-@ABS(B13)))
>I13:/F$@LOOKUP(H13,O7...O18)
>K13:/F$@IF(H13<0,@ERROR,@IF(@AND(H13=0,@ISNA(I13)),0,(I13*J13)))
>P13:/F$+M13*@IF(@AND(D15>=1,D15<=5),1,@IF(@OR(D15>=6,D15<=10),.9,@IF(D15>11,.8,@ERROR))
>A14:@LOOKUP(C14,N7...N18)
>B14:@IF(@ISNA(A14),0,C14-A14)
>H14:@IF(B14=0,C14,(C14*(-@ABS(B14)))
>I14:/F$@LOOKUP(H14,O7...O18)
>K14:/F$@IF(H14<0,@ERROR,@IF(@AND(H14=0,@ISNA(I14)),0,(I14*J14)))
>P14:/F$+M14*@IF(@AND(D16>=1,D16<=5),1,@IF(@OR(D16>=6,D16<=10),.9,@IF(D16>11,.8,@ERROR))
>A15:@LOOKUP(C15,N7...N18)
>B15:@IF(@ISNA(A15),0,C15-A15)
>H15:@IF(B15=0,C15,(C15*(-@ABS(B15)))
>I15:/F$@LOOKUP(H15,O7...O18)
>K15:/F$@IF(H15<0,@ERROR,@IF(@AND(H15=0,@ISNA(I15)),0,(I15*J15)))
>P15:/F$+M15*@IF(@AND(D17>=1,D17<=5),1,@IF(@OR(D17>=6,D17<=10),.9,@IF(D17>11,.8,@ERROR))
```

Appendix III

Formulas for Template in Chapter 10

```
>S54:(@INT(L57/100)/1000)
>V54:@IF(L56<>1,@LOOKUP(S54,A2...A136),@LOOKUP(S54,D3...D54))
>W54:/FR"*
>T56:@IF(@AND(V54<=4,L56<>1),@CHOOSE(V54,0,@LOOKUP(L58,F2...F52),
                @LOOKUP(L58,H2...H52),@LOOKUP(L58,J2...J52)),0)
>U56:@IF(@AND(V54>=5,V54<=7,L56<>1),@CHOOSE(V54-4,@LOOKUP(L58,L2...L52),
                @LOOKUP(L58,N2...N52),@LOOKUP(L58,P2...P52)),0)
>V56:@IF(@AND(V54=8,L56<>1),@LOOKUP(L58,R2...R52),0)
>T57:@IF(@AND(V54>9,V54<=11),@CHOOSE(V54-8,@LOOKUP(L58,T3...T51),
                @LOOKUP(L58,V3...V51),@LOOKUP(L58,X3...X51)),0)
>U57:@IF(V54=12,@LOOKUP(L58,Z3...Z51),0)
>V57:@IF(V54>12,@LOOKUP(L58,Z3...Z51),0)
>O58:/F*@IF(@OR(V54=15,V54=14,V54=13),6,0)
>O62:/F$@IF(L62=1,1.5,0)
>O63:/F$@IF(L63=1,1.5,0)
>O64:/F$@IF(L64=1,.26,0)
>O66:/F$.25*(@INT(L66-100/100)+@IF(+L66-100/100<>@INT(L66-100/100),1,0))
>J67:@IF(L76<>1,(L58),0)
>O67:@IF(L56<>1,@SUM(S56...V56),0)
>J68:@IF(L76=1,(L58),0)
>O68:@IF(L56=1,@SUM(S57...V57),0)
>O70:@SUM(O62...O69)
>H73:/F*@IF(L62=1,4,0)
>O73:@IF(H72=0,0,O70+O72)
```

Key Formulas for Template in Chapter 11

```
>E6:/FR1+E5
>F6:/F$.13+F5
>G6:/FR1+G5
>H6:/F$.75+F6
>E7:/FR1+E6
>F7:/F$.13+F6
>G7:/FR1+G6
>H7:/F$.75+F7
>A8:"CLASS----
>B8:"-------->
>C8:/FL2
>E8:/FR1+E7
>F8:/F$.13+F7
>G8:/FR1+G7
>H8:/F$.75+F8
>C9:/FL
>E9:/FR1+E8
>F9:/F$.13+F8
>G9:/FR1+G8
>H9:/F$.75+F9
>A10:"COST (CALC
>B10:"CULATED):
>C10:/F$(C6*(@CHOOSE(C8,@LOOKUP(C4,E5...E12),@LOOKUP(C4,G5...G12))
>E10:/FR1+E9
>F10:/F$.13+F9
>G10:/FR1+G9
>H10:/F$.75+F10
>C11:/--
>E11:/FR1+E10
>F11:/F$.13+F10
>G11:/FR1+G10
>H11:/F$.75+F11
>E12:/FR1+E11
>F12:/F$.13+F11
>G12:/FR1+G11
>H12:/F$.75+F12
```

Appendix III

Key Formulas for Template in Chapter 12

```
>C8:/FI+C6*C7
>D8:/FI+D6*D7
>E8:/FI+E6*E7
>F8:/FI+F6*F7
>C11:/FI(C8*C9)
>D11:/FI(D8*D9)
>E11:/FI(E8*E9)
>F11:/FI(F8*F9)
>C18:@SUM(C13...C17
>D18:@SUM(D13...D17
>E18:@SUM(E13...E17
>F18:@SUM(F13...F17
>C21:/FI(C6*C18)
>D21:/FI(D6*D18)
>E21:/FI(E6*E18)
>F21:/FI(F6*F18)
>C24:/FI@SUM(C20...C23)
>D24:/FI@SUM(D20...D23)
>E24:/FI@SUM(E20...E23)
>F24:/FI@SUM(F20...F23)
>C28:/FI(C22)/((C11-C21)/C11)
>D28:/FI(D22)/((D11-D21)/D11)
>E28:/FI(E22)/((E11-E21)/E11)
>F28:/FI(F22)/((F11-F21)/F11)
>C29:/FI(C28/C9)
>D29:/FI(D28/D9)
>E29:/FI(E28/E9)
>F29:/FI(F28/F9)
>C31:/F$((C11-C28)/C11)*100
>D31:/F$((D11-D28)/D11)*100
>E31:/F$((E11-E28)/E11)*100
>F31:/F$((F11-F28)/F11)*100
```

Key Formulas for Template in Chapter 13

```
>H18:@IF(@SUM(G14...G18)<>1,@ERROR,1)      >H29:@IF(@SUM(G22...G29)<>1,@ERROR,1)
>H35:@IF(@SUM(G33...G35)<>1,@ERROR,1)      >H42:@IF(@SUM(G39...G42)<>1,@ERROR,1)
>H47:@IF(@SUM(G46...G47)<>1,@ERROR,1)


>J57:+G14*J14        >K57:+G14*K14        >J58:+G15*J15          >K58:+G15*K15
>J59:+G16*J16        >K59:+G16*K16        >J60:+G17*J17          >K60:+G17*K17
>J61:+G18*J18        >K61:+G18*K18        >J63:@SUM(J57...J61)   >K63:@SUM(K57...K61)
>J65:+G22*J22        >K65:+G22*K22        >J66:+G23*J23          >K66:+G23*K23
>J67:+G24*J24        >K67:+G24*K24        >J68:+G25*J25          >K68:+G25*K25
>J69:+G26*J26        >K69:+G26*K26        >J70:+G27*J27          >K70:+G27*K27
>J71:+G28*J28        >K71:+G28*K28        >J72:+G29*J29          >K72:+G29*K29
>J74:@SUM(J65...J72) >K74:@SUM(K65...K72) >J76:+G33*J33          >K76:+G33*K33
>J77:+G34*J34        >K77:+G34*K34        >J78:+G35*J35          >K78:+G35*K35
>J80:@SUM(J76...J78) >K80:@SUM(K76...K78) >J82:+G39*J39          >K82:+G39*K39
>J83:+G40*J40        >K83:+G40*K40        >J84:+G41*J41          >K84:+G41*K41
>J85:+G42*J42        >K85:+G42*K42        >J87:@SUM(J82...J85)   >K87:@SUM(K82...K85
>J89:+G46*J46        >K89:+G46*K46        >J90:+G47*J47          >K90:+G47*K47
>J92:@SUM(J89...J90) >K92:@SUM(K89...K90) >L92:@SUM(L89...L90)   >H101:+G12
>J101:+H101*J63      >K101:+H101*K63         >P101:@AVERAGE(J101...N101)
>Q101:((+P101^2*(-5))+((J101^2)+(K101^2)+(L101^2)+(M101^2)+(N101^2)))/5^.5
>H102:+G20      >J102:+H102*J74        >K102:+H102*K741     >P102:@AVERAGE(J102...N102)
>Q102:+P102^2*-5+(J102^2)+(K102^2)+(L102^2)+(M102^2)+(N102^2)/5^.5
>H103:+G31      >J103:+H103*J80        >K103:+H103*K80      >P103:@AVERAGE(J103...N103)
>Q103:+P103^2*-5+(J103^2)+(K103^2)+(L103^2)+(M103^2)+(N103^2)/5^.5
>H104:+G37      >J104:+H104*J87        >K104:+H104*K87      >P104:@AVERAGE(J104...N104)
>Q104:+P104^2*-5+(J104^2)+(K104^2)+(L104^2)+(M104^2)+(N104^2)/5^.5
>H105:+G44      >J105:+H105*J92        >K105:+H105*K92      >P105:@AVERAGE(J105...N105)
>Q105:+P105^2*-5+(J105^2)+(K105^2)+(L105^2)+(M105^2)+(N105^2)/5^.5
>H107:@IF(@SUM(H101...H105)<>1,@ERROR,1)
>J107:@IF(@ISERROR(H107),@ERROR,@SUM(J101...J105))
>K107:@IF(@ISERROR(H107),@ERROR,@SUM(K101...K105))
>H118:+G118*H101   >J118:+H118*J63        >K118:+H118*K63      >P118:@AVERAGE(J118...N118)
>Q118:+P118^2*-5+(J118^2)+(K118^2)+(L118^2)+(M118^2)+(N118^2)/5^.5
>H119:+G119*H102   >J119:+H119*J74        >K119:+H119*K74      >P119:@AVERAGE(J119...N119)
>Q119:+P119^2*-5+(J119^2)+(K119^2)+(L119^2)+(M119^2)+(N119^2)/5^.5
>H120:+G120*H103   >J120:+H120*J80        >K120:+H120*K80      >P120:@AVERAGE(J120...N120)
>Q120:+P120^2*-5+(J120^2)+(K120^2)+(L120^2)+(M120^2)+(N120^2)/5^.5
>H121:+G121*H104   >J121:+H121*J87        >K121:+H121*K87      >P121:@AVERAGE(J121...N121)
>Q121:+P121^2*-5+(J121^2)+(K121^2)+(L121^2)+(M121^2)+(N121^2)/5^.5
>H122:+G122*H105   >J122:+H122*J92        >K122:+H122*K92      >P122:@AVERAGE(J122...N122)
>Q122:+P122^2*-5+(J122^2)+(K122^2)+(L122^2)+(M122^2)+(N122^2)/5^.5
>G124:@IF(@OR(@SUM(G118...G122)>1.05,@SUM(G118...G122)<.95),@ERROR,1)
>H124:@IF(@OR(@SUM(H118...H122)>1.05,@SUM(H118...H122)<.95),@ERROR,1)
>J124:@IF(@ISERROR(H124),@ERROR,@SUM(J118...J122))
>K124:@IF(@ISERROR(H124),@ERROR,@SUM(K118...K122))
>P124:@AVERAGE(J124...N124)
>Q124:+P124^2*-5+(J124^2)+(K124^2)+(L124^2)+(M124^2)+(N124^2)/5^.5
>F135:+J107        >G135:+K107        >H135:+L107        >I135:+M107
>J135:+N107        >F138:+J124        >G138:+K124        >H138:+L124
>I138:+M124        >J138:+N12         >F140:@AVERAGE(F135...F138)
>G140:@AVERAGE(G135...G138)  >H140:@AVERAGE(H135...H138)  >I140:@AVERAGE(I135...I138)
>J140:@AVERAGE(J135...J138)  >F146:/F*@IF(F140=@MAX(F140...J140),5,0)
>G146:/F*@IF(G140=@MAX(F140...J140),5,0)    >H146:/F*@IF(H140=@MAX(F140...J140),5,0)
>I146:/F*@IF(I140=@MAX(F140...J140),5,0)    >J146:/F*@IF(J140=@MAX(F140...J140),5,0)
```

Appendix III

Key Formulas for Template in Chapter 14

```
>D21:@SUM(D10...D19
>D63:@SUM(D37...D40,D42,D44,D46,D48...D61
>D82:@SUM(D71,D73...D79)
>D89:@SUM(D85...D87)
>D91:+D82+D89
>D103:@SUM(D96...D101)
>D106:+D103+D91+D63+D32
>AB10:@SUM(D10...Z10)
>AB11:@SUM(D11...Z11)
>AB12:@SUM(D12...Z12)
>AB13:@SUM(D13...Z13)
>AB14:@SUM(D14...Z14)
>AB15:@SUM(D15...Z15)
>AB16:@SUM(D16...Z16)
>AB17:@SUM(D17...Z17)
>AB18:@SUM(D18...Z18)
>AB19:@SUM(D19...Z19)
>AB21:@SUM(D21...Z21)
>AB25:@SUM(D25...Z25)
>AB26:@SUM(D26...Z26)
>AB27:@SUM(D27...Z27)
>AB28:@SUM(D28...Z28)
>AB30:@SUM(D30...Z30)
>D32:+D21+D30
>AB32:@SUM(D32...Z32)
>AB37:@SUM(D37...Z37)
>AB38:@SUM(D38...Z38)
>AB39:@SUM(D39...Z39)
>AB40:@SUM(D40...Z40)
>AB41:@SUM(D41...Z41)
>AB42:@SUM(D42...Z42)
>AB43:@SUM(D43...Z43)
>AB44:@SUM(D44...Z44)
>AB45:@SUM(D45...Z45)
>AB46:@SUM(D46...Z46)
>AB47:@SUM(D47...Z47)
>AB48:@SUM(D48...Z48)

>D63:@SUM(D37...D40,D42,D44,D46,D48...D61
>AB82:@SUM(D82...Z82)
>D106:+D103+D91+D63+D32
>E106:/FR
>F106:+F103+F91+F63+F32
>H106:3876.72
>AB106:@SUM(D106...Z106)
```

Key Formulas for Template in Chapter 16

```
>I4:@COUNT(A6...A15)
>L4:/F$@AVERAGE(A6...A15)
>I5:@SUM(A6...A15)
>L5:/F$@AVERAGE(B6...B15)
>E6:/FI(A6*A6)
>F6:(B6*B6)
>G6:(A6*B6)
>I6:@SUM(B6...B16)
>L6:/F$@SQRT((-I5*I5/I4+I7)/(I4-1))
>E7:(A7*A7)
>F7:(B7*B7)
>G7:(A7*B7)
>I7:@SUM(E6...E15)
>L7:/F$@SQRT((-I6*I6/I4+I8)/(I4-1))
>B8:/F$+B7-14
>E8:(A8*A8)
>F8:(B8*B8)
>G8:(A8*B8)
>I8:@SUM(F6...F15)
>K8:"SLOPE M
>L8:/FG(I9-(I5*I6/I4))/(I7-(I5*I5/I4))
```

```
>A9:576
>B9:/F$+B8-21
>E9:(A9*A9)
>F9:(B9*B9)
>G9:(A9*B9)
>H9:/FR"SUM XY
>I9:@SUM(G6...G15)
>K9:"Y INTERCE
>L9:/FG(-L8*I5+I6)/I4
>A10:684
>B10:/F$+B9-23
>E10:(A10*A10)
>F10:(B10*B10)
>G10:(A10*B10)
>K10:"CORR.COE
>L10:/F$(L8*L6/L7)
>A11:923
>B11:/F$+B10-14
>E11:(A11*A11)
>F11:(B11*B11)
>G11:(A11*B11)
```

```
>K11:/-#
>L11:/-#
>A12:1006
>B12:/F$+B11-15
>E12:(A12*A12)
>F12:(B12*B12)
>G12:(A12*B12)
>K12:"X GUESS
>L12:+B17
>A13:1487
>B13:/F$+B12-16
>E13:(A13*A13)
>F13:(B13*B13)
>G13:(A13*B13)
>K13:"Y PREDICT
>L13:/F$(L8*L12+L9)
>A14:1983
>B14:/F$+B13-27
>E14:(A14*A14)
>F14:(B14*B14)
>G14:(A14*B14)
```

```
>K14:/--
>L14:/--
>A15:2005
>B15:/F$+B14-12
>E15:(A15*A15)
>F15:(B15*B15)
>G15:(A15*B15)
>K15:"Y GUESS
>L15:/F$+B19
>K16:"X PREDICT
>L16:/FI(L15-L9/L8)
>A17:"ENTER X->
>B17:400
>K17:/--
>L17:/--
>A19:"ENTER Y->
>B19:/F$235
```

Appendix III

```
Key Formulas for Template in Chapter 17

>O26:/F$+B26
>P26:+C26
>Q26:@LOOKUP(P26,B1...M1)
>R26:@IF(P26/4=@INT(P26/4),@LOOKUP(O26,B6...M6),@LOOKUP(O26,B11...M11)
>S26:+O26-@INT(O26)*100-1
>T26:+Q26+R26+S26
>T30:+T26
>D31:@INT(C31/5)*7+C31-(5*@INT(C31/5)
>E31:@IF(-7*@INT(4+D31+T30/7)+4+D31+T30<(-7*@INT(4+T30/7)+4+T30),2,0)
>F31:+T30+D31+E31
>G31:@LOOKUP(F31,B2...M2)
>H31:+F31-@LOOKUP(G31,B1...M1)
>I31:@IF(G31/4=@INT(G31/4),@LOOKUP(H31,B7...M7),@LOOKUP(H31,B12...M12)
>J31:@IF(G31/4=@INT(G31/4),H31-@LOOKUP(I31,B6...M6),H31-@LOOKUP(I31,B11...M11)
>O31:/F$+I31+(J31/100)
>P31:+G31
>Q31:@LOOKUP(P31,B1...M1)
>R31:@IF(P31/4=@INT(P31/4),@LOOKUP(O31,B6...M6),@LOOKUP(O31,B11...M11)
>S31:+O31-@INT(O31)*100-1
>T31:+Q31+R31+S31
>D32:@INT(C32/5)*7+C32-(5*@INT(C32/5)
>E32:@IF(-7*@INT(4+D32+T31/7)+4+D32+T31<(-7*@INT(4+T31/7)+4+T31),2,0)
>F32:+T31+D32+E32
>G32:@LOOKUP(F32,B2...M2)
>H32:+F32-@LOOKUP(G32,B1...M1)
>I32:@IF(G32/4=@INT(G32/4),@LOOKUP(H32,B7...M7),@LOOKUP(H32,B12...M12)
>J32:@IF(G32/4=@INT(G32/4),H32-@LOOKUP(I32,B6...M6),H32-@LOOKUP(I32,B11...M11)
>O32:/F$+I32+(J32/100)
>P32:+G32
>Q32:@LOOKUP(P32,B1...M1)
>R32:@IF(P32/4=@INT(P32/4),@LOOKUP(O32,B6...M6),@LOOKUP(O32,B11...M11)
>S32:+O32-@INT(O32)*100-1
>T32:+Q32+R32+S32
>D33:@INT(C33/5)*7+C33-(5*@INT(C33/5)
>E33:@IF(-7*@INT(4+D33+T32/7)+4+D33+T32<(-7*@INT(4+T32/7)+4+T32),2,0)
>F33:+T32+D33+E33
>G33:@LOOKUP(F33,B2...M2)
>H33:+F33-@LOOKUP(G33,B1...M1)
>I33:@IF(G33/4=@INT(G33/4),@LOOKUP(H33,B7...M7),@LOOKUP(H33,B12...M12)
>J33:@IF(G33/4=@INT(G33/4),H33-@LOOKUP(I33,B6...M6),H33-@LOOKUP(I33,B11...M11)
>O33:/F$+I33+(J33/100)
>P33:+G33
>Q33:@LOOKUP(P33,B1...M1)
>R33:@IF(P33/4=@INT(P33/4),@LOOKUP(O33,B6...M6),@LOOKUP(O33,B11...M11)
>S33:+O33-@INT(O33)*100-1
>T33:+Q33+R33+S33
```

Appendix III

Key Formulas for Template in Chapter 18

```
>B7:+K7+T7+AC7+AL7            >C7:+L7+U7+AD7+AM7            >D7:+M7+V7+AE7+AN7
>E7:+N7+W7+AF7+AO7            >F7:+O7+X7+AG7+AP7            >G7:+P7+Y7+AH7+AQ7
>H7:+Q7+Z7+AI7+AR7
>AS7:@SUM(K7...P7,T7...Y7,AC7...AH7,AL7...AQ7)
>AT7:+H7-AS7
>B8:+K8+T8+AC8+AL8            >C8:+L8+U8+AD8+AM8            >D8:+M8+V8+AE8+AN8
>E8:+N8+W8+AF8+AO8            >F8:+O8+X8+AG8+AP8            >G8:+P8+Y8+AH8+AQ8
>H8:+Q8+Z8+AI8+AR8
>AS8:@SUM(K8...P8,T8...Y8,AC8...AH8,AL8...AQ8)
>AT8:+H8-AS8                  >B9:+K9+T9+AC9+AL9            >C9:+L9+U9+AD9+AM9
>D9:+M9+V9+AE9+AN9            >E9:+N9+W9+AF9+AO9            >F9:+O9+X9+AG9+AP9
>G9:+P9+Y9+AH9+AQ9            >H9:+Q9+Z9+AI9+AR9
>AS9:@SUM(K9...P9,T9...Y9,AC9...AH9,AL9...AQ9)
>AT9:+H9-AS9                  >B10:+K10+T10+AC10+AL10       >C10:+L10+U10+AD10+AM10
>D10:+M10+V10+AE10+AN10       >E10:+N10+W10+AF10+AO10       >F10:+O10+X10+AG10+AP10
>G10:+P10+Y10+AH10+AQ10       >H10:+Q10+Z10+AI10+AR10
>AS10:@SUM(K10...P10,T10...Y10,AC10...AH10,AL10...AQ10)
>AT10:+H10-AS10               >B11:+K11+T11+AC11+AL11       >C11:+L11+U11+AD11+AM11
>D11:+M11+V11+AE11+AN11       >E11:+N11+W11+AF11+AO11       >F11:+O11+X11+AG11+AP11
>G11:+P11+Y11+AH11+AQ11       >H11:+Q11+Z11+AI11+AR11
>AS11:@SUM(K11...P11,T11...Y11,AC11...AH11,AL11...AQ11)
>AT11:+H11-AS11               >B12:+K12+T12+AC12+AL12       >C12:+L12+U12+AD12+AM12
>D12:+M12+V12+AE12+AN12       >E12:+N12+W12+AF12+AO12       >F12:+O12+X12+AG12+AP12
>G12:+P12+Y12+AH12+AQ12       >H12:+Q12+Z12+AI12+AR12
>AS12:@SUM(K12...P12,T12...Y12,AC12...AH12,AL12...AQ12)
>AT12:+H12-AS12               >B13:+K13+T13+AC13+AL13       >C13:+L13+U13+AD13+AM13
>D13:+M13+V13+AE13+AN13       >E13:+N13+W13+AF13+AO13       >F13:+O13+X13+AG13+AP13
>G13:+P13+Y13+AH13+AQ13       >H13:+Q13+Z13+AI13+AR13
>AS13:@SUM(K13...P13,T13...Y13,AC13...AH13,AL13...AQ13)
>AT13:+H13-AS13               >B15:+K15+T15+AC15+AL15       >C15:+L15+U15+AD15+AM15
>D15:+M15+V15+AE15+AN15       >E15:+N15+W15+AF15+AO15       >F15:+O15+X15+AG15+AP15
>G15:+P15+Y15+AH15+AQ15       >H15:+Q15+Z15+AI15+AR15
>AS15:@SUM(K15...P15,T15...Y15,AC15...AH15,AL15...AQ15)
>AT15:+H15-AS15               >B17:@SUM(B7...B13)           >C17:@SUM(C7...C13)
>D17:@SUM(D7...D13)           >E17:@SUM(E7...E13)           >F17:@SUM(F7...F13)
>G17:@SUM(G7...G13)           >H17:@SUM(H7...H13)           >K17:@SUM(K7...K13)
>L17:@SUM(L7...L13)           >M17:@SUM(M7...M13)           >N17:@SUM(N7...N13)
>O17:@SUM(O7...O13)           >P17:@SUM(P7...P13)           >Q17:@SUM(Q7...Q13)
>T17:@SUM(T7...T13)           >U17:@SUM(U7...U13)           >V17:@SUM(V7...V13)
>W17:@SUM(W7...W13)           >X17:@SUM(X7...X13)           >Y17:@SUM(Y7...Y13)
>Z17:@SUM(Z7...Z13)           >AC17:@SUM(AC7...AC13)        >AD17:@SUM(AD7...AD13)
>AE17:@SUM(AE7...AE13)        >AF17:@SUM(AF7...AF13)        >AG17:@SUM(AG7...AG13)
>AH17:@SUM(AH7...AH13)        >AI17:@SUM(AI7...AI13)        >AL17:@SUM(AL7...AL13)
>AM17:@SUM(AM7...AM13)        >AN17:@SUM(AN7...AN13)        >AO17:@SUM(AO7...AO13)
>AP17:@SUM(AP7...AP13)        >AQ17:@SUM(AQ7...AQ13)        >AR17:@SUM(AR7...AR13)
```

Appendix III

249

```
Key Formulas for Template in Chapter 19
>B9:/F$@IF((AB9*100-@INT(AB9*100)=A2),(AB9-(A2/100)),999999999
>C9:/F$@IF((AC9*100-@INT(AC9*100)=A2),(AC9-(A2/100)),999999999
>D9:/F$@IF((AD9*100-@INT(AD9*100)=A2),(AD9-(A2/100)),999999999
>E9:/F$@IF((AE9*100-@INT(AE9*100)=A2),(AE9-(A2/100)),999999999
>F9:/F$@IF((AF9*100-@INT(AF9*100)=A2),(AF9-(A2/100)),999999999
>G9:/F$@IF((AG9*100-@INT(AG9*100)=A2),(AG9-(A2/100)),999999999
>H9:/F$@IF((AH9*100-@INT(AH9*100)=A2),(AH9-(A2/100)),999999999
>I9:/F$@IF((AI9*100-@INT(AI9*100)=A2),(AI9-(A2/100)),999999999
>J9:/F$@IF((AJ9*100-@INT(AJ9*100)=A2),(AJ9-(A2/100)),999999999
>K9:/F$@IF((AK9*100-@INT(AK9*100)=A2),(AK9-(A2/100)),999999999
>L9:/FI
>AA9:/FL220
>AB9:/F$109
>AC9:/FG0
>AD9:/FG113.4502
>AE9:/FG309.0003
>AF9:/FG484.1406
>AG9:/FG0
>AH9:615.1303
>AI9:737.1505
>AJ9:842.1001
>AK9:966.3005
>A10:/FL(A9+50)
>B10:/F$@IF((AB10*100-@INT(AB10*100)=A2),(AB10-(A2/100)),999999999
>C10:/F$@IF((AC10*100-@INT(AC10*100)=A2),(AC10-(A2/100)),999999999
>D10:/F$@IF((AD10*100-@INT(AD10*100)=A2),(AD10-(A2/100)),999999999
>E10:/F$@IF((AE10*100-@INT(AE10*100)=A2),(AE10-(A2/100)),999999999
>F10:/F$@IF((AF10*100-@INT(AF10*100)=A2),(AF10-(A2/100)),999999999
>G10:/F$@IF((AG10*100-@INT(AG10*100)=A2),(AG10-(A2/100)),999999999
>H10:/F$@IF((AH10*100-@INT(AH10*100)=A2),(AH10-(A2/100)),999999999
>I10:/F$@IF((AI10*100-@INT(AI10*100)=A2),(AI10-(A2/100)),999999999
>J10:/F$@IF((AJ10*100-@INT(AJ10*100)=A2),(AJ10-(A2/100)),999999999
>K10:/F$@IF((AK10*100-@INT(AK10*100)=A2),(AK10-(A2/100)),999999999
>AA10:/FL(AA9+50)
>AB10:110.2801
>AC10:/FG284.1406
>AD10:/FG134.1803
>AE10:/FG0
>AF10:/FG415.1303
>AG10:/FG584.1406
>AH10:/FG0
>AI10:715.1303
>AJ10:834.1505
>AK10:/FG0
>A11:/FL(A10+50)
>B11:/F$@IF((AB11*100-@INT(AB11*100)=A2),(AB11-(A2/100)),999999999
>C11:/F$@IF((AC11*100-@INT(AC11*100)=A2),(AC11-(A2/100)),999999999
>D11:/F$@IF((AD11*100-@INT(AD11*100)=A2),(AD11-(A2/100)),999999999
>E11:/F$@IF((AE11*100-@INT(AE11*100)=A2),(AE11-(A2/100)),999999999
>F11:/F$@IF((AF11*100-@INT(AF11*100)=A2),(AF11-(A2/100)),999999999
>G11:/F$@IF((AG11*100-@INT(AG11*100)=A2),(AG11-(A2/100)),999999999
>H11:/F$@IF((AH11*100-@INT(AH11*100)=A2),(AH11-(A2/100)),999999999
>I11:/F$@IF((AI11*100-@INT(AI11*100)=A2),(AI11-(A2/100)),999999999
>J11:/F$@IF((AJ11*100-@INT(AJ11*100)=A2),(AJ11-(A2/100)),999999999
```

Key Formulas for Template in Chapter 20

```
>Q10:(D10-@SUM(J10...P10))-(E10-@SUM(F10...I10)
>Q11:(D11-@SUM(J11...P11))-(E11-@SUM(F11...I11)
>Q12:(D12-@SUM(J12...P12))-(E12-@SUM(F12...I12)
>Q13:(D13-@SUM(J13...P13))-(E13-@SUM(F13...I13)
>Q14:(D14-@SUM(J14...P14))-(E14-@SUM(F14...I14)
>Q15:(D15-@SUM(J15...P15))-(E15-@SUM(F15...I15)
>Q16:(D16-@SUM(J16...P16))-(E16-@SUM(F16...I16)
>D190:@SUM(D7...D189)
>E190:@SUM(E7...E189)
>F190:@SUM(F7...F189)
>G190:@SUM(G7...G189)
>H190:@SUM(H7...H189)
>I190:@SUM(I7...I189)
>D193:@SUM(D7...D189)-@SUM(J190...P190)
>E193:@SUM(E190...E190)-@SUM(F190...I190)
>E202:(F190)
>I202:@IF(G202>E202,0,E202-G202)
>J202:@IF(G202>E202,G202-E202,0)
>E203:(G190)
>I203:@IF(G203>E203,0,E203-G203)
>J203:@IF(G203>E203,G203-E203,0)
>E204:(H190)
>I204:@IF(G204>E204,0,E204-G204)
>J204:@IF(G204>E204,G204-E204,0)
>E205:(I190)
>I205:@IF(G205>E205,0,E205-G205)
>J205:@IF(G205>E205,G205-E205,0)
>E207:@SUM(E202...E206)
>I208:@IF(I207>J207,I207-J207,0)
>J208:@IF(J207>I207,J207-I207,0)
>E212:(J190)
>I212:@IF(G212>E212,0,E212-G212)
>J212:@IF(G212>E212,G212-E212,0)
>E213:(K190)
>I213:@IF(G213>E213,0,E213-G213)
>J213:@IF(G213>E213,G213-E213,0)
>E214:(L190)
>I214:@IF(G214>E214,0,E214-G214)
>J214:@IF(G214>E214,G214-E214,0)
>E215:(M190)
>I215:@IF(G215>E215,0,E215-G215)
>J215:@IF(G215>E215,G215-E215,0)
>E216:(N190)
>I216:@IF(G216>E216,0,E216-G216)
>J216:@IF(G216>E216,G216-E216,0)
>I217:@IF(G217>E217,0,E217-G217)
>J217:@IF(G217>E217,G217-E217,0)
>E218:(P190)
>I218:@IF(G218>E218,0,E218-G218)
>J218:@IF(G218>E218,G218-E218,0)
>E220:@SUM(E212...E219)
>I221:@IF(I220>J220,I220-J220,0)
```

Appendix III

Formulas for Template in Chapter 21

```
>F10:@IF(C10<99,F8+D10,F8-D10)
>G10:1
>H10:@IF(E10=H6,D10,0)
>I10:@IF(E10=I6,D10,0)
>J10:@IF(E10=J6,D10,0)
>K10:@IF(E10=K6,D10,0)
>L10:@IF(E10=L6,D10,0)
>M10:@IF(E10=M6,D10,0)
>N10:@IF(E10=N6,D10,0)
>O10:@IF(E10=O6,D10,0)
>P10:@IF(E10=P6,D10,0)
>Q10:@IF(E10=Q6,D10,0)
>R10:@IF(@AND(C10>99,G10<>1),D10,0)
>S10:@IF(@AND(C10<99,G10<>1),D10,0)
>A11:/FR"FEB
>B11:/FL7
>C11:/FL1529
>D11:46
>E11:1
>F11:@IF(C11<99,F10+D11,F10-D11)
>G11:1
>H11:@IF(E11=H6,D11,0)
>I11:@IF(E11=I6,D11,0)
>J11:@IF(E11=J6,D11,0)
>K11:@IF(E11=K6,D11,0)
>L11:@IF(E11=L6,D11,0)
>M11:@IF(E11=M6,D11,0)
>N11:@IF(E11=N6,D11,0)
>O11:@IF(E11=O6,D11,0)
>P11:@IF(E11=P6,D11,0)
>Q11:@IF(E11=Q6,D11,0)
>R11:@IF(@AND(C11>99,G11<>1),D11,0)
>S11:@IF(@AND(C11<99,G11<>1),D11,0)
>F33:(F31)
>H33:@SUM(H10...H32)
>I33:@SUM(I10...I32)
>J33:@SUM(J10...J32)
>E42:(E38+E39-E40)=E41
>E44:(E41-(E38+E39-E40))
>A45:/F*@IF(E44<>0,@IF(@INT(E44/9)=(E44/9),6,0),0)
>B45:/F*@IF(E44<>0,@IF(@INT(E44/9)=(E44/9),6,0),0)
```

Key Formulas for Template in Chapter 22

```
>C7:(+C4*((C5/100)/12))/(1-((1+((C5/100)/12))^(-C6*12)))
>A9:/F*@IF(C6>10,7,0)
>B9:"MAX YRS=10:
>C9:"ERROR IF>10
>A14:/FI1
>B14:@IF(C6>10,@ERROR,C4)
>C14:(C4*((C5/100)/12)
>D14:@IF(C14<.005,0,(C7-C14))
>E14:@IF(C14<.005,0,(C14+D14))
>A15:/FI@IF(@OR(A14+1>(C6*12),A14=0),0,A14+1)
>B15:@IF((B14<.005),0,(B14-D14)
>C15:(B15*((C5/100)/12))
>D15:@IF(C15<.005,0,(C7-C15))
>E15:@IF(C15<.005,0,(C15+D15+E14))
>A16:/FI@IF(@OR(A15+1>(C6*12),A15=0),0,A15+1)
>B16:@IF((B15<.005),0,(B15-D15)
>C16:(B16*((C5/100)/12))
>D16:@IF(C16<.005,0,(C7-C16))
>E16:@IF(C16<.005,0,(C16+D16+E15))
>A17:/FI@IF(@OR(A16+1>(C6*12),A16=0),0,A16+1)
>B17:@IF((B16<.005),0,(B16-D16)
>C17:(B17*((C5/100)/12))
>D17:@IF(C17<.005,0,(C7-C17))
>E17:@IF(C17<.005,0,(C17+D17+E16))
>A18:/FI@IF(@OR(A17+1>(C6*12),A17=0),0,A17+1)
>B18:@IF((B17<.005),0,(B17-D17)
>C18:(B18*((C5/100)/12))
>D18:@IF(C18<.005,0,(C7-C18))
>E18:@IF(C18<.005,0,(C18+D18+E17))
>A19:/FI@IF(@OR(A18+1>(C6*12),A18=0),0,A18+1)
>B19:@IF((B18<.005),0,(B18-D18)
>C19:(B19*((C5/100)/12))
>D19:@IF(C19<.005,0,(C7-C19))
>E19:@IF(C19<.005,0,(C19+D19+E18))
>A20:/FI@IF(@OR(A19+1>(C6*12),A19=0),0,A19+1)
>B20:@IF((B19<.005),0,(B19-D19)
>C20:(B20*((C5/100)/12))
>D20:@IF(C20<.005,0,(C7-C20))
>E20:@IF(C20<.005,0,(C20+D20+E19))
>A21:/FI@IF(@OR(A20+1>(C6*12),A20=0),0,A20+1)
>B21:@IF((B20<.005),0,(B20-D20)
>C21:(B21*((C5/100)/12))
>D21:@IF(C21<.005,0,(C7-C21))
>E21:@IF(C21<.005,0,(C21+D21+E20))
>A22:/FI@IF(@OR(A21+1>(C6*12),A21=0),0,A21+1)
>B22:@IF((B21<.005),0,(B21-D21)
>C22:(B22*((C5/100)/12))
>D22:@IF(C22<.005,0,(C7-C22))
>E22:@IF(C22<.005,0,(C22+D22+E21))
>A23:/FI@IF(@OR(A22+1>(C6*12),A22=0),0,A22+1)
>B23:@IF((B22<.005),0,(B22-D22)
>C23:(B23*((C5/100)/12))
>D23:@IF(C23<.005,0,(C7-C23))
>E23:@IF(C23<.005,0,(C23+D23+E22))
```

Appendix III

```
Key Formulas for Template in Utility 1

>D8:@IF(D5=A8,D5,0)
>E8:@IF(E5=A8,1,@IF(D8<1,0,D8+1))
>F8:@IF(F5=A8,1,@IF(E8<1,0,E8+1))
>G8:@IF(G5=A8,1,@IF(F8<1,0,F8+1))
>H8:@IF(H5=A8,1,@IF(G8<1,0,G8+1))
>D25:@IF(D8<=5,B25*@LOOKUP(D8,R5...R19),B25)
>E25:@IF(E8<=5,B25*@LOOKUP(E8,R5...R19),B25)
>F25:@IF(F8<=5,B25*@LOOKUP(F8,R5...R19),B25)
>G25:@IF(G8<=5,B25*@LOOKUP(G8,R5...R19),B25)
>D34:(@SUM(D25...D32)
>E34:(@SUM(E25...E32)
>F34:(@SUM(F25...F32)
>G34:(@SUM(G25...G32)
>H34:(@SUM(H25...H32)
>I34:(@SUM(I25...I32)
>J34:(@SUM(J25...J32)
>K34:(@SUM(K25...K32)
>L34:(@SUM(L25...L32)
>M34:(@SUM(M25...M32)
>N34:(@SUM(N25...N32)
>O34:(@SUM(O25...O32)
>P34:@SUM(P25...P32)
```

Key Formulas for Template in Utility #2

>C11:+B11*.0254
>H11:+G11*.03937
>C12:/F$+B12*2.54
>H12:+G12*.3937
>C13:/F$+B13*30.48
>H13:+G13*3.937
>C14:/F$+B14*.3048
>H14:+G14*3.2808
>C15:/F$+B15*.9144
>H15:+G15*32.808
>C16:/F$(B16*5280)*.3048
>H16:+G16*328.08
>C17:/F$+B17*1.609
>H17:+G17*.621
>H18:+G18*6.21

>C21:+B21*(1/1549.9)
>C22:+B22*(1/119.6)
>H22:/FG+G22*1549.9
>C23:+B23*(1/2.471)
>H23:/FG+G23*119.6
>C24:+B24*(1/.386)
>H24:/FG+G24*2.471
>H25:/F$+G25*.386
>C28:+B28*.0648
>C29:+B29*28.3495
>H29:+G29*.1543
>C30:/F$+B30*453.59
>H30:+G30*1.5432
>C31:+B31*45.36
>H31:+G31*15.432
>C32:/F$+B32*907.18
>H32:+G32*.3527
>H33:+G33*3.5274
>H34:+G34*2.2046
>H35:+G35*22.046
>C36:+B36*.2366
>H36:+G36*220.46
>C37:+B37*.4732
>H37:+G37*2204.6
>C38:+B38*.9464
>C39:+B39*3.7854
>H41:+G41*.338
>H42:+G42*3.38
>C43:/F$+B43-32*5/9
>H43:+G43*1.0567
>H44:+G44*2.64
>H45:+G45*26.418
>H46:+G46*264.18
>H50:/F$(G50*9/5)+32

Appendix III

Key Formulas for Template in Utility #3

```
>C14:@CHOOSE(C12,@LOOKUP(C4,D14...D38),@LOOKUP(C4,F14...F38),
     @LOOKUP(C4,H14...H38),@LOOKUP(C4,J14...J38),@LOOKUP(C4,K14...K38))
```

>D15:+D14+50	>G21:8785	>J27:+J26+50
>E15:+E14+20	>H21:+H20+50	>K27:+K26+19
>F15:+F14+50	>I21:+I20+22	>D28:+D27+50
>G15:8680	>J21:+J20+50	>E28:11014
>H15:+H14+50	>K21:+K20+19	>F28:+F27+50
>I15:+I14+22	>D22:+D21+50	>G28:8908
>J15:+J14+50	>E22:+E21+20	>H28:+H27+50
>K15:+K14+19	>F22:+F21+50	>I28:+I27+22
>D16:+D15+50	>G22:8803	>J28:+J27+50
>E16:+E15+20	>H22:+H21+50	>K28:+K27+18
>F16:+F15+50	>I22:+I21+22	>D29:+D28+50
>G16:8698	>J22:+J21+50	>E29:11037
>H16:+H15+50	>K22:+K21+18	>F29:+F28+50
>I16:+I15+22	>D23:+D22+50	>G29:8925
>J16:+J15+50	>E23:+E22+20	>H29:+H28+50
>K16:+K15+18	>F23:+F22+50	>I29:+I28+22
>D17:+D16+50	>G23:8820	>J29:+J28+50
>E17:+E16+20	>H23:+H22+50	>K29:+K28+19
>F17:+F16+50	>I23:+I22+22	>D30:+D29+50
>G17:8715	>J23:+J22+50	>E30:11059
>H17:+H16+50	>K23:+K22+19	>F30:+F29+50
>I17:+I16+22	>D24:+D23+50	>G30:8943
>J17:+J16+50	>E24:+E23+21	>H30:+H29+50
>K17:+K16+19	>F24:+F23+50	>I30:+I29+22
>D18:+D17+50	>G24:8838	>J30:+J29+50
>E18:+E17+20	>H24:+H23+50	>K30:+K29+18
>F18:+F17+50	>I24:+I23+22	>D31:+D30+50
>G18:8733	>J24:+J23+50	>E31:11082
>H18:+H17+50	>K24:+K23+18	>F31:+F30+50
>I18:+I17+22	>D25:+D24+50	>G31:8960
>J18:+J17+50	>E25:10947	>H31:+H30+50
>K18:+K17+18	>F25:+F24+50	>I31:+I30+22
>D19:+D18+50	>G25:8855	>J31:+J30+50
>E19:+E18+20	>H25:+H24+50	>K31:+K30+19
>F19:+F18+50	>I25:+I24+22	>D32:+D31+50
>G19:8750	>J25:+J24+50	>E32:11104
>H19:+H18+50	>K25:+K24+19	>F32:+F31+50
>I19:+I18+22	>D26:+D25+50	>G32:8978
>J19:+J18+50	>E26:10969	>H32:+H31+50
>K19:+K18+19	>F26:+F25+50	>I32:+I31+22
>D20:+D19+50	>G26:8873	>J32:+J31+50
>E20:+E19+20	>H26:+H25+50	>K32:+K31+18
>F20:+F19+50	>I26:+I25+22	>D33:+D32+50
>G20:8768	>J26:+J25+50	>E33:11127
>H20:+H19+50	>K26:+K25+18	>F33:+F32+50
>I20:+I19+22	>D27:+D26+50	>G33:8995
>J20:+J19+50	>E27:10992	>H33:+H32+50
>K20:+K19+18	>F27:+F26+50	>I33:+I32+22
>D21:+D20+50	>G27:8890	>J33:+J32+50
>E21:+E20+20	>H27:+H26+50	>K33:+K32+19
>F21:+F20+50	>I27:+I26+22	

Formulas for Template in Chapter Utility #4

```
>C1:@IF(B24=0,0,C1+1)
>C3:@IF(B24=0,0,@LOOKUP(C1,D43...D52))
>H9:@IF(B24=0,0,@IF(D43=C1,@LOOKUP(E43,E9...E19),H9))
>E10:@IF(D9=C3,D9+1,0)
>H10:@IF(B24=0,0,@IF(D44=C1,@LOOKUP(E44,E9...E19),H10))
>E11:@IF(D10=C3,D10+1,0)
>H11:@IF(B24=0,0,@IF(D45=C1,@LOOKUP(E45,E9...E19),H11))
>E12:@IF(D11=C3,D11+1,0)
>H12:@IF(B24=0,0,@IF(D46=C1,@LOOKUP(E46,E9...E19),H12))
>E13:@IF(D12=C3,D12+1,0)
>H13:@IF(B24=0,0,@IF(D47=C1,@LOOKUP(E47,E9...E19),H13))
>E14:@IF(D13=C3,D13+1,0)
>G43:/F$@IF(F43=0,0,@IF(H9=0,0,@CHOOSE(H9,I9...I18)
>I43:/F$+F43*G43
>D44:+D43+1
>G44:/F$@IF(F44=0,0,@IF(H10=0,0,@CHOOSE(H10,I9...I18)
>I44:/F$+F44*G44
>D45:+D44+1
>G45:/F$@IF(F45=0,0,@IF(H11=0,0,@CHOOSE(H11,I9...I18)
>I45:/F$+F45*G45
>D46:+D45+1
>G46:/F$@IF(F46=0,0,@IF(H12=0,0,@CHOOSE(H12,I9...I18)
>I46:/F$+F46*G46
>D47:+D46+1
>G47:/F$@IF(F47=0,0,@IF(H13=0,0,@CHOOSE(H13,I9...I18)
>I47:/F$+F47*G47
>D48:+D47+1
>G48:/F$@IF(F48=0,0,@IF(H14=0,0,@CHOOSE(H14,I9...I18)
>I48:/F$+F48*G48
>I54:/F$@SUM(I43...I48
>I55:/F$.054*I54
>I57:/F$(I54+I55)
>I60:/F$(I57-I58)
```

Appendix III

```
Key Formulas for Template in Utility #5

>C18:@EXP(C10*(C9/100))*C8
>D18:@IF(@AND(D9=0,D10=0,D11=0),0,@EXP(@LN(D11)-(D10*(D9/100))))
>E18:/F$@IF(@AND(E8=0,E10=0,E11=0),0,(@LN(E11/E8)/E10)*100)
>F18:/F$@IF(@AND(F8=0,F9=0,F11=0),0,@LN(F11/F8)/(F9/100))
>C19:(C9/100)/360+1^(360*C10)*C8
>D19:@IF(@AND(D9=0,D10=0,D11=0),0,@EXP(-360*@LN((D9/100)*D10/360+1)+@LN(D11))
>E19:/F$@IF(@AND(E8=0,E10=0,E11=0),0,(@EXP(@LN(E11)-@LN(E8)/360)-1*360/E10)*100)
>F19:/F$@IF(@AND(F8=0,F9=0,F11=0),0,@EXP(@LN(F11)-@LN(F8)/360)-1*360/(F9/100))
>C20:(C9/100)/12+1^(12*C10)*C8
>D20:@IF(@AND(D9=0,D10=0,D11=0),0,@EXP(-12*@LN((D9/100)*D10/12+1)+@LN(D11))
>E20:/F$@IF(@AND(E8=0,E10=0,E11=0),0,(@EXP(@LN(E11)-@LN(E8)/12)-1*12/E10)*100)
>F20:/F$@IF(@AND(F8=0,F9=0,F11=0),0,(@EXP(@LN(F11)-@LN(F8)/12)-1*12/(F9/100))
```

Index

A

ABS, 87
Account Codes, 184
ACOS, 44
Adding Sensitivity, 120
Adjust, 64
Amortization, Loan, 99
AND, 1, 88, 96, 186
Angles, Triangle Calculation, 38
ASIN, 40
Ask, 64
Asterisk (*), 97, 102
ATAN, 44
Automated,
    Invoice system, 205
    Mini-Ledger, 181
AVERAGE, 122, 143, 146

B

Balance Sheet, 49, 52
BASIC, 124
Blue Label-UPS, 89
Boolean, 1
Break-even Analysis, 108
Bricklin, Dan, 124

C

Calculating Dates, 151
Calculator,
    Break-even, 108
    Interest, 213
Calendar Management, 150
Cash Flow, 75
    Rental, 71

Check for a Little Bit, 105
Checkbook Manager, 175
Checkbook Register, 19
CHOOSE, 43, 88, 95, 202, 205
Circular References, 50, 54
Columnar LOOKUP, 79
Commission,
    Calculator, 137
    Statements, 136
Comparison List, 79
Completion Tests, 49
Consolidate, 181
Consolidation, 159, 159, 181
Conversion, English/Metric, 197
Coordinate Calls, 19
COPY, 25
    Down, 25, 188
    From, 25, 188
COS, 40
Cosines, Law of, 43
COUNT, 43, 143, 145
CP/M, 1
Criterion, 9, 115

D

Data Load, 124, 125
//Data Management, 8
Data Save, 124, 125
Database,
    Management, 115
    Spreadsheet, 1
DATE, 25, 157, 157
DBMS, 115
DELTA(), 49

Index

Depreciation, 74
Deviation, Standard, 123
DIF, 124, 124, 161, 179
Discounted Cash Flow, 75
Display Security System, 168

E

EDIT, 21
Either/Or, 2, 109
English/Metric Conversion, 197
ERROR, 51, 55, 67, 82, 102, 115
Estimating, 27
EXP, 215
eXternal,
    File Link, 123, 134
    USE, 167, 167, 181
Extract, 9

F

FALSE, 1, 178
Field Names, 9
FIND, 9, 15
Formula, Check for Little Bit, 105
Forward References, 49
Frankston, Bob, 124
Functions, Trig, 36

G

Game, Math Exerciser, 51
General Ledger, 174
Greater Than (>), 170
Guidelines for LOOKUP, 81

H

HIDE, 37, 62, 69
Home Budgeting, 175
Horizontal Recalculation, 50
Household Accounts, 175

I

IF, 2, 31, 67, 88, 102, 122,
Income Statement, 49, 52
Income Tax Record, 131
INDEX, 45
Input, 9
INT, 48, 96, 151, 172, 188
Interest Calculator, 213, 213
Investment Evaluator, 73
Invoicing, 27, 205
IRA, 60
IRA Analysis, 60
Iteration, 49, 54, 57, 210
ITERCNT(), 210
IterS (SC3), 59

L

Law of Cosines, 43
Law of SINEs, 41
Leap Year, 152
Ledger Accounting, 175
Ledger System, 174
Linear Regression, 142, 142
    Formula, 145
Linking Spreadsheet Files, 159
LN, 215
/Load Part, 135
Loan Calculator, 99
LOCK, 25, 82
LOOKUP, 27, 78, 91, 138, 151, 194,

M

Math,
    Exerciser Game, 51
    Operators, 108, 114, 197
MAX, 11, 74, 122
Metric/English Conversion, 197
MIN, 11
Mini-General Ledger, 180
Monthly Expense Record, 124

Multiparameter Subj. Analysis, 114

N

NA, 28, 84, 136, 138, 195
NAME, 70, 123
Natural Order Calculation, 50, 205
Nested LOOKUP, 88
Net Present Value, 71
(N)o, 4
No Adjust, 64
Notes Payable, 52
NPV, 71

O

Operators, Math, 114
OR, 1, 102
Output, 10
Overlays, 159
Oversize Values,
   (##), 173
   (>>), 173

P

Payment Function (SC3), 107
Payments Formula, 101
Period, Searching for, 215
PI, 39
PMT, 107
Price List, 78
Principal, 101
   Searching for, 215
Print Shop, 27
Project Scheduling, 149
Property Purchasing, 71
/Protect, 82, 190

Q

Quota Forecasting, 160

R

Radian, 38
Ranking Utility, 17
Ranking, 11
Recalculate, 155
!Recalculation, 59, 200
Recalculation,
   Horizontal, 50
   Vertical, 50
References
   Circular, 50
   Forward, 9
Regression, Linear, 142
Relative, 69
Rental Cash Flow, 71
/Replicate, 4
Result List, 79
ROUND, 106, 107

S

Salary Finder, 168
Sales Territory. Management, 159
Scheduler, Startup, 191
Scheduling, Project, 149
Scoreboard, 12
Scoring, Weighted, 114
Secure Displays, 168
Self-calls, 50, 58
Sides, Triangle Calculation, 38
SINE, 40
SINES-Law of, 41
Sort, 18
Spreadsheet Users Group, 61
SpreadTip,
   Auto-Recalc Off, 151
   Blanking Formats, 166
   Block Replication, 117
   Bulk Erasure, 156
   Column Width, 21
   Concealing Data, 61
   Displaying Blanks, 185
   Dissimilar Formulas, 66

Index

Formatting, 68
Formula Building, 32
Naming DIF Files, 133
Non-Range SUMming, 129
Protected Cells, 82
Relationships, 64, 70
Replicate vs. Copy, 117
Shorter Iterations, 55
SUMming, 23
Switch Diagnostics, 63
Using /Edit, 151
Using DIF, 122
Using MOVE, 126
Utilities, 17
Window Design, 37
Window Displays, 143
SQRT, 40, 123, 142, 147
Square Root, 143
Standard Deviation, Formula, 120, 123
Startup Schedule, 191
STDEV, 123, 148
SUM, 23, 96, 115, 129, 139, 146
Switch, Variable, 62

T

TAB, 106, 109
Tax Formulas, 131
Tax Tables, 201
Textual Values, 34, 106,107,123,181
Textual Values, 79, 107, 123, 181

Transposition Error Trap, 187
Triangle Solver, 36
Trig Functions, 36
TRUE, 1, 178
Two-dimensional LOOKUP, 201

U

United Parcel (UPS), 88

V

Validation, data, 79
Value, Textual (see Textual), 34
Variable Switch, 62, 72
Variables, 100
Vertical Recalculation, 50

W

WDAY, 158, 158
Weighted Scoring, 144
Weighting, 117
What-if, 60, 191
Windows, 36, 142

Y

Yearly Expense Record, 131
Yield, Searching for, 215

Z

ZIP Codes, 89
Zone Chart-UPS, 89